KILLING
WILLIS

From Diff'rent Strokes *to the Mean Streets*
to the Life I Always Wanted

TODD BRIDGES

with Sarah Tomlinson

A TOUCHSTONE BOOK

Published by Simon & Schuster
New York London Toronto Sydney

Touchstone
A Division of Simon & Schuster, Inc.
1230 Avenue of the Americas
New York, NY 10020

First Touchstone hardcover edition March 2010

TOUCHSTONE and colophon are registered trademarks
of Simon & Schuster, Inc.

For information about special discounts for bulk purchases,
please contact Simon & Schuster Special Sales at
1-866-506-1949 or business@simonandschuster.com.

The Simon & Schuster Speakers Bureau can bring authors to your
live event. For more information or to book an event contact the
Simon & Schuster Speakers Bureau at 1-866-248-3049
or visit our website at www.simonspeakers.com.

Designed by Claudia Martinez

Manufactured in the United States of America

1   3   5   7   9   10   8   6   4   2

Library of Congress Cataloging-in-Publication Data
Bridges, Todd.
Killing Willis : from Diff'rent Strokes to the mean streets to the
life I always wanted / by Todd Bridges with Sarah Tomlinson.
p.   cm.
1. Bridges, Todd. Television actors and actresses—United States—
Biography. I. Tomlinson, Sarah. II. Title.
PN2287.B6924A3 2010
791.4502'8092—dc22
[B]
2009039130

ISBN 978-1-4391-4898-3

This book is dedicated to my mom Betty Bridges for giving birth to me when no one else could, to my brother Jimmy Bridges and my sister Verda Bridges Prpich, for being my best friends, and to all three of them for standing by me when no one else would.

And to my kids Spencir and Bo. Never give up on life. Always remember to keep trying, and all of your dreams will come true.

AUTHOR'S NOTE

Except for my family members and people I worked with during my television career, the names and some identifying details of the other people in this book have been changed.

CONTENTS

Contents

KILLING WILLIS

EVERYBODY'S GOT A SPECIAL KIND OF STORY

FROM THE TIME that I was five years old, I thought I knew how my story was going to go. All I ever wanted as a kid was to be a famous TV star. Just a few years later, my dream came true, when I was lucky enough to land the role of Willis Jackson on the hit show *Diff'rent Strokes*. If only everything in life happened exactly like we wanted it to, right? I thought I had it made, and for a little while, I did. But I didn't know that God had other plans for me. As most people are very well aware, if they happened to check out their groceries anywhere near a tabloid, or turn on a TV entertainment show, anytime in the early '90s, many of the other stories I barely lived through weren't quite so happy. They featured drug addiction, devastating personal loss, and more than one trip to jail. Most painful and humbling of all, they all happened because of decisions I made for myself.

After ten years of struggle, I was finally able to forgive myself and reach the point where I can honestly say that I wouldn't change anything in my life. Well, maybe I wouldn't have worn those Jordache jeans for so long into the '90s. But, as we've established, there were a few years when I wasn't in my right mind. Seriously, I would not change a single thing about my life. Because if I fixed even one bad thing that happened to me, it would change everything; I wouldn't have my wife, or my son, or my daughter. I wouldn't be the person I am today. And that's the person who was inspired to write this book and tell you my real story. It's a story about forgiveness—forgiving others, and most importantly, forgiving ourselves. It's a story that will hopefully entertain and move people, which is what I've wanted all along.

1

SUICIDE BY COP

SUICIDE BY COP. It was my only way out. I couldn't see any other solution. I didn't care enough about myself or anything else to find another answer. Officers from the Burbank Police Department had pulled me over on a residential street. I was on my way back from scoring drugs for a girl I knew, and I had a sixteenth of speed in the hiding place in my car. Their squad cars were parked close behind my Mercedes, with their lights flashing, sirens blaring. They were out of their cars now, coming up on me, their weapons drawn and held steady, right at my head.

I reached for my gun.

This was December 29, 1992, and I was worn out. It'd been a long time coming. I'd been using and dealing on and off for six years, and even though I'd been trying to get my act cleaned up, it clearly wasn't working. I decided to give the cops what I knew they wanted, the chance to say they'd taken down Todd Bridges, the former child star turned drug dealer, whether they got me with bullets or with bars.

I never would have let myself get caught with drugs in my car before. When I was a serious dealer of crack and methamphetamine, I dealt to supply my own addiction to both. Being high made me more alert, and I was high all the time. Sometimes things got real weird, and I felt like I was living in one of the movies I had acted in during my old life. But I always knew when the cops were watching me, and I kept my stuff well hidden.

The drugs and dealing had been exciting for a while. But more importantly, they had kept me numb. They made me forget all of the bad things that had happened to me as a child. On the outside, I'd had it all, living the life I'd always dreamed of as a TV star with a lead part on the hit shows *Fish* and *Diff'rent Strokes*. But that wasn't the whole story.

On the inside, I'd been left with dark memories that overpowered the good. I didn't want to feel the pain I'd carried with me from my childhood into adulthood, and so I didn't want to stop using drugs. But I couldn't keep on going like I was. I kept trying to do the right thing, like my mom had taught me, like I had been told in church when I was growing up, like I knew I should. But my life was so crazy that any attempt I made to be a decent human being only seemed to land me in another whole mess of trouble.

A few months before my run-in with the Burbank Police, I'd met this girl, Tiffany. With me, there was always a girl involved somehow. There was something nice, almost normal, about this particular girl. She was mulatto, medium height, and curvy. She had this reddish hair that she wore short and spiked. She started hanging around, and pretty soon we were dating. I guess that's what you'd call it. I wasn't exactly the kind of guy who sent flowers back then. But we were together a lot, just doing whatever. And even though she was using drugs herself, she was supportive, in her own way, of the fact that I was trying to get my life together.

I was done with how crazy the drugs made me: the paranoia, the hallucinations, the feeling that maybe if I had to draw my gun on somebody, and then, if he drew his gun and shot me to death, it'd be for the best. I didn't think my mind or my spirit could take much more.

I quit meth. I quit crack. I basically quit selling drugs. I had a little money that my mom had kept safe for me during the years I had gotten heavily into drugs, and I just tried to live something like a normal life.

But getting out wasn't that easy. Not after I'd been so deeply involved for as long as I had been. On the day of my run-in with the Burbank Police, I was in my house in Sun Valley when I got a phone call from this other girl, Joelle, I'd hung around with for a month or so, about seven months earlier. I knew I shouldn't be taking calls from other girls when I was seeing someone, so I went into the other room to keep Tiffany from hearing my conversation.

There was no way I was going to not take this call. Joelle was something else. She was the one who got me hooked on methamphetamine. The first time she ever shot me up with meth, the high was so good, I came. I was hooked on the drug, and I was hooked on her. She was a pretty girl—blond and very voluptuous, with a great body for a drug addict—and very wild, sexually, just nasty and crazy. It was always real intense with her, real on the edge, and I never knew what was going to happen next. So when I heard her voice on the phone that day, all sexy and suggestive, that's all it took to get me excited.

I knew Joelle was dangerous, but I wasn't thinking too clear right then.

"Can you get me a sixteenth of speed?" she asked.

"No, I'm not doing that anymore," I said, keeping my voice down.

"Well, can you just go find somebody to get it for me?"

Her voice was real flirty-like. I knew if I did her a favor, I'd get something good in return. Girls who needed drugs would do anything. That's how I liked it.

"Yeah, okay," I said. "Where do you want me to meet you at?"

We worked out a plan where I would meet her in Burbank to get the cash to buy the drugs, go buy them, and then hook back up with her in Burbank. If there was one thing I had learned, it was to never buy drugs for someone without getting the money up front. People were always trying to pull something. And if she didn't pay me for the speed once I bought it, it would be worthless for me to hold out on giving it to her, since I wasn't using anymore. What I cared about was how she was planning to say thank you. I had a few ideas in mind.

Like I've already said, I wasn't really dealing anymore, so I didn't have any drugs on me. I called a friend of mine and arranged to meet him at his place in North Hollywood to get some speed for Joelle. Then I drove from my house to meet her, and then, from there, to my buddy's house. While I was driving, I totally forgot about the cops who were following me.

This was not easy to do. The cops had been a constant force in my life since I was fifteen. That's when my family moved to the San Fernando Valley. The police force started harassing me, pulling me over, calling me a nigger, and finding any excuse they could to hassle me until I came to hate the color of my own skin, almost as much as I hated the police. They'd arrested me plenty of times since I'd gotten into drugs, and they'd been following me pretty much nonstop for the past two years. In fact, my good friend Shawn Giani, who was my neighbor in Sun Valley for many years, had called me and tipped me off that the cops had asked if they could watch my house from his bushes.

At the height of my meth use, I got so messed up on drugs that I went out to their undercover van and started banging on it, shouting, "I know you're in there!" There was a guy in there, all right. He took one look at me, climbed up into the driver's seat, and drove away. But that wasn't the last I saw of him.

Whatever I was doing, I could count on the fact that there was always a cop somewhere nearby. When I was on meth, no matter how high I was, I knew the police were out there. And I was always able to avoid them. Even when I was doing fourteen grams of meth a day, and so high I was having hallucinations, driving around with drugs and loaded guns in my car, dropping off and picking up the girls I had working the streets for me, the cops never caught me.

But on that day in December, I smoked some pot, and pot made me stupid, real stupid. It was the only thing I was doing since I'd quit crack and meth. It should have been an improvement, right? It would have been, except for the fact that on pot, I was a total moron. That made me an easy target. I didn't care that the cops were following me because I didn't know. I had forgotten that cops even existed.

Get this, though. Even though I was driving around in the stupidest marijuana haze possible, the cops somehow managed to lose me. Maybe that says something about all of the times the police didn't catch me when I was doing something illegal. After they got separated from my Mercedes, they pulled their squad car off the road and two officers ran into a Ralph's grocery store, looking for any sign of me.

They happened to stop a lady who knew my mother.

"Have you seen Todd Bridges in here?" they asked her, thinking she'd be able to recognize me from TV, not knowing she was a family friend.

"No," she said. "He hasn't been here."

After checking the store, the officers jumped back into their squad car and drove away. As soon as they were out of sight, that lady ran to a pay phone and called my mom. "They're looking for your son," she told my mom.

My mom wasn't at all surprised to receive a call like that. She'd prayed, and cried. She'd come to family therapy sessions when I was in rehab. She'd bailed me out of jail when she could, and visited me in jail when I was denied bail. But nothing had done anything to turn me around. At the time, I was so far gone that I couldn't register anything beyond how low I was feeling about myself, and how the drugs—whether it was crack or speed or pot—made this pain go away. I couldn't hear what she was saying when she begged me to get sober, and I certainly couldn't understand how much I was hurting her. But no matter how dark my life got, my mom never gave up on me. When she learned that the cops were after me, she called my house. And when she got the machine, she left a message for me.

"Whatever you're doing, stop it now. The police are looking for you."

I didn't ever get that message.

By that point I was on the way back from my friend's house with a sixteenth of speed, totally ignorant of all of the excitement I'd been causing across the San Fernando Valley. I had the drugs, and I was going to see a sexy girl who would be very glad to get them. That's all that mattered to me. My gun was in the secret hiding place I'd made in the dashboard of my car. It was right below the radio. There was a button that looked like it controlled the car alarm, but when you pushed it, a secret compartment dropped down. I was good at hiding places. There were plenty of times the police searched different cars I owned over the years, but they never found my drugs or my gun.

The police hadn't given up searching for me. Far from it. They picked me back up. As soon as I heard the siren, I knew they had me. I pulled over. They came out of everywhere. And they made it clear—they weren't playing.

"Get out of the car, right now!" one of the officers yelled at me, his gun drawn.

Behind him, the officers from the other squad cars and the undercover van stood at the ready, legs wide, guns drawn. A drug dog barked and tugged at its leash. I had been through this before. My trial for attempted murder in '89 was big news. The headlines that ran on TV and in the tabloids were plenty nasty. I'd had to go through it again a year later, when they retried the case.

I couldn't face it all over again. I was totally demoralized.

I hit the button and opened the secret compartment where my gun was hidden. I had a 9mm Beretta in there, and I put my hand on the grip.

"Forget it," I thought. "Just kill me now, because I'm tired of this life anyway."

I was ready for it all to end. I was done with the hurt and the shame I felt over the abuse and racism I had experienced as a child, the feeling I had that my life wasn't worth anything, and that because I was a drug addict, I didn't deserve any better anyhow.

The cops were ready, too. They watched me closely.

But then something spoke to me from deep inside of myself, maybe God, maybe some part of me that had somehow managed to survive all of the bad stuff I had been through and wasn't ready to give up, no matter how much pain I was in.

"Don't reach for it," the voice said. "Just let it go."

It was a hard choice. Suicide by cop was easy compared to what I had in front of me. I had gone from being a teen idol to a tabloid joke. I was broke, and I didn't have any prospects of getting my career back. I had been to rehab five times. I usually didn't last more than a few days. It never once stuck for longer than a few months. I had spent almost a year in jail while awaiting trial and vowed I would never go back. I had tried, and failed, to block out all of the things that had been written about me in the press before. I had felt pain and self-hatred so deep and raw that the only way to silence it was with drugs.

But this was not how I wanted to end it. I wanted to live. I let go of my gun and closed up the secret compartment.

Now that I didn't want to die, I was scared that they were going to kill me. The cops in the San Fernando Valley had abused me so much as a teenager that I finally filed a police harassment lawsuit in the mid-'80s. It only made them hate me more. And now they had their guns drawn and plenty of reasons to use them.

I kept my hands visible as I opened the car door slowly, careful not to spook them. I got out of the car, trying to act cool. Everything went crazy after that. The sirens ripped through my skull. The drug dog leaped toward me, barking even louder. I rested my hands on the back of my head to show I was cooperating and backed up toward them, trying not to imagine being shot in the back. The police were all over me. They rushed up, shouting orders, their guns at close range.

The undercover officer whose van I'd ambushed when I was out of my mind on drugs came up and put his gun to my head.

"I've got you now, motherfucker," he said.

I wasn't exactly in a position to argue.

They grabbed me, got me onto the ground, and held me there. They patted me down and let the dog go over me. I was wearing baggy Cross Colours clothes, which young black men were really into at the time, and they checked all of the pockets for weapons and drugs. When they cuffed my arms behind my back, I knew it was all over. As they put me in the back of a squad car, I actually felt a sense of relief. I hated my old way of living so much that I had been ready to die. And now I had a chance at something better, if I could only hold it together this time.

I didn't realize it then, but it was ironic that the Burbank Police Department was the one to arrest me and, ultimately, save my life. When I was at the height of my career as one of the stars of *Diff'rent Strokes*, I received a plaque on October 13, 1979, "In Appreciation for Services Rendered to the Burbank Police Officers' Association." Nothing could be a clearer symbol of how far I'd fallen since then. Gone was the cute kid who had made people laugh on TV and used his fame for good by visiting veterans, children's hospitals, and public schools. In his place was a shell of a man who was so sick in body and mind that he had almost given the officers who had honored him a good reason to shoot him to death.

When the cops searched my Mercedes, they found my gun and the speed. They knew right where to look. Not too many people were aware of my secret hiding place. But Joelle knew. I was sure she had set me up.

I wanted to kill her. I would have, too, if I'd seen her right then. My mind was still all screwed up from the drugs and everything I'd been through.

But I was tired of feeling like that, of living in a world of drugs and guns, where surviving meant getting the other person before he could get me. I felt lucky that I had made it out alive. I was going to at least try to stay that way. I basically told the officer everything. Ironically, there wasn't much to tell, not like if they had arrested me a year earlier. Since I had quit using hard drugs, and pretty much quit dealing, my life was fairly tame. But there was enough to keep me in jail.

I called up my lawyer, Johnnie Cochran, who went on to make his name defending O. J. Simpson during his murder trial. Johnnie came down and sat next to me in the cell. He rolled his ring around on his finger, thinking, before he spoke.

"I'm going to tell you what," he said. "This is the last time I'm going to help you with anything. If you don't straighten your life out, I'm done. Don't call me. Don't be my friend. I don't need you in my life if you can't straighten yourself out."

Johnnie had always been there for me. My family and I first hired him to represent me in my lawsuit against the LAPD. This was after their years of discrimination came to a head when they tried to arrest me for supposedly stealing my own car. He had represented me in my attempted-murder trial in '89. And when my own father didn't visit me, even once, while I was in jail for nine months leading up to that trial, Johnnie had been like a father to me. The thought of not having him there to help me anymore filled me with panic.

"You know, Johnnie," I said, "I'm ready to stop. I just need to know how."

"Well, you need to figure out how to do it," he said.

That was the problem. I didn't even know how to start.

I was bailed out of jail a few hours later. I went home, and even though I had the desire to turn my life around, I couldn't. I started getting high again right away, and not only on marijuana either. I was back on meth and crack. Like I had told Johnnie: I didn't know how to stop. I stayed high for the next few months, until I had to go back to court. I probably would have felt bad about letting Johnnie down, and about letting myself down, and about letting my mother and everyone else in my life down. But when I was high, I didn't feel anything. That was the whole point.

Finally, I went to court in Pasadena. My mom was there, sitting next to this old guy I had never seen before. I looked at the judge's bench, and I saw this circle with a triangle in it. I knew it was from AA, and I knew that it meant unity, strength, and hope. I was looking at it as the judge was talking to me and thinking about how I'd never been able to stay sober for longer than a few months at a time.

"I'll tell you what I'm going to do, Mr. Bridges," he said. "Two things can happen. I'll either send you to jail tonight, or you can go to rehab tonight. What do you want to do?"

I wasn't about to go back to jail.

"I want to go to rehab," I said.

"Okay, well, you need to show up there by eight o'clock tonight," he said. "If you do not show up there, I will put a bench warrant out for your arrest."

"Oh, no, I'll be there," I said.

I turned around and looked at my mom. I knew that she was behind the rehab deal, and I was angry at her for doing this to me. She had set it all up with the guy sitting next to her. He worked over at this rehab called CPC Westwood, and he made deals with the court system so people like me, who needed help getting sober, could go to rehab instead of jail. I should have been glad that I didn't have to go to jail. I should have felt lucky that my mom hadn't given up on me, even though I'd put her through hell for the past seven years. But I didn't want to kick. I had done it before; I had sweated it out and been sick with diarrhea and the shakes and the worst cravings I'd ever known in my life. I did not want to do it again. I did not want to go to rehab. Being sober allowed me to feel way more pain than I could bear. And I hadn't been taught anything to help me manage my pain during those five other times I had gone to rehab. I couldn't believe it would be any different now.

But at the same time, I was already turning away from my old ways. I didn't want to continue being nothing but an addict and a dealer. I knew I had to get over the anguish that tormented me from my childhood and dig my way out of this hole.

I went back home, and I called a friend I knew I could trust.

"Look," I said. "Come pick me up at seven o'clock. No matter what, you have to be here at seven o'clock. You have to take me to this rehab place."

I decided that I wasn't going to give myself any excuse to want to use drugs ever again. I went out and spent my last bit of money on crack and weed and meth. I brought it home and sat down on my living room couch and spread it all out in front of me. And then I just went for it. I smoked about $200 worth of crack. I shot about $300 worth of meth. I smoked a bunch of weed in one of the homemade bongs I was always building from PVC pipe and whatever else was lying around. I did all of the drugs I had bought before it was time for my buddy to come pick me up. That way I wouldn't be able to say, "I didn't do this or I didn't do that."

I didn't want to leave myself any excuses. I was tired of excuses.

My friend showed up to get me at seven o'clock, and we drove over to CPC Westwood. Even before we got there, all of the paranoia I used to feel when I was shooting a lot of meth came rushing back on me like no time had passed. I was chain smoking and looking every which way, sure everyone was after me.

I got myself checked in, and not only was I paranoid, but I was furious, too. It was a really nice place, with beautiful grounds and a pool. But I did not want to be there. Right away, I went from wanting to get sober to being angry that I had to stop using or go to jail. It was not fair that it had to go down like this. I was mad at everybody. I called my mom, and when I got her on the phone, I didn't thank her for standing by me for all of those years, or for getting me into a safe place in the end. No, instead I said, "I hate you, and I never want to talk to you ever again."

I wore my shades, because I hated everybody. I wouldn't talk to the nurses, because I hated everybody. I fell asleep without unpacking or even getting under the covers, because I hated everybody. I didn't

want to hear anything they had to say. When I woke up in the morning, I had sobered up, so my attitude was even worse. I was furious that
I was still in rehab. I should have felt lucky that I wasn't coming to in a
jail cell at that very moment. But I was too mad to be grateful.

A nurse came in and smiled at me.

"You've got to go to a meeting," she said.

"I'm not going to no meeting," I said. "Screw you."

All of my anger erupted then. It was like when I was in school and
a bully pushed me too far, and I started releasing this pure rage built
up from everything bad that had happened to me in my home life.
There was no stopping me until I let it all out of me. I stormed into
the bathroom, ripped the shower rod down from the wall, and held
it up like a weapon as I ran back into my bedroom.

"Come on!" I shouted. "Any of you guys come in here, I'm going
to hit you all with this shower rod."

I didn't care how many staff members they sent in after me. The
anger had a hold on me, and I was going to fight them all.

I heard them sound some sort of alarm out in the hall.

I stood there with my shower rod in the air, wondering what was
going on.

"I don't care," I thought. "What are they going to do? Send all of
their guys in here? Let them. I'm going to beat the crap out of all
their guys. Come on!"

And then I heard BOOM, BOOM, BOOM coming down the hall
toward me.

That got my attention.

"What the hell is that?" I thought. "Sounds like a big guy."

This huge, black, bald-headed guy came in. He was so big, he had
to duck under the doorway to get inside my room. He looked at me,
sized up my lifetime of anger and my shower rod, and I could tell
that he was not impressed.

"This can be hard, or this can be easy," he said.

That was enough to convince me.

"Easy," I said.

I dropped the shower rod, and it made a pathetic clinking sound when it hit the ground. But their definition of "easy" wasn't exactly the same as mine. They grabbed me and took me upstairs to the psych ward. They put me in a diaper, and they strapped me down in four points. It was the same thing they had done to me back in county jail in '89. I guess I hadn't learned all that much in the meantime. Talk about demoralizing.

"This is a far cry from Willis Jackson," I kept thinking.

For three days, they kept me strapped down like that. It was the worst way to kick drugs. I was super-aware of every inch of my body, and it all felt sick. My skin itched. I was sweaty, and shaking with chills, all at the same time. My mouth was dry. My stomach cramped up, and I had the worst diarrhea right there in my diaper. But there was nothing I could do to stop it from happening, or to clean myself up. The whole time, I couldn't stop thinking how simple it would be to just smoke some crack or shoot some meth and make it stop. That's all it would take to make the bad feelings go away. Not only that, but I'd feel good. I'd feel better than good. I'd feel invincible. When I wasn't thinking about drugs, I was obsessed by thoughts about the girl who had ratted me out, and how I'd like to make her pay for what she'd done. But I was trapped there, and so I had no choice but to get through it.

While I was lying there, I could hear these kids playing outside the building, laughing and shouting and having the best time. I wondered what game they were playing, maybe jump rope or tag. It reminded me of the huge street football games my brother and I used to get together outside our house in Baldwin Hills, my friends and I facing off against him and the older guys. Those games had been so much fun, but that was a long time ago now. There was no way it could ever be that easy to be happy again, not after everything I'd been through. But those kids sure sounded happy. I couldn't stop thinking about them. I kept wondering, "Who are these people?"

Finally, they released one arm. I was exhausted, and my anger was starting to fade, so I didn't make a fist and punch any of the orderlies in the face. Instead, I scratched my itches and held on to my stomach when it hurt and kept listening to those kids. They were my link to the outside world and the possibility of a better life. A full day went by, and then they released the other arm. The whole thing had been pretty humbling, and I wasn't really feeling angry anymore, so I didn't threaten anyone. The next day, they released a leg. On the fourth day, when they felt confident that I wasn't going to hurt myself or anyone else, they released my other leg.

Finally, when they let me up off the table on which I'd been restrained, I was able to look out the window. The voices I had heard belonged to normal kids who lived in the neighborhood. There was nothing special about them or their circumstances. I was the one who had been given the charmed life, and the chance to live my dream of being an actor from the time I was seven years old. But they had something I had never had: They were happy, and they felt good about themselves. Now that I could see happiness right there in front of me, I wanted it for myself.

"God, I want what they have," I said.

It was the first thing I had wanted in a long time, other than to be dead, or to have all of the drugs and sex I needed to keep myself from feeling how unhappy and ashamed I was inside. It was the first time I had talked to God in even longer. My faith and my recovery were linked from then on, and I really credit God with helping me to find my way back. After that, I focused on trying to feel the same kind of happiness I had heard out my window while I was restrained. It's what got me through those first days I was in rehab.

CPC Westwood had great services, too. I went to see my psychiatrist, Dwayne, every day. He was a black guy in his late thirties who had a small Afro and a goatee and always wore suits. I talked to him about what I was feeling. I wanted to get released from the psych ward, and go back down to the ground floor, so I could go outside and be near those happy people. Then, I thought, I could have a chance at being a normal, happy person myself.

But I had to get off the psych ward first.

"I want to get down there" I kept saying, over and over again.

"Nobody wants you down there," Dwayne replied every time. "None of the counselors wants to deal with you. They think you're out of control and violent."

I could see why they would think that, based on my past record, and even how I had acted on my first day in rehab. I had been out of control and violent. But I didn't feel that way anymore. I felt like maybe I was ready to change. I wanted to try.

"Please, just let me down there, even on a temporary basis," I said. "Let me prove to them that I can do this."

Dwayne was working on getting me to where I could leave the psych ward. He had figured out that my impulse-control mechanism was damaged, and so he put me on Depakote, which calms the brain when a person gets angry. It helped me be able to do what I call "add and subtract in my head," so I stopped going all nuts on people, and I could think about the consequences of something before I did it.

But even with the Depakote, I had a lot to live down, and they weren't convinced I was ready yet. So I stayed where I was.

And then, one day, I was sitting on my bed upstairs in the psych ward, and all of a sudden, a light hit me. I felt the power of something bigger than me—I don't know what this life force is for other people, but for me, it was God—and He spoke right to me.

"Your life is going to change," He said. "But you have to stop listening to yourself and start listening to others. I will put the right people in your life to lead you away from the drugs and the pain and to make you happy again."

That's all I wanted. It had taken those kids outside to make me realize it, but I wanted what everybody else in the world had, even when they were going through a bad day. I wanted to be happy to be alive. I wanted to be happy about me. I wanted to be happy about my life. I wanted to be happy about my surroundings. Because, for so many years, I wasn't happy, even though I had everything that was supposed to make me happy—money, fame, women, and the chance to live out my dream as a successful actor on a hit TV show. Since I was a kid, I'd been sad about who I was. The world had taught me that the color of my skin meant I could expect to be called names and threatened and hated. For years I was sad about what had been done to me when I was young. I kept blaming myself for that and for everything else, too.

But then it hit me. The only thing I really had to take responsibility for was using drugs. None of that other stuff was my fault. After that moment, they told me I could go downstairs. This real sweet redheaded woman named Judy said she would be my counselor in rehab, this meant she believed in me, and she thought I had a chance at staying sober. I was scared that I would let her down. I had tried this so many times before. I knew that without the drugs to keep me numb, I was going to start feeling all of the things I'd been trying to outrun for so many years. I knew that no matter how much I wanted to change, my first instinct was going to be a return to the drugs to dull the pain. I didn't know if I was capable of anything else.

But slowly I was starting to think that maybe I was. Because, for the first time in a long time, I did something different than I had done before. When I got downstairs, and I started working with Judy, I finally knew enough to just shut up and listen. I took in everything she and everyone else had to say. It started to make sense. I wasn't happy yet, but at least I wasn't dead. I wasn't even as unhappy as I had been before. I started thinking about what had happened to knock me so far down in life, because I sure didn't want to go back to those depths ever again. What I wanted was to be the good person I knew I could be. What I wanted was to stop feeling guilty about getting people strung out on drugs, and making my family worry, and letting myself down. No matter how painful it ended up being, I made up my mind to remember. I vowed to face everything that had driven me to become a drug addict, finally let it go, forgive myself, and move on with my life. I could tell it wasn't going to be easy. But for the first time in a long time, I was determined to try.

2

"I WANT TO BE JUST LIKE HIM WHEN I GROW UP"

WHEN I WAS A KID, the thing that scared me the most wasn't sharks or zombies. It was the sound of the garage door opening. We lived in San Francisco in one of the trilevel houses that were very common there. On a typical school night, my brother Jimmy, my sister Verda, and I would be playing down in the finished basement, which was set up like a family room, with couches and a television. Or we'd be upstairs by the fireplace in the living room, listening to my mom singing. My favorite song was always "Stormy Weather." No matter what we were doing, we'd always be laughing and having a great time, being together, the way families were supposed to be.

And then we heard the familiar noise of the garage door jerking open, and the fun was over. What came next happened so many times that it's hard to remember one bad night from another, but they all went something like this.

My mom scrambled to get everything together. She straightened our clothes and fixed our hair, making sure all of us kids looked very presentable. We helped her put away the Monopoly board and any toys we had pulled out after school. By tidying up around us, she tried to make it seem like we weren't doing anything wrong, which of course we weren't. But I felt like I'd been bad anyhow. I had a sick, worried feeling in my stomach, like when something scary happened on TV.

I looked back and forth between my mom, who was fussing over her own hair now, and the door that led from the garage into the house. The car engine shut off. There was a moment of silence, and then the car door slammed shut. The panic rose from my stomach into my chest. A set of keys jingled. The smoke from a burning cigarette drifted under the door. I looked at Jimmy and Verda. They were older, but they seemed scared, too. My mom came over and stood by us. I was the baby of the family, and she rested her hand on my shoulder to comfort me. But there was nothing any of us could do to make it better. My dad, James Bridges, was home.

Maybe this time it would be different. Maybe he'd kiss my mom and ask my brother and me if we wanted to go throw the football around in the yard. Hope would flicker up beneath the fear inside me. He was my dad, and I loved him.

He swung the door open and slammed it behind him. Everything he did was louder and more forceful than it needed to be. He had stopped at the bar after work, and he was drunk. A compact man with a mustache, he didn't care much for his appearance, but he cared about being respected. And he always felt like I needed to be schooled in that area. He glared at us and then got up close enough to me that I could smell the booze and cigarettes on his breath.

"Why-didn't-you-do-your-damn-chores-like-I-asked-you-to-Todd?" he said, grabbing my arm and yanking me away from my mom. He talked fast and ran his words together, especially when he was drunk. He was always drunk, so I could never understand what he was saying. That just made him madder.

"Ain't-you-gonna-answer-me-boy?" he said. "I'll-teach-you-some-respect."

And then, *WHAP*, he slapped me on the back of my head. I hated that. Not only being hit, but how unfair it was that he punished me when I hadn't even done anything wrong.

"Stop it, James, you haven't even been in his room," my mom said.

"Shut up, woman," my dad said, looking like he might slap her, too.

"Let me heat up some dinner for you, James," my mom said.

She moved to stand between my dad and us and nodded for us to go to our rooms, where we'd be out of his sight, so if he got mad at anybody it would be her.

"I'm not hungry," my dad said.

From that moment on, the rest of the night was ruined. Even if he just sat in his recliner, drinking brandy and smoking cigarettes while he watched television, he found a way to make the rest of us miserable. No matter how good we were, or how hard we tried to make him happy, it was never good enough.

That was probably my first experience of acting, pretending to be the perfect kid who was a part of the perfect family, when my dad walked in the door every night. What's funny about our need to perform for my dad is that everything pretty much was perfect when I was growing up, except for him.

Even though my dad drank a lot, he always worked hard, and we were middle class in the late '60s, at a time when that was a very difficult thing for a black family to be. My dad was proud of this fact. He had been forced to start working at fifteen to help support his own family, and it gave him satisfaction to know that we were better off than his family had been. My family was poor in the early years, when my brother James Jr. (Jimmy) and my sister Verda were born. But my mom had done well in college and gotten a job in a bank after she graduated. And my dad was a manager at a local Mayfair department store before becoming a longshoreman. And because they both believed in working hard, and my mom was really good with money, the family was doing all right by the time I came along on May 27, 1965.

And even though there weren't many other middle-class black families in our neighborhood, everyone got along really well. San Francisco was such a melting pot, even back in the late '60s, I didn't know what racism was until we moved to Los Angeles. Our best friends were white, black, Latino, and East Indian. When my mom had parties, they were always very well mixed, and everyone had a good time together, no matter what color their skin. We had a great life in San Francisco.

From a very young age, my favorite thing was to take apart anything and everything I could get my hands on. I just loved breaking things into pieces, trying to figure out how they worked, and then seeing if I could put them back together.

The Christmas I was four years old, my mom and dad bought me a gas-powered airplane that could really fly. They tried to assemble it on Christmas Eve, so it would be waiting as a surprise for me in the morning, but they couldn't figure out how to put it together. They finally had to give up and go to bed.

The next morning, I got up before they did, and I put that airplane together, without the instructions or anything. Once I had it assembled, I took it out behind our house; we called that whole area the Rocky Mountains, because it was covered with these little pieces of broken rock. I was happy as could be, flying my new airplane all around the backyard with Jimmy and Verda. The sound of the engine finally woke up my parents. They came running outside because they didn't know what they were hearing. When they saw me flying that plane, they couldn't believe it. I was afraid I was going to get in trouble for putting the gas in by myself, because I knew I was supposed to wait for them to do stuff like that. But they were so impressed with me that they couldn't even be that mad. Pretty soon after that, they decided they would only give me toys that had to be assembled. They had already stopped buying me anything mechanical because I would just tear it apart and use the pieces for something else.

When my dad wasn't home, the rest of my family loved to hang out at the house together. One of our favorite things to do was to listen to my mom sing. She was also a fantastic artist, and she used to draw pictures of all of us kids. She had grown up with eight brothers, so she was great at sports, too. She would always play basketball and baseball with us. My dad couldn't be bothered to spend the time, but my mom more than made up for it. She was very patient, and she taught us how to do so many things.

We spent many happy afternoons out in front of our house after school. One of the best days of all was when I got my first bike. I already loved to go everywhere with Jimmy. Once I could ride my own bike, I would be able to keep up with him and his friends, no matter where they went. I was so excited.

My mom held on to the back of my new bike and helped me to balance it without wobbling too much from side to side.

"Come on, baby, you can do it," she said.

I started pedaling. She didn't even have to hold me up or tell me what to do.

"That's right, just like that," she said.

I pedaled harder, and the next thing I knew, I was riding a bike for the first time. It felt so amazing, like I could ride forever. After that, I was always off on my bike with my brother or my friends. Those were different times. We went off by ourselves for the whole day, and our parents never had to worry.

They'd just say, "Be home before the streetlights come on."

Among Jimmy and Verda and me, and all of our friends, there were always plenty of kids around for all different kinds of games, and we had such a good time playing together. We used to play baseball back behind our house in that area we called the Rocky Mountains. Let me tell you, there was no sliding into base during one of those baseball games. If one of us fell, it was curtains for our arms.

Because our house was so much fun, all of the neighborhood kids loved to come over after school. My dad was always on his best behavior when we had other kids around, so we were glad when the house was full. All of the kids looked up to him because most of them didn't have a father at home. Strangely, he was a really good father to all of the kids who didn't have dads. They saw a different side of him than I ever did. Like, one time, some people started a football league in the neighborhood, and some of the kids couldn't afford shoes, so my dad went out and bought cleats for them.

It was hard for me sometimes, seeing how great he was with other kids, when he barely paid any attention to me. But being jealous was way better than having him all to myself, when he'd just be yelling at me or hitting me anyhow.

The neighborhood kids looked up to my mom, too. And everybody called them Mom and Dad. The house was full all of the time, and there was always somebody spending the night. Some of those kids stayed pretty much the whole summer, plus we had cousins from my mom's family in San Diego who came to stay with us during the summer, too. There were even kids who stayed with us during the school year. The more guests, the better. When there were a lot of people there, it may have seemed noisy and chaotic to the outside eye. But because my dad was being nice, we felt like the house was in a state of peace.

In many ways, I was just a normal kid who happened to have a complicated home life. But my dreams were a lot bigger than that. Even at five years old, I knew I was going to be a star. All I had to do was find the vehicle to get me there. That came through my mother. After college, she studied acting at American Conservatory Theater, which was a big acting school in San Francisco. When my mom graduated from ACT, one of her teachers encouraged her to get an agent, and so she did. Even though there weren't a lot of production companies in San Francisco, she landed three or four commercials right away, and she had to quit her job at the bank.

Jimmy, Verda, and I loved going to Mom's performances. Seeing her onstage and on television was really cool, and it made acting seem like something I could do, too. But I first knew for sure that I wanted to be an actor while I was watching my favorite TV show one night.

I used to watch a lot of TV, including all of the usual shows that everyone loved back then. I was a big fan of *The Little Rascals*, *The Three Stooges*, and this Japanese show called *Ultra Man*. The biggest thing for us to do on Saturdays was to watch *Kung Fu Theater*. We planned our whole day around it.

But the show I loved most was *Sanford and Son*.

I would always be right there when it was about to start. I'd get into my pajamas with the feet on them and curl up on the couch with my mom and Verda and Jimmy. There was no moment during the week that I loved more. I think I was about five years old on the night that I made up mind about what I wanted to be.

I turned to my mom.

"I want to be just like him when I grow up," I said.

"What do you mean?" she asked.

"I want to be an actor like him," I said, pointing at Redd Foxx.

From that moment on, my mom was determined to help me realize my dream. She expected me to be determined, too. She always taught us that once we started something, we couldn't quit. Even if it got hard, we always had to go forward with it. Not that acting ever felt hard to me. It was fun.

My mom was an acting teacher as well as an actress. She started giving Jimmy and Verda and me acting lessons, and she eventually taught us everything she had learned at ACT.

She taught us how to cold-read, which meant reading from a script that we hadn't practiced before. Sometimes we would read from scripts she had written, or she would take an old script from a part she had done and we'd go over it together. I've read a lot of scripts over the years, so I can't exactly remember any one of those lessons, but they always went something like this. She would gather Jimmy and Verda and me together in the living room and give us each a copy of the script.

"Now, Todd, in this scene, you're upset because you got in trouble for breaking a window with your baseball. Try saying the line at the top of the page."

"It was an accident, I swear," I read.

"Good job, baby," she said. "But this time I want you to think about something that makes you sad and say it again."

With the man that I had for a dad, there were plenty of sad memories to choose from. I thought about him slapping me in the back of the head, and I could feel all over again how angry and frustrated I had been when it happened.

"It was an accident, I swear," I said again. This time my voice shook a little.

"That's wonderful," she said. "Now come on over here toward me."

I walked across the rug toward where she was standing.

She laughed, but not in a mean way.

"You're thinking too hard," she said. "You don't want to get all stiff or else you'll come off looking like a robot. You've got to move like how you do normally."

My mom took a few steps to show me, and it wasn't like she was in a scene at all. She was just a woman walking through her living room. I moved like her.

"You've got it now," she said, giving me a hug.

There's a lot more to being an actor than just acting, and my mom prepared us for all of that, too. She taught us how to interview, and by the time I was going out on a lot of auditions, I was really good at it. She got us to the point where we were completely comfortable with how the whole process worked. Even when I was going up for big jobs, I never got nervous.

After my mom booked her first commercial jobs, we were excited to give it a try, too. We begged her to let us do a commercial. When she finally thought we were ready, she got us an agent in San Francisco, and we started going out on commercial auditions. The first job I ever booked was a family job. It was a Jell-O brand gelatin commercial. My mom went for the audition first, and they narrowed it down to about ten women to possibly play the part of the mom. Then they had all of the ladies bring in their families, and we ended up getting it.

I was seven at the time, and I had one line. My mom worked with me so I'd be ready on the day of the shoot. When it came time to go in front of the cameras, I actually did better than my mom did. I remembered my line, and she kept messing hers up. In fact, I calmed her down between takes.

"Don't worry, Mom," I said. "You can remember. Take your time. And just think about the dialogue. Remember what you told us?"

Finally we all nailed our parts. And I got to deliver my line. That was a long time ago now, and I've delivered thousands of lines since then, but my mom and I remember it being something like this: "Mom, what are you going to do with the Jell-O?" I had this squeaky, high-pitched voice back then, and everyone just thought that was the cutest thing ever.

After that, we did a Tide commercial as a family, too. And then my first big commercial was a United Airlines ad starring Carl Weathers and featuring their old jingle "Fly the Friendly Skies." My mom was in that one, too, and Carl played my dad. That was the third or fourth commercial in which Carl had been cast as my mom's husband. My dad did not like that one bit. He was very jealous of any successful black man, and he dealt with it like he did everything else; by being drunk and mean.

I did my best to avoid his abuse, but there was no escaping it completely. It started to affect me outside of the house, too. After my dad hit my mom, I always seemed to get into a fight or get in trouble at school. I was the smallest kid growing up, so other kids thought they could pick on me. What they couldn't see was that I was also one of the toughest kids. I had all of this anger toward my dad that was banging around inside me, and it didn't take much for it to rear up. If someone started something with me, I went nuts.

Plus, I knew how to fight from my older brother and my cousins. The first time I ever got jumped, I was six or seven, and these two brothers started in on me. One of them stuck his finger in my nose, and it started bleeding. I came home crying. Jimmy looked me over. He wasn't really a fighter. He was a good guy who could talk his way out of anything. But when he got angry, he could really hurt somebody. Well, he grew up in the same house as me, so it's not surprising that he had some anger, too. Anyhow, he knew what I needed to do to save my reputation.

"You're going to go back, and you're going to fight these kids," he said.

Jimmy was pretty much my hero growing up, and he has been my best friend ever since. I'm lucky he was a nice guy, because I would have done anything he told me to do. I went back, and I ended up beating up both of those kids. It was like something came over me, and everything I had pushed down inside me came rushing up and made my fists fly. In a way, it felt good to get it out.

I was really emotional, probably because of everything I was seeing at home, and I never picked on anyone. I knew how bad it felt to endure unfair abuse, and I couldn't have done that to someone else. But I was not the kid to pick on. There was already a fire burning inside me. And if someone started with me, they faced the consequences. Sometimes I even went overboard and hurt the other person more than he deserved, just because I couldn't contain my rage.

After that, I was always up for a fight. If someone messed with me, it was on. There wasn't ever a doubt in my mind that I wasn't going to fight. I got in trouble a lot at school. My mom knew that I was only acting up because I was upset about my dad. But she still always tried to get me to do the right thing.

Most of my friends at school were the rejects, who normally got picked on. They liked being friends with me because they knew I'd stand up for them. I always seemed to hang around with the smart kids, because they were the ones who needed protection. It worked out well for me, too, because being around them made me smarter.

My grades were actually pretty good, and I think it's because all of my friends helped me with my schoolwork. School was hard for me because I'm dyslexic. I have trouble making sense of numbers when they're written down. And when I read, my brain skips over some of the words, so I have to double-read things to make sure I don't miss anything. That was very frustrating as a child, because they didn't really know what dyslexia was back then or understand how it worked.

I was always very talkative and hyper, sort of like I am now. Of course, now, it's a good thing because running my mouth earns me a good living. But back then it was a problem, because my teachers wanted me to be quiet in class. The school even told my mom they wanted to put me on Ritalin. At first she considered it because she was worried about the behavioral problems I was having at school. But then, one day, she went to my school and saw this kid who was on Ritalin, and he was basically drooling on himself. My mom was not going to go for that. She told them they were going to have to learn how to deal with me the way I was. I don't think the Ritalin would have done anything for the real cause of my behavioral problems anyhow. Luckily, my grades were good enough that they let me get away with a lot over the years, because they knew my schoolwork would be straight.

After we had done those first few commercials, my mom decided that we had outgrown San Francisco and needed to move. She realized that the only way to be successful in the entertainment business was to go to Los Angeles. It was a big decision, but her family was very supportive of her, and that helped. My uncles Eugene and Robert had gone to see her in a Shakespeare play that was staged at ACT, and they told her that she was talented and needed to go where the big stuff was. She wanted more opportunities for us kids, too.

Not surprisingly, my dad didn't want to move. But my mom knew how important it was for the whole family.

"Well, we're moving, so you're either moving with us or you're staying here," she said to my dad.

That was probably the only time I ever saw my mom stand up to him. He ended up coming with us.

When we got to LA, my mom got a job right away, and when she showed up on the first day, Carl Weathers was there to play her husband. My dad went ballistic when he found out. He tried to say that Carl and my mom must have had something going on. Of course, they were just friends who were happy to see each other because they had both coincidentally moved to LA at about the same time. But there was no talking sense to my dad when he was mad about something.

My mom got Jimmy and Verda and me interviews with a bunch of different agents, and we were taken on by the Mary Grady Agency, which is called MGA Talent now. They're not as big today, but they were one of the biggest kid agencies there was back then. As soon as we signed with them, my career just took off.

I was very fortunate that when I came into the business, I was extremely different from all the other kids, so I stood out at auditions. I was black, for one thing, and there weren't a lot of black child actors back then. Also, my mom had trained me, so I had a lot more experience than most kids my age. I really wanted to succeed as an actor, which meant I was determined. Plus, I was very emotional. As a child actor, I had to cry in most of the shows I appeared on. It wasn't hard for me. I could cry just like that. I liked the fact that when I was acting, I didn't get in trouble for expressing myself, like I did when I dealt with my emotions in unhealthy ways at school. It was a relief to be given a part where it was okay to cry, or yell, or act out.

There was a lot that was hard and painful about growing up in my house. But all of the emotion I saw there was great for me as an actor. Over the years, I've found that most good actors are very emotional people, and they often have volatile families. Actors need somewhere to dig from. Let me tell you, I had plenty to dig from.

It was about to get a lot worse. When we moved to Los Angeles, it was great for my acting career. But Los Angeles was also where the real problems started. It was in LA that I experienced racism for the first time. I didn't get it at first. I was only eight years old. So how could I understand why the color of my skin suddenly meant that I wasn't as good as everyone else? It had always been perfectly fine up until then. Even if I was confused by what was happening and why, I grasped that people hated me for reasons that didn't make any sense to me. And it hurt.

We first experienced racism as a family right when we got to Los Angeles. My parents found a house they wanted to buy in a neighborhood called Culver City. When my mom called the real estate agents, they told her over the phone that the house was available. Now, I know some people aren't going to like this, but my mom sounds like a white person on the phone because she's educated and very well spoken. For whatever reason, the real estate agent clearly didn't think my mom was black, because when my parents went to see the house in person, they got a whole different story.

"Oh, we're sorry, we just sold that house," the real estate agent said to them.

They went home. But my mom had this feeling that something just wasn't right. It was too hard to believe that they had just sold the house. She called again. This time she was really specific. She mentioned the street address, and the ad she had seen in the newspaper, and then she asked if the house was available.

"Of course," the real estate agent said.

"How much are you asking for it?" my mom asked.

The real estate agent told her the price. My mom and dad went over to look at the house again. As soon as they showed up, they were told the house had just been sold. My mom even called back a third time, and she made her voice sound very refined, and she asked if the house was available. The real estate agent said it was, and my mom made an appointment to go see it. Of course, every time she went back, the real estate agent put her off again by telling her the house had just sold.

A friend later told my mom that she should have gotten a white couple to go look at the house. If the real estate agent showed them the house, my mom could have proven that the real estate agent was being discriminatory and sued. But my mom didn't think to do that. She was too shocked to think that clearly. After having lived in San Francisco for so many years, she wasn't used to experiencing racism like that anymore.

Of course, my mom had been exposed to racism her whole life. I later heard her tell a story about being thrown off the sidewalk in Texas by a white lady who told her she wasn't supposed to walk on the curb while whites were walking there. But she had chosen not to tell her children about those experiences when we were little. I think she didn't want to make us jaded. Instead of taking away our innocence by telling us about how hateful people could be, she instilled in us the idea that we were just as good as anyone else, even if others didn't see it that way. The only thing she did tell us about race was that because we were minorities, we couldn't afford to make the same mistakes that the white kids were able to make. She warned us that if we made mistakes, we would be held accountable for them for the rest of our lives, and we would find that people weren't quick to give us a second chance. She was definitely right about that, as I would later learn. But as a child, she protected us from the worst the world was capable of, and I didn't ever know what racism was until I started seeing it firsthand in Los Angeles.

I had more problems at school in LA than I had ever had in San Francisco, and I think much of that was because of racism, too. Sure, I had been involved in fights and gotten in trouble in San Francisco. But there, a scuffle was just two kids who didn't get along. It wasn't until I moved to LA that any kids called me a nigger.

I soon had a reputation, again, as the kid who nobody wanted to pick on. I still got along with most of my classmates and never started fights, but I was finding that I had more reason to fight than ever before. The more bad stuff that happened to me—receiving even worse abuse from my dad at home as he vented his unhappiness about the move to LA, experiencing racism at school—the angrier I got. By this time, if someone picked on me, I unleashed the hounds of hell on him. I got suspended from school a lot for fighting.

Moving to Los Angeles was definitely an adjustment in a lot of ways. But it could have been a lot worse. My career took off as soon as we got settled, and that meant I didn't have to go to the regular elementary school anymore. And so I didn't get involved in as many fights as I would have otherwise. I honestly don't know how long I would have lasted in school if I had gone full-time. As much as I have reason to look back and regret aspects of my life, I feel very lucky that I had the opportunities I did. In many ways, my childhood dreams really saved my life.

3

SKY'S THE LIMIT!

MY DREAM OF BEING ON TV was quickly becoming a reality. One of the biggest national commercials I got was for this brand of margarine called Parkay. They had a famous ad campaign in the late '70s and all through the '80s, with a talking tub of Parkay. I was in one of their earliest commercials. I can still remember it. There was a white kid with glasses, and then there was me, and we were sitting next to each other with this container of Parkay in front of us.

The lid on the Parkay tub lifted, and this voice said, "Parkay."

"Did you say that?" I asked the other kid.

"I didn't say that," the other kid said.

"Yes, you did." I said.

I always booked a lot of commercials. After that, I did a couple of McDonald's commercials. I did milk commercials. I did a Manwich commercial. I would say I've probably done forty or fifty commercials in my lifetime, if not more. Even if it was only one line, I was always glad to be working. I was very proud of the fact that I had a job and that I was good at it. I understood that I got paid well for the commercials, but money wasn't a big deal to me. Because my parents were already middle-class, and I already had everything I wanted and needed, my increasing success didn't change our lifestyle at all. My mom put my money away for me, and she was very careful to make sure I didn't get spoiled or think I was better than my siblings or the other neighborhood kids because of it.

It definitely wasn't just a job to me, though. I loved acting. I loved the whole experience of going to the set and collaborating with everyone else on the job. And I loved not having to be at school, dealing with racism and bullies.

Once my commercial career was rolling, I started doing a lot of movies of the week. And then, in 1975, I booked my first role on a television show. It was an episode of *Barney Miller*. I played a kid called Truman Jackson, and I held up Mrs. Miller in the elevator with a pointed stick. They put me in jail with the real criminals to teach me a lesson, which is ironic, given how my life later turned out. Some things we just have to learn firsthand.

I was only on one episode of *Barney Miller*, but one of the show's executive producers, Danny Arnold, decided that I had talent and he was going to help me. I can remember him pulling me aside after I was done shooting the episode.

"I want you to be on a TV show," he said. "And I'm going to find it."

I did a TV pilot called *The Orphan and the Dude* in 1975. I remember I was so excited when I found out that I got the part, and the whole time that we were shooting I couldn't believe I was going to have a regular part on a TV show. But my excitement was short-lived. The pilot aired, but the show never got picked up.

That same year, I was cast in one of many TV movies I did as a child. It was called *The Radical*, and it starred Sissy Spacek and Henry Winkler. Sissy Spacek played this privileged young woman who started fighting for social justice and got caught up with this whole radical scene. I had only a small part, but it was great to work with such established actors, and Sissy Spacek and Henry Winkler both treated me well.

Almost all of the older, experienced actors I worked with over the years were really great to me. They were patient and kind, and I had the chance to learn so much just by watching them. There always has to be an exception, though. In 1976, I got a job on a commercial that had a Bicentennial theme. The basic setup was that there was a kid playing a drum, a kid playing a flute, and a kid carrying a flag, like that famous image of the fife and drum corps from the Revolutionary War. I can't remember for sure anymore, but I think I was playing the drum.

The commercial's star was Henry Fonda, who was a legend. His career had included everything from *The Grapes of Wrath*, which earned him an Academy Award nomination, to *How the West Was Won*. He was also Jane and Peter Fonda's dad.

Well, we shot the commercial up by where the Magic Mountain amusement park used to be, and the hill we were told to walk down was really steep and rough. There were holes everywhere, and cow patties, too. We were doing our best, but we kept stumbling and falling. Henry Fonda was walking behind us, delivering his lines about the Bicentennial. But the director kept making him stop because one of us kids would mess up, or fall down, and we'd have to start all over again.

Finally, Henry Fonda had had enough. He turned around and lost it on us.

"You motherfucking kids," he said. "Goddamn you, get this shit right. I don't want to be here all fucking day."

And then he stormed off.

We were little kids, and we were terrified. So we all started to cry. Our parents got really mad when they saw how upset we were, and they told the producers they were going to take us home unless he came back and apologized. The set was really tense while we waited to see what would happen. But, finally he came back out and walked over to where we were waiting with our parents.

"Sorry," he said. "Sorry."

We were still scared of him, but we managed to get through the commercial after that. I was sure glad when that job was over. Henry Fonda was not a nice man. No matter what kind of a day he was having, or how far this commercial was from the films he did at the height of his career, he should not have cussed at kids.

Experiences like that were rare, though, and I truly loved everything else I did. I was living my dream, and I could not have been happier. It didn't matter to me if I was doing a commercial or a bigger part. I liked them all.

Looking back, I would have to say that one of the most important moments of my acting career came early on, when I was hired for a part in the adaptation of Alex Haley's *Roots*, which aired in 1977. I was eleven years old at the time, and it was a really special experience to find myself working with all of those gifted black actors, such as LeVar Burton, Cicely Tyson, John Amos, George Stanford Brown, and Louis Gossett Jr. I was used to being one of the only blacks on the set, if not the only black on the set. And so it felt amazing to be around all of that black talent while working together on a project that celebrated where we all had come from as a people. The role of Bud was actually one of my biggest challenges as an actor, too, because the way that my character spoke was completely foreign to me. My mother had to teach me how to speak poorly in order to play that part. I got to stretch myself as an actor, and the shoot was a really positive experience all around.

Of course, we didn't know what a huge cultural phenomenon *Roots* was going to be until it aired. It was a different time back then, and it was hard for us to imagine that a miniseries about black people and their experience would even find an audience, let alone be one of the highest-rated miniseries in TV history.

I didn't even really know what slavery was until I did *Roots*. We weren't taught about it in school. This was long before Black History Month and Barack Obama. Blacks and black culture weren't visible in the same way they are today. Growing up, I never thought history contained any black heroes. It wasn't until I was older that I learned how much black Americans have done for our country, and not just in areas such as music and sports, where they receive a lot of recognition now. Blacks have contributed to our culture in so many ways that have transformed how we live. Even with *Roots*, it was hard not to feel like being black was a bad thing, especially with all of the racists I encountered making me think that it was.

Roots had a major impact when it aired, and I definitely think it helped me to gain recognition as an actor. But it didn't change the fact that blacks were still a minority in Hollywood, just like they were everywhere else. I was still one of the only black actors on most of the shows I was doing at the time. I was among the first, if not the first, blacks on *Little House on the Prairie*. That was a great show to do. Michael Landon was one of the nicest people I ever worked with, and he treated me with the utmost respect. But there was always this feeling of being different. I was among the first blacks on *The Waltons*, too, and even though I went on to be a recurring character, that feeling of not quite fitting in stayed with me.

It was exciting to be one of the first, and it certainly helped my career to grow quickly, as I became the go-to young black actor for TV parts in my age range. But it wasn't easy being a minority in the industry, especially at such a young age. It bothers me today when I see shows about blacks in the entertainment business, and my name never seems to be mentioned. It's like no one takes me seriously as an actor because I achieved my greatest success, so far, as a kid, and because I went on to become a tabloid joke by getting into trouble when I was older. No one seems to remember that for years I was one of the only young black actors who was getting roles, and for years I was on everything.

Being overlooked upsets me because I'm so proud of the work I did back then, and because I paid a personal cost for the experience. I can't say that I was ever subjected to overt racism in Hollywood. But I was always aware of being black, of feeling like I had to work even harder than the white actors to prove that I belonged on the set. That's a lot of pressure for a kid, on top of the fact that I wanted to do a good job so I could keep my career going.

My mom and I also noticed little things that weren't quite fair, like my trailer would be the farthest away from where we were shooting. Or during one project, my mom came to find out that the white kid who only had five lines was making more money than I was. Well, she certainly wasn't going to stand for that, not as my manager or my mother. She went to the producers and set them straight.

"How are you going to tell me that my son's the lead in the show, the show's about him, and you're paying this kid three times more than you're paying him?" she said. "You're going to make a change in the contract."

They changed the contract, but that kind of injustice was hard to ignore. And experiences like that added up over the years. Coupled with the racism I was experiencing at school and in my community, these snubs started to eat away at my sense that I had value as a person. The abuse I received from my father wasn't helping any, either. As I began to suffer from a lack of self-respect and self-esteem, I was primed for the problems I experienced later in my life, and these are issues I have struggled with until very recently.

Luckily, my mom was my manager throughout my career. She both stood up for me on the set and always let me know that I was a talented young actor and a special young man who deserved love and respect. I wasn't always able to hear this message, but I would have been in much worse shape if it weren't for her.

No matter what happened at home, or at school, or on the set, or how bad it made me feel about myself, I kept right on working. I loved acting, and I wasn't going to let anything get in the way of the career I had wanted more than anything else since I was five. Suddenly there was more work to do. I was starting to become an in-demand actor, and the parts kept getting better and better.

Danny Arnold kept his word and found me a show. In 1977 they made a spin-off of *Barney Miller* that was called *Fish*. It starred Abe Vigoda as Detective Phil Fish, who was this cranky old police detective. He and his wife, who was played by Florence Stanley, had decided to take in five foster kids. And I was one of those kids. My name was Loomis, and I was this angry little guy. Whenever I'd get mad at Mr. Fish, I'd lock myself in the basement and say, "You're a mean, old white man."

"Oh, come out," Detective Fish would say in this exasperated tone of voice.

I never wanted to come out.

But of course I always did.

And then, on the next episode, we'd go through it all over again.

That was a very exciting time for me. Being on *Fish* was great. I loved acting, and I was thrilled to go to the set every day. *Fish* was soon a top-rated show, and I was starting to get recognized when I went places with my family. That was a lot of fun. Even better, I was starting to have quite a few female fans.

I was still at the age where I was more into riding bikes with my friends than spending time thinking about having a girlfriend or anything like that. But I was definitely starting to notice girls, too. It felt pretty cool having girls my age go nuts when they saw me on the street or at the mall.

My career was really starting to take off. At about that time, my dad met a man who wanted to help us take it even farther. His name was Ronald Rayton, and he was a talented musician and gospel singer who was friendly with the most elite members of black Hollywood. When we first got to know Ronald, he told us that he had recently finished working for the Jacksons, and he introduced my family to Joe Jackson. As I became more in demand, my family was just beginning to move into the world of successful black entertainers. Ronald's connections were desirable, especially for my dad, whose insecurities made him eager to be accepted by the people he admired.

The weird thing about Ronald Rayton, given the impact he ended up having on my life, is that I'm not even sure how he and my dad came to know each other. My mom can't exactly recall, either. She just remembers my dad bringing him back to the house one day during the time I was on *Fish*.

In my own memory, my family met Ronald through the Reverend James Cleveland. And I know that connection would have definitely made an impression on my dad. At that time, the reverend was one of the most successful black gospel musicians and preachers in the world. He led the Southern California Community Choir at the LA New Temple Missionary Baptist Church, which he founded and which grew to thousands of members at the height of his popularity. Many people say the reverend was the first person to give gospel music the pop sound that has made it as big as it's become today.

So the fact that Ronald was a musician who the reverend knew and respected would have meant a lot to my family. Church was an important part of our life when I was growing up. We went to services every Sunday. My mom taught me to believe in a God who loves each and every one of us, and who watches over us at all times. Even during my dark years, when I felt about as far away from God as a person can be, some part of me knew that He still had an eye on me and was keeping me safe. I know I would have been lost without my faith, even if I didn't see the role it was playing in my life during the times I needed it the most.

No matter how we actually did meet him, there's no doubt that Ronald made quite an impression. He was over six feet tall and handsome and a great dresser. He always made an effort to look sharp. Even if he was just coming over to my family's house, he'd be dressed well, in flared trousers and a fitted vest over a tailored shirt. His shoes were always polished to a shine. He was very charismatic, and he charmed everyone.

Ronald wanted to be my publicist, and he made it clear that he had the connections and the know-how to make the most of my growing popularity. He told us he was going to make me an even bigger star than I had become on my own. I liked the sound of that. We were excited to have him take an interest in me. So even though he wasn't working as a publicist for anyone else at that point, we hired him.

Full of ideas and energy, Ronald always had something in the works. He spent a lot of time with my family and me, helping my mom and dad manage my career, and just hanging out at the house. It felt good to be around him. He was funny and he was really good at doing impressions of other people. But what I liked the most about him was that he thought I was special. He told me again and again that he thought I was talented. And he liked to spend time with me.

Ronald was like a dad to me. He gave me all of the affection that I had never received from my own father. I wanted so badly for my dad to be proud of me, or even just to take an interest in me. But my dad just didn't have the capacity to be a good father. Spending time with Ronald quickly became the next best thing. Unlike my dad, Ronald was always up for doing things with me.

My dad's idea of taking my brother and me fishing was to bring us down to the docks near where he was a longshoreman, drop us off there, and then go to the bar to drink with his buddies. He never once picked up a rod and spent the afternoon casting a line with us. He couldn't be bothered.

But Ronald was different. Ronald was more like what I'd always wanted a dad to be. He had this saying "Sky's the limit!" I loved hearing those words from him because he really seemed to believe they were true. He thought I could do anything. So when I was around him, I felt like I could do anything, too. I loved that Ronald went out of his way to make me feel special.

The time I spent with Ronald tends to blend together in my memory. But I do remember him asking me if I wanted to go throw the football around in the yard. He wasn't exactly a natural athlete, but that was one of my favorite things to do, so I was always up for a game with him. A typical afternoon with him would have gone something like this.

Ronald draped an arm around my shoulders and gave my Afro an affectionate rub with his fist while we walked out to the backyard. We smiled at each other and spread out, so we could throw the ball back and forth.

"Does your dad play catch with you?" Ronald asked.

"No, never," I said.

He threw me a pass and smiled at me when I landed it. I beamed back at him, so excited for the attention he was giving me.

"Any time you need someone to be there for you, I'll be there," Ronald said.

I stood with the ball in my arms, taking in what he had just said.

It was exactly the kind of thing I had always wished my dad would say to me instead of yelling at me or slapping me on the back of my head. But if I couldn't get affection from my dad, getting it from Ronald felt pretty good, too.

"Let's see what you've got," Ronald said.

I wanted so badly for Ronald to keep on liking me and wanting to do things with me. In fact, his friendship was as important to me at that point as the things he was doing to help my career. I definitely didn't want to let him down or drive him away. I concentrated hard on launching the best spiral I could throw.

"Sky's the limit!" Ronald said as he caught the ball. "With an arm like that, you could even play for the NFL someday."

When he said it like that, anything seemed possible.

"Go deep," he said as he prepared to throw me a long pass.

I took off running, looking over my shoulder to keep my eye on the ball as he threw it. The football landed in my hands as I skidded to a halt to avoid the wood fence that ringed our yard. Elated, I spiked the ball into the ground and did my best touchdown boogie. Ronald laughed at my dance and scooped up the ball.

"Good game, little man," he said, smacking me on the butt as we went inside.

Ronald used to give me presents, too. One time, he surprised me by buying me a $300 bike. It was the kind of fancy Schwinn cruiser that all of the kids were asking their parents for at the time. I wanted one as much as everyone else did, but my mom wouldn't buy it for me because she thought it was too expensive. Even though I was making good money on *Fish*, she didn't want me to become spoiled. When Ronald showed up at my house with my new bike, I couldn't believe it. Even better, he went outside with me and hung out while I rode it. Once again, he was showing up for me in all of the ways that my dad never did.

Even though I was starting to think of Ronald almost like my new dad, my own father didn't care enough to be jealous of how much time Ronald was spending with me. My dad was impressed with how well connected Ronald was, and he didn't care about anything else. It made my dad feel like a high roller, too.

My dad had decided he wanted to be a talent agent, and he was pushing to make this happen. I think he'd always been jealous of my mother. She was doing really well in Los Angeles, where she was getting regular parts in commercials and on TV, and her career as an actor's manager was taking off. So my dad was determined to make it, too. Ronald thought my dad had a shot and kept encouraging him to open his own agency and represent me. With the major roles I was landing, Ronald figured it would be easy for my dad to get other clients. Ronald promised to bring in big-name clients, too. He kept saying he'd make my dad "the biggest nigga in town." Of course my dad ate that up.

During that whole time, my acting career continued to boom. When we were on hiatus from *Fish*, I kept busy doing more commercials and Movies of the Week. I did one TV movie called *A Killing Affair* with O. J. Simpson. I'm not even making that up. It starred Elizabeth Montgomery and Rosalind Cash, too.

I worked with Rosalind Cash a bunch of times. She always played my mother. Most people probably don't remember her anymore, but she was one of the most successful black TV actresses of her day. She appeared on everything from *Mary Tyler Moore* to *Kojak* at least once, and she was always really nice to me.

It was during this time that I started appearing on *The Waltons*, too. And I even did a guest spot on *The Love Boat*. That was a lot of fun.

While I was on *Fish*, I received an exciting opportunity to expand my career beyond acting, too. One day, my mom got a call from someone at a record label run by Maurice White of Earth, Wind & Fire, which had scored big hits with their songs "Shining Star" and "Reasons." The people at the label had seen me on TV. They thought I was a cute kid, and they were interested in seeing if they could turn me into the next Michael Jackson.

I had grown up listening to my mom practice numbers from the musicals she did back in San Francisco. And I was finding that I had inherited not only her passion for music but also her talent for singing. I was thrilled by the idea of making a record, especially if it meant working with Maurice White.

The deal did happen. I was given a big advance, and I worked with Maurice on a regular basis during that time. I loved it. It was so much fun. I was really excited by the whole experience. We finished the album and even shot the cover art and everything. But it never got released. Maurice had a disagreement with the record label he had his imprint through, and they took everybody's albums and refused to release anything. I was really disappointed, but there was so much else happening in my career that it didn't slow me down for long.

People have always assumed that being a child star was too much pressure at such a young age and that the experience must have screwed me up. But my career was actually a great escape for me, given how much trouble I had in school.

During *Fish*, I went to school on the set, which I liked better than regular school. I didn't have to struggle because of my learning disability and behavior problems, or be on guard in case someone started something with me. I loved being on set, where I felt like I belonged, and I knew I was good at my job. If I hadn't had the chance to channel my emotions into acting, I probably would have gotten expelled from school eventually, and things would have turned out for me a lot worse than they did.

Show business actually saved me in a lot of ways. And no matter how much I was working, I never got tired of acting. I was an actor. That's who I was. To me, acting was more fun than anything else.

As I've said, my mom was my manager, but she wasn't like those stage moms I've run into so many times during my years in the business. She thought it was really important that I had the chance to be a normal kid when I wasn't working. Even though I was starring on a hit TV show, I was like any other boy my age. I played Little League baseball and Pop Warner football and spent a lot of time in my neighborhood.

During the years that I was on *Fish*, my family moved from Culver City to Baldwin Hills, which was an upper-middle-class area on the southwestern side of Los Angeles and which has sometimes been called the black Beverly Hills.

The majority of my friends weren't actors. They were just normal kids who grew up nearby. My three best friends were Juan, Mitch, and Garth, and we were always off on some kind of adventure, riding our bikes to go play pinball or get a soda or ice cream at the store. Our favorite thing to do was to ride up into the mountains near our houses and catch snakes. We got so good at it that we started a business called Snakes, Inc. During that time, my brother and I were always organizing these big street football games on Sunday afternoons, too.

Even when I had an audition, my mom thought it was more important that I had the chance to run around outside and have fun after I had been at school or on the set, than showing up looking totally perfect. She didn't prep me like the other kids I saw on auditions, who were all stiff and done up just so, like these little robots. If my shirt was dirty, my mom didn't care. She figured that's how real kids looked, right? No matter what the part was, I was supposed to be playing a real kid.

I think her approach actually helped me to get a lot of jobs. I looked just like a regular kid, which was what the casting directors wanted. And because auditions didn't seem like that big of a deal to me, I didn't feel any more pressure than other kids did when they were going about their normal school days. Her relaxed attitude also meant that auditions and the acting jobs I landed were fun for me. The same definitely cannot be said for many of the child actors I met over the years.

Although my mom didn't worry about the superficial side of Hollywood, she was a great manager and acting coach. She worked with me to prepare whenever I had an audition or a big day of shooting, and she was always really supportive.

Even when my career took off, all of us kids were considered equal. I was never treated like I was better than anyone else, just because I was starring on *Fish*. My brother and sister were starting to have some success as actors, too. Jimmy did a few episodes of a show called *James at 15* in 1978. Verda also landed regular commercials and parts on different TV movies and shows, including *Charlie's Angels*.

It was a very exciting time for the whole family. It seemed like someone was always going on an audition or a callback. My mom would help us get ready, and we helped each other, too. We often read scripts and rehearsed together.

Usually things were very harmonious around the house, and there was no competition among us kids. My mom had raised us better than that, and we all got along too well to let our careers spoil our friendships. I do remember this one time, though, when my mom was trying to work with Verda on the script for a show she had booked. My mom was trying to get her ready, but she wasn't listening to anything my mom was saying. I watched all of this go down.

"That's probably why I've got a series and you don't," I said. "You're not listening."

I know, I probably sounded like the brattiest little brother ever. But there was no denying the truth. After that, Verda and Jimmy both started listening more. My mom still laughs about that story to this day.

Unfortunately, not everyone in my family was so supportive of my success. My dad had always had a hard time with black men who were better off than he was. Even though I was only twelve at the time, he suddenly started to have a problem with me, too. He honestly got jealous of his own kid, and his anger and frustrations came out in the usual way. He started drinking more, and he started yelling more. It got so bad that my mom and my sister felt the need to become my protectors. If my mom woke up in the morning and saw that my dad was already awake and out of bed, she would jump up and run downstairs. She knew that if my dad was downstairs alone with me for even ten minutes, he was going to hit me.

I can remember so many times when he came down the stairs in the morning, and that was it, he just hauled off and whacked me in the back of the head.

"I didn't do anything," I said. "I didn't do anything."

"It's the way you look at me," he said. "You think you're something because you make all that money."

I didn't even know how much money I was making, and I wouldn't have cared anyhow. What I cared about was my dad's respect. If he had been proud of me, it would have meant more to me than any paycheck or success.

Now that I'm a parent myself, I can see how messed up he must have been to feel competitive toward me like that. I can't imagine being anything but thrilled by my kids' success. I want them to achieve everything they can dream and more. But my dad was a bully, and it wasn't only my budding fame that set him off. Every time he walked into a room, I tensed up and waited for the moment when he would turn on me. I was scared of him. He could go nuts over anything. We had a dog when I was growing up, and one of my chores was to clean the dog poop up from the backyard. I remember, this one time, I hadn't taken care of it like I was supposed to have done. Well, my dad came home at midnight, and when he looked at the backyard, he was just furious. He came storming up to the room my brother and I shared, and he banged open the door and turned on the light.

I was awake in an instant, my heart racing, but it took me a minute to figure out what all the noise was about and why my dad was so mad. He came over to my bed and got right in my face, his breath hot and stinking of booze.

"I-told-you-to-clean-up-that-yard, Todd," he said.

"I didn't get to it," I said.

"I-don't-care-who-you-think-you-are-you've-got-to-learn-to-show-me-some-respect," he said.

He dragged me out of bed, and he made me go downstairs to take care of it.

There was no talking sense to my dad when he was like that. I learned the hard way that there was no standing up to him, either. One time, when I was about nine or ten, he was hitting me on the back of the head, and I finally got tired of it. I balled up my fist, and I held it right in his face.

"You're not going to hit me anymore," I said.

He hit me even harder, right in the middle of my chest. He knocked the wind right out of me and nearly caved my chest in. It really scared me, and I didn't talk back to him again after that.

At the same time that my show business career made my dad more abusive because of how jealous he felt, it also took my mom and me out of the house, which actually saved us from a lot of abuse. When we were anywhere in his line of vision, there was no telling what reason he would come up with to yell, or hit, or both. He'd always find something we'd done wrong, or some way we had disrespected him. But once I was starring on *Fish*, I was working five days a week. As long as we were at the studio, we were free from his abuse. It was such a relief.

4

HOLLYWOOD TEEN

THOSE WERE THE DAYS when teenage girls loved to read magazines such as *16*, *Teen Beat*, *Tiger Beat*, and *Right On!*, which was a favorite with black teens. All were filled with pictures of and stories about their favorite teen idols. Many of these young stars had gotten famous by appearing on the day's popular television shows. It seemed like every show had a lead actor the girls totally loved. And since *Fish* was one of the top-rated shows on television, I was becoming a teen idol myself. Not only that, but I was one of the only black teen idols at that time. I had adoring female fans of all races. It was weird at first, having girls scream when they saw me at the mall or on the street, and having both kids and adults come up and ask for my autograph or tell me how much they loved the show. But I started to like the attention, especially from the girls. What teenage boy wouldn't?

I was asked to be a part of this traveling talent show called the Hollywood Teen Tour, which featured some of the hottest young entertainers of the day. The group included Scott Baio, who had made a name for himself even before landing his most famous role as Chachi on *Happy Days*, when he starred in this kids' gangster film *Bugsy Malone* in 1976. It also featured Lou Ferrigno, otherwise known as the Incredible Hulk, and Willie Aames, who was Tommy on *Eight Is Enough*.

We toured across America on and off for three years, flying to different cities on weekends and when our television shows were on hiatus. My mom always traveled with me, and we loved it when the Hollywood Teens took off for a few days, because we didn't have to worry about my dad hitting us or being nasty. We'd sit there on the airplane or in our hotel and say, "This sure is peaceful, huh?"

The guys on the tour with me varied from year to year, but Scott Baio was always involved, and we became close friends. The whole group of us would make appearances at malls and amusement parks, and packs of teenage girls would crowd around us, screaming and trying to rip off our clothes. Nice work if you can get it. As you can imagine, we were in heaven. I was only twelve when we first started doing the show, but that was plenty old enough to appreciate the attention. The rest of the guys were about sixteen or seventeen.

We all had a talent in the show. Mine was singing and dancing. I performed "Greased Lightnin'," from *Grease*. I would get up on the stage and sing.

"Greased Lightnin',
Go Greased Lightnin'."

I danced while I sang, doing all of the moves from the number that had been choreographed for John Travolta in the film. Now, I don't want to hurt anybody's feelings, but I have to be honest about this: I was always the best dancer out of everyone. Scott Baio was my very good friend, and we still talk to this day. But it must be said: He was a horrible dancer. Sorry, Scott.

Scott and I always had fun when we traveled together. Even though we were acting on hit shows, making good money, and getting attention from female fans, we were really just teenage boys. We loved nothing more than to goof off. As soon as we got to the airport, we'd find ourselves some wheelchairs and kill time until our flight by racing up and down the length of the terminal. We figured out how to get on the intercom, so we could be heard everywhere across the whole airport. We used to say all sorts of silly things, but this was one of our favorite announcements to make: "Paging Me Off. Last name, Me Off. First name, Jack. Paging Me Off. Paging Jack Me Off." We could barely get the words out, we were laughing so hard. We thought that was hilarious.

It wasn't all fun and games, though. This was the mid-'70s, and the country was still very much divided by race. There still weren't many successful blacks in any arena, and I was one of only a few popular black entertainers at the time. Other than Michael Jackson, I was the only black teen idol. This made me especially popular in black households. There were plenty of girls of all races who showed up and screamed my name at my appearances. But the more popular I got, the more it opened me up to attacks from people who had a real problem with seeing a black kid get famous and rich. There were plenty of them out there. Like when I experienced racism for the first time in Los Angeles, it was hard for me to understand how my skin color could upset people that much and make them be so cruel to me. I may not have understood, but I was definitely affected by it.

All of this, both the good and the bad, was a lot to handle at an age when most kids weren't dealing with anything more complicated than their paper routes and first dates. On the one hand, I got a lot of special treatment because I was a popular actor. Even though my mom made sure I didn't get too full of myself, it was hard not to feel different from other kids my age. I was on television, just like my idol Redd Foxx was. I didn't know exactly how much money I was making, but I knew it was a lot. People did things for me and took care of me when I was on the set or making a public appearance. I knew there was something special about me.

On the other hand, I was a symbol of something dangerous for a lot of racist people who didn't want to see blacks in our country get too uppity or expect too much in the way of equality. They couldn't stand the thought that this little black kid was making more money than they were. I heard some pretty nasty things. It didn't happen everywhere we went, but it happened a lot in the South and the Midwest, and it always went something like this.

I'd be onstage with the Hollywood Teens, and we'd all be having fun, playing off each other and getting amped up by the crowd's energy. When it was my turn to sing "Grease Lightning," I held my mic loosely in my hand and bounded up to the front of the stage, feeling cool and confident. I was getting paid to do what I loved most in the world, and I was good at it. As soon as I got close to the audience, all of these girls started screaming my name and reaching out for me, trying to rip off a piece of my clothing, or even just to touch my leg or my hand. I started singing, and then they really went crazy. I could see every different kind of girl in the crowd—some black girls and Asian girls and Latino girls—but they were mostly white girls. It wasn't a big deal to me that white girls thought I was cute. I didn't see people in terms of their skin color, and it didn't seem like most of them did, either. Not that girls couldn't be racist, but when race came up at school or in my neighborhood, it was mostly boys who got in my face about it, because they knew it was a taunt that would start a fight. But a lot of kids my age made friends with and dated people of all different races. We were a new generation, and most of the girls didn't seem to care that I was black, any more than I cared if a girl I had a crush on happened to be black or white or Asian. But, of course, not everyone was so open-minded, and a lot of white guys did not like it when their girls got excited about a black guy.

I felt amazing, being up onstage, dancing and singing and basking in all of that attention. I launched into the next verse and raised my arm, moving it across the front of my body and pointing at the girls in the front row, just like John Travolta did in the movie. They screamed louder, and the sound made my smile even bigger. I was about to bring it on home with the song's big finale.

"Get off the stage, nigger!" a man's voice boomed out from the crowd.

It was like the air got knocked out of me. I was up onstage, and there was nowhere to hide, and all I could think was that everyone was looking at me and thinking I was nothing but a nigger. It crushed me. In an instant, I went from being proud of myself to hating myself because my skin color made people think I wasn't good enough to be performing, or even to be alive. I wanted to run far away from all these people so I wouldn't have to be judged and hated. And then I got angry. As I've already said, it didn't take much to set me off back then, and I wanted nothing more than to storm off the stage and beat that racist loudmouth to a pulp. But, of course, I couldn't do any of these things. I was a professional. I had to keep dancing and singing and, hardest of all, keep smiling. We all pretended like nothing had happened when I got offstage, but it really shook me up.

Being heckled wasn't even the worst instance of racism that occurred during the Hollywood Teens tours. I learned about this next incident only a few years ago. Scott Baio knew the whole story, but he never told me what happened because he was my very good friend, and he didn't want to upset me. I wouldn't have had any reason to remember the night otherwise, because it was like any other we experienced on tour. We had done a show in Alabama, and Scott and I were hanging out in my hotel room afterward. We were sitting on the beds, watching TV and goofing around, talking about bikes, and girls, and music, and whatever else we were into back then. The phone rang, and Scott was closer to it, so he answered. He put the receiver to his ear, and then he got this weird, scared look on his face, and he slammed down the receiver without saying anything.

"I've got to go," he said to me. And he left.

I didn't understand why he was acting so odd, but I didn't think much about it beyond that. Finally, a few years ago, Scott and I were talking about the old days. He told me that when he picked up the receiver, there was a man on the other end.

"This is the Ku Klux Klan," the man said. "Give me that nigger, Todd Bridges."

Imagine that, a grown man calling to harass and terrify a teen-age boy. It's probably a good thing that Scott didn't tell me what happened at that time. I would have been one more reason for me to begin hating the world in which we lived and the skin in which I lived in it. And I would already struggle with more than enough anger in the years to come.

I may have been among a minority population, both in Holly-wood and beyond, but the black entertainers of the day had their own little world. Within that world, we were very supportive of each other. From a very early age, I was encouraged and championed by many of the day's most revered black actors.

But no one ever took more of a shine to me than Sammy Davis Jr. From very early on in my career, I had heard that he was a fan of my work. Everyone always said that if I ever ran into Sammy Davis Jr., he was going to cook for me.

Well, I finally got to meet him and experience his hospitality firsthand while I was traveling with the Hollywood Teens. We were in Detroit and Sammy found out that I was staying at the same hotel as he was.

He told the people at the check-in, "When you see Todd Bridges, I want you to tell him that I want him to come up to my room."

When we came back from the appearance we had done, I had this amazing message from Sammy Davis Jr. waiting for me. Of course, when the other people in our group heard the name Sammy Davis Jr., they all wanted to meet him, too. My mom had the hotel clerk call up to Sammy's room and ask him if all of the Hollywood Teens could come by to say hello.

He was such a nice man. He invited us up to his room, just like that. I was a little nervous as we rode up in the elevator and walked down the hallway to his room. And then, before I knew it, I was standing right in front of him, and he was smiling at me. How could I not be impressed when I met him? He was Sammy.

He was incredibly gracious when he was introduced to all of us. And then it got even better. It was Sammy and me, talking together like old friends. He looked right at me, and I tried to keep my cool while wondering what he was going to say.

"Young man," he said, "do you know I have a copy of everything you've ever done? You are one of the finest young actors I have ever seen."

It was pretty much the greatest compliment I've ever received in my life.

Sammy invited all of the Hollywood Teens to a Fourth of July party at his house in Detroit, and my mom and Lou Ferrigno and I went. I had never seen anything like his house before. It was huge and really fancy. He cooked some of the best BBQ I've ever eaten. Then he took me down to his basement, where he had a full-size home theater. He showed me this whole wall of movies—that was back when BETA tapes had just come out, before VHS, and way before DVDs—and he pointed out that he had everything I'd ever done. Not many people had access to this technology yet, so I was impressed that his industry connections had allowed him to gain use of it. He had taped every episode of *The Waltons*, every TV movie I'd had even the smallest part in, every episode of *Fish*. It was one of the best moments in my career.

For me, the greatest honor I could imagine was having my heroes, the people I had watched on television and in the movies, back when I was just dreaming of being a star, welcome me as one of their own. By the time *Fish* was well into its first season in 1977, there wasn't a black entertainer who was in my league who I hadn't worked with or didn't know personally.

I'm so glad it's more equal in Hollywood today, and that blacks and whites mix more freely, especially since my son Spencir is starting to build his own career, and I don't want him to ever have to think about the color of his skin. But the downside is that we've forgotten our sense of unity as a people. I think this change really came to pass when we lost all of the members of the old establishment—people such as Sammy Davis Jr. and Redd Foxx, who had so graciously welcomed and encouraged the performers below them. When they passed away, no one stepped in to take their place. We stopped looking out for each other, and that's a shame. I think it's also prevented us from rising as high as we could in the industry because we don't have the same insider network that the whites do, and we're more likely to be competing for a job than to be creating work for each other. I hope this can change, though, and that we can start to be more aware of our group identity and power.

During that first season of *Fish*, I was traveling a lot, performing with the Hollywood Teens, and often working on several projects at once. Ronald was still working as my publicist, and he had promised us that he could capitalize on my growing popularity by booking public appearances that would earn me a lot of money. He landed me an autograph-signing gig at Tower Records, and he told my father they would pay $1,000. He didn't exactly live up to his promise on that one. He actually exceeded it. He got us a deal for $2,000. My father measured everything in terms of money, so he liked Ronald even more after that.

Ronald booked me a lot of appearances at Tower Records and other record shops in Los Angeles and the neighboring San Fernando Valley in 1977, so they've all sort of run together in my mind. But they usually went down something like this. We rode to the record store together in a big black limousine. Ronald was well dressed, as always, in a white suit and black-framed sunglasses like those worn by all of the coolest cats from Motown. I was looking good, too, in my flared jeans and Nikes. And I was feeling good. I was starting to get used to having fans who wanted to meet me. I had fun when I got to do appearances, especially when Ronald was with me. He always made me feel like I deserved special treatment because of how exceptional I was.

When we pulled up outside the record store, an interracial pack of female fans swarmed the car and began shrieking. Ronald kept close by me as I hurried into the store and sat down behind the table that was set up for my signing. It was unbelievable. The line stretched out the door, onto the sidewalk, and into the parking lot. Some of these girls were going crazy.

Ronald stood close behind me, keeping an eye on everything. By the time all of the girls had gotten their autographs signed and headed back out into the sunny afternoon, my hand was cramped, and I was feeling woozy from the marker fumes. But it was definitely not a bad way to spend a Saturday afternoon. It was certainly a lot better than being at home doing chores. Yes, I still did chores.

When the signing ended, Ronald led me back out to the limo. As we were about to reach the waiting car, a handful of girls came out from behind it. One of the girls, who had a cute face but was on the heavier side, rushed straight for me. I started to back away. Ronald stepped between us and pushed me into the limo before climbing in behind me. As he closed the door, our chauffeur drove away and left a small crowd of girls waving their arms behind us.

"You okay, Todd?" Ronald asked me. He was watching me closely.

"Yeah, I'm good," I said. "Thanks for saving my life. Not to be mean, but that girl could have crushed me."

Ronald and I laughed at that one.

"Well, you handled yourself very well today," he said. "I'm proud of you."

I loved hearing that. It was something my dad had never said to me.

"It was fun," I said. "And some of those girls were fine."

I was just starting to get into girls, and it still made me feel kind of weird to talk about it out loud, so I looked down at the floor as I said this.

"What do you know about girls being fine?" he said in a teasing voice.

I smiled with embarrassment, feeling even shier. Ronald laughed harder.

"I don't know," I said.

"Aw, man, don't tell me you're going girl-crazy on me," he said. He was giving me a really intense look. I felt nervous, and I wasn't sure why.

"Nah, it's just that some of them were cute, is all," I said.

"Well, let me tell you," he said. "Girls are not what it's made up to be."

"What do you mean?"

"I mean you shouldn't get carried away with all that," he said. "You're becoming quite a young star. You should enjoy yourself."

I nodded at him. I loved having these conversations with Ronald. It felt so good to have someone I could talk to about this stuff. My brother, Jimmy, was my best friend. But he was five years older than I was, and suddenly that age gap meant a lot more than it had in the past. When he went on his first dates, I wanted to go with him, like I'd gone everywhere with him my whole life. He had to make my mom explain why it wouldn't be right for me to tag along. I can't say I totally got it, even after that. Since Jimmy was already dating, and I didn't want to look stupid by admitting how much I didn't know about girls, I didn't talk to him much about my newfound interest. But I felt like I could tell Ronald anything. And because he was older, and he knew so much about everything, I believed anything he told me.

"Let me tell you something else," he said. "You can get the same feeling from boys that you can from girls."

"Really?" I asked. I didn't know what to make of this. When one of the girls had brushed up against me at the autograph signing, I had felt excited. But I never felt that way if a guy touched me when we were playing football.

"It's just all about feeling good," Ronald said.

I wasn't sure what he meant by that, but I felt weird, so I didn't ask.

Ronald was always really good at giving me attention and encouragement. But then, after about six months, when I had come to think of him not only as the publicist who was helping me to achieve my dreams, but also as one of my best friends, he started saying other things. He would point out how my parents didn't care about me as much as he did. After he gave me my new bike, he made sure to remind me how expensive it was and how lucky I was that he had given it to me.

"Your mom wouldn't buy you that bike," he said. "But I got you that bike."

I loved that bike. It meant a lot to me that he had bought it for me. And I knew that what he had said about my mom was true. I started to wonder if maybe he was right; that he did care about me more than my own parents did, even my mom.

Or when we were alone, he'd say things about my dad.

"Your dad's too hard on you," he said. "I'm not hard on you like he is."

Well, that was definitely true.

Then he started making me afraid that he might leave me.

"No other publicist will take you because you're black," he said. "But I'm black, too, so I'll work with you."

As he liked to remind me, if he decided to stop working with me, I wouldn't have anyone who cared about me, not like he did, and I certainly didn't want that.

5

EVERYTHING CHANGES

ONE DAY, Ronald was driving me home from an autograph signing at a record store in the San Fernando Valley. He had a big Cadillac with one of those long bench seats. We were sitting side by side, kind of close to each other. He pulled the car over on a quiet side street without any traffic and looked at me with that intense look I was starting to recognize from past conversations.

"I'm telling you, it can be the same with boys as it is with girls," he said, watching me closely. "If you just try it, you'll like it."

"I don't know," I said, looking out the window. I suddenly wished I was at home in the kitchen, eating Jell-O with my mom, or riding bikes with my brother. I didn't know what to think about what he'd just said. I'd recently turned twelve, and I wasn't even sure it was possible for me to feel good in the way he described.

"Believe me, you'll like the feeling," he said. "It feels better than anything else in the whole world."

I have to admit that I was curious. And obviously I really liked Ronald and wanted to make him happy. Even more than that, I didn't want to disappoint him. He had done so much for me. I didn't want him to go away, like he had said he might. Then the autograph signings and special appearances would go away. He wouldn't be there to ride bikes and play football, or tell me he was proud of me.

"Come on, Todd," he said. "You'll like it. I promise."

Ronald put his hand over my crotch. I squeezed my legs together and looked at him, still unsure.

He smiled at me like he had so many times before.

But he looked different to me now.

"You trust me, right?" he asked.

"Yeah," I said. I did trust him. But I felt weird and a little scared, too.

"I want to show you that a man's mouth can feel just the same as a woman," he said. "There's no difference."

He was watching me closely. He looked excited. But I still couldn't understand why, or what was happening.

"Pull your pants down," he said.

I didn't want to lose everything he had given me. And so I did.

He put his mouth on me. I got hard. I didn't know where to look or how to feel. I squirmed against the back of the seat. He kept on going, getting into it.

I hoped it would be over fast.

Then it happened. I came.

As confused and upset as I was, I liked the feeling. I didn't think about whether it was wrong that a man had done that to me. I held on to the fact that it felt good. In the moment of pleasure, I had forgotten about everything stressful and upsetting in my life, about

Ronald, and my dad, and the kids at school who wanted to fight me, and the people out in the world who called me a nigger. The feeling was a way to avoid all of the bad things in my life, this latest bad thing now included. From that moment on, sex became one of the escapes I turned to throughout my life; I wanted to block out the pain I felt inside me, and so I wanted as much as I could get of anything that would help to make me numb.

I didn't know what to say or how to look. I pulled my pants back up. Ronald smiled at me just like it was any other day, and we were hanging out like normal.

"You okay?" he asked, rubbing my thigh.

"I guess," I whispered, still not wanting to look at him.

As we pulled up in front of my house, I wanted to be out of his car and away from him as quickly as possible. I was already gripping the door handle. Ronald put his hand on my shoulder before I could climb out of the car.

"Remember, Todd, this is our secret, right?" he said.

I didn't say anything.

"You've got another autograph signing in Agoura Hills next weekend," he said. "I already told your mom that I can take you. We'll have fun, right?"

He extended his clenched fist to give me a pound. I didn't know what else to do, so I pounded him back. Then I slid out of the car and ran into the house, slamming the front door behind me as hard as I could.

I was nervous around Ronald after that because I never knew if he was going to do that to me again. But he acted as if everything was normal—better than normal, even. But things were far from fine for me. No one had ever talked to me about sex before. They definitely hadn't told me anything about what Ronald had done to me. But somehow I knew it was wrong for a man to do that to a boy. And the thought that I had done something wrong, without even meaning to, made me scared.

I was really confused, too, because having an orgasm had felt good. I wanted to feel that way again, but I also felt guilty about my desire. I didn't think I wanted it to happen with Ronald again, because I had felt so weird while he was doing it to me. But I wasn't totally sure. Maybe he was the only person who could make me feel that way. No one else had ever made me feel that way before.

I was so afraid that my mom and dad would find out because I didn't know how they'd react. Maybe they'd be mad at me, or maybe they'd be disgusted. I didn't want anyone else to know, either, because I didn't want people to think I was gay. It was a much less tolerant world back then, and I was afraid that if the kids in my neighborhood found out, they would think I was some kind of a freak and make fun of me. Or, what if no one believed me, and they all thought I was lying? My mom had taught me that lying was wrong. I already felt bad enough about it as it was.

Mostly I tried not to think about what Ronald had done to me. Luckily, I was working a lot during that time. Nothing made forgetting easier than going to work and pretending to be someone else for a few hours.

When the second season of *Fish* came to an end, Abe Vigoda demanded more money to do a third season. Back then, the producers had full control, and they didn't go for that kind of behavior. It wasn't like in recent years, when the actors on shows such as *Friends* and *Seinfeld* were able to demand $1 million an episode. But in 1978, if the producers didn't want to pay, they pulled the plug. And so the final episode of *Fish* aired in June 1978, right after my thirteenth birthday.

I had really liked doing *Fish*, but I wasn't worried when it got canceled. By that time I always seemed to be working. I quickly landed interviews for two great parts: *The Mickey Mouse Club*, which was an established hit at that point, and *The Mork and Mindy Show*, which was shooting its pilot. The original concept for *Mork and Mindy* was that the show would be called *Mork from Ork*. It was going to focus on Mork, an extraterrestrial being who had come to Earth and was living in this black kid's attic. That seemed like a big part to get, and I was really excited about the audition.

After the last episode of *Fish* aired, I went on vacation with my family. We were on a cruise ship when my mom got a shore-to-ship call from my agent.

"As soon as you get back from vacation, you and Todd have got to go to NBC Studios," she said. "The very next day. They want to see Todd."

When we got home from vacation, the script for the first episode of *Diff'rent Strokes* was waiting for me. My mom worked with me on it that night, just like it was any other audition. The next day, we went straight to NBC. They had already lined up Conrad Bain, who played my adoptive father, Philip Drummond, on the show. And they had cast Gary Coleman as Arnold Jackson. The show's story line was that Philip Drummond was a rich businessman living in Manhattan who adopted the child of his African-American maid when she died. But Conrad felt that the show wouldn't work unless there was an older brother, too. And they needed an actor to play the older brother, Willis Jackson.

Barbara Biglioti, who worked at NBC, knew that *Fish* had just been canceled and that I was available, so she pushed for me to get the part. They had already shot a pilot for an earlier version of the show without me, but no one had been happy with it. When they finally brought me in, something about the three of us together in those roles just worked, and it was on. They didn't even reshoot the pilot. We just went in and performed scenes from the script at a meeting. When the network saw us do this twenty-minute presentation from the pilot script, they bought twenty-six episodes right then and there. That never happened in TV production. From the beginning, there was something special about that show.

The producers of *Mork and Mindy* ended up changing their concept to the show that everyone came to know and love. And the black character I had auditioned for was only in about ten episodes. So looking back, I'm glad I chose *Diff'rent Strokes*. But at the time there was no way to know what would be a hit and what wouldn't. I was only thirteen years old, and I went with the part of Willis because I wanted to be an older brother.

I did feel like Gary Coleman's older brother in the beginning. He was three years younger than I was, and he was totally unseasoned as an actor. That's what made the show great. He was so cute and funny that people just loved him immediately. Even though he was still learning how to deliver a joke, he was surrounded by all of these veteran actors who knew how to be his straight man.

After NBC bought the first season, we interviewed actresses to play the part of Kimberly Drummond, my adoptive sister on the show. As soon as I met Dana Plato, I knew she was the girl. She was so bubbly and alive and fun. Plus she was cute, which definitely mattered to me at thirteen. Of course, she got the role, and I don't think anyone could imagine the show without her.

The first episode of *Diff'rent Strokes* aired on November 3, 1978. We shot an episode every week. We rehearsed Monday through Wednesday, and then we'd do a run-through with cameras on Thursday and tape in front of a live studio audience on Friday. *Fish* had been filmed in front of a live studio audience, too, so I wasn't nervous about performing in front of a crowd. In fact, I liked it.

We filmed at MetroMedia on Sunset Boulevard, so we were right in the middle of Hollywood. Many shows filmed on the same lot, so

I got to know the actors from *Silver Spoons*, *The Jeffersons*, *One Day at a Time*, *The Facts of Life*, and, most exciting for me, the show that first inspired me to be an actor, *Sanford and Son*.

The mood on the set was really great. Conrad was the sweetest man in the world. From the very beginning, he was like a father to me. He was always very caring and supportive, which, of course, was really important to me, especially at that point in my life. It was such a relief to be around a kind, generous man who wanted nothing from me and who did nothing but love and nurture me.

Gary and I had a great time together, too. He was really intelligent, I think because he had been around adults his whole life. He was born with nephritis, a congenital kidney disease, which stunted his growth and required him to receive daily dialysis on the set, in spite of kidney transplants in 1973 and 1984. I don't know if it was because of this, but his parents never let him play with other kids, so he was advanced for his age. Gary and I spent a lot of time together during the first two years we worked on the show. We were always playing. We'd build these big cardboard houses on the set, with all of these rooms that were connected to each other. If the people on the set were looking for us to rehearse a scene, they'd have to climb through all of the cardboard and figure out where we were.

We loved to play tricks on people, too. One of the best pranks we ever pulled was on Gerren Keith, who directed me on the show for a good eight years. It seemed like everyone used to smoke cigarettes on the set back then, and he always had a lit cigarette in his hand. Well, I went to a magic store and bought some of those little triggers you put into cigarettes to make them blow up. Gary and I would take turns distracting him, and we'd shove one of those into every one of his cigarettes. So he'd be smoking, and all of the sudden, "Pow!" It would blow up and really scare him.

Gary and I would start laughing like crazy.

And he'd go, "You kids."

But he never really got mad at us. In fact, he ended up quitting smoking in the end. He was at home one night, and he had a pack of cigarettes he thought was safe. But we had gotten to that one, too, and when a cigarette blew up on him, he was like, "That's it, I quit."

And he did.

Gerren and I still get together and laugh about those days. He's another person who was like a father to me. I feel so lucky that I had a few people in my life, like him and Conrad, who could do a little to counterbalance all the bad that was happening to me elsewhere. I can imagine how much worse off I would have been without them, and I'm sure it would have gotten even uglier than it eventually did.

For the most part, the whole crew was like one big family. Everyone was great, down to the wardrobe and makeup people. During the first season, though, there were two problems that had to be handled. I think the first one says something about how few black actors there were in TV then. The hairdresser we had when the show started did not know how to do black hair at all. My mom would come into the makeup area and see the woman just sort of patting my hair, or Gary's hair.

"No, you've got to put the pick in there and pull it up," my mom told her.

But that lady saw the kinks in our hair, and it was like she did not even want to touch it. She had no idea what to do. We had to have her replaced with a black hairdresser named Joanne Chainley, who knew how to do black hair. Joanne did a great job on everyone's hair, black and white, for the rest of the show's run.

Unfortunately, the second problem was much more serious. One of the producers the first season was this man named Herbert Kenwith. He loved to make Dana and me feel like dogs. He had been in the industry for a long time, so you would think he would have been more professional than that. He had even directed my mom in an episode of *Good Times*. But he was nothing but trouble on the set of *Diff'rent Strokes*. He would sit Gary in his lap and fawn all over him.

"See, you're a good actor," he said to Gary. "Those little brats, they can't act their way out of a paper bag."

He would look right at Dana and me while he was saying it.

One time he was so nasty to me that I ran off the set and out onto the lot. My mom happened to come by to see me, and she found me standing outside in the rain, crying. She asked me what was wrong, and I told her how mean he was. She went right in there and chewed him out left and right.

"You do not hurt my child," she said. "You do not do that. That's one thing I am not going to tolerate."

She was so mad that she called Alan Horn, who was the producer in charge of the show. I don't know how it all went down, but Herbert did not come back for the second season. I think Conrad had him fired because he was upsetting us kids or our parents said we weren't coming back if he stayed.

Other than that, everything else was great. Not only was the show fun to work on, but it was clear from the beginning that it was going to be a hit. It had something for everyone. Gary was the little comedian. I was the one the girls liked. And the guys all liked Dana.

More than that, though, the story line about a white family who adopted two little black kids was something people had never seen before. It's true that *Fish* had a mixed-race cast, too. But *Diff'rent Strokes* was something new. It was a comedy, but it wasn't just about laughs. For the first time on television, black characters were seen telling a white character they loved him. Even more important, for one of the first times on television, black characters were presented as the equals of white characters.

The show became popular with both black and white audiences. That meant that a lot of people were watching it every week. We were soon at no. 27 in the Nielsen ratings.

Not everyone was ready for the races to mix so freely, though. We got a lot of nasty letters, and even some death threats. People used to write Conrad letters that said things like, "Why are you hugging those niggers?" We also got letters from black people that said, "Why are you hugging those white people?"

When the show became a hit, I started getting recognized more frequently, but this wasn't always a good thing. One day I was on my way somewhere with my mom, and we stopped at a store in a suburb of Los Angeles. When we walked in, the woman who worked there started screaming at me.

"What's wrong?" my mom asked her.

"He's always coming in here, stealing from me," the woman said.

At first I felt nervous, like I was going to get in trouble. Of course, I'd never been in that store, or that town, before in my life. But the woman was really mad, and it was hard not to be affected by having her yell at me. Luckily, my mom was not the type of person to stand for someone talking to her son like that.

"Ma'am, you're not recognizing him from coming in here," my mom said. "This is the first time we've ever even been over here. You recognize him from television."

The woman looked at me more closely. But she wasn't convinced.

"Well, who is he?" she asked.

"Have you ever seen the kid from *Diff'rent Strokes*?" my mom said. "Willis."

"Oh, my God, it *is* Willis," the woman said.

After that, she couldn't have been nicer to me. But it definitely upset me. When a woman thought a black kid looked familiar, her first thought was that I had come in the day before and done something bad, not that she might recognize me for a positive reason. I'm sure the idea that I was a successful actor could not have been farther from her mind. As I said, being famous was fun, but it also meant that I had to deal with a lot of stuff that was pretty complicated for a kid my age.

All of a sudden, though, plenty of people knew exactly who I was when they saw me on the street. This was way beyond anything I had experienced during *Fish*. I became way more famous than I had been before, and the girls got a lot crazier. I couldn't go anywhere. If I went to the mall, I got mobbed. All of the girls started chasing me, and parents brought their kids up to ask me for autographs. I couldn't do anything by myself anymore. It was just too crazy.

I even had my own fan club. That was a pretty strange concept for a kid to handle. But again, my mom made sure I never got too full of myself. She made me read all of the letters I received and write back little notes to send out with my signed headshots. To this day, people still come up to me and tell me they were in my fan club. I feel very lucky that my mom raised me to be polite, so even when I was just a kid, I always treated people well when they came up to talk to me. The good manners I displayed during this time would later change my life forever. But I wouldn't know that for many years.

When I was asked to do appearances, which was happening more and more often, my mom or Ronald would always go with me. It was at one of these events that I knew things had really changed. I was doing a parade in Watts, and Kim Fields, who played Tootie on *The Facts of Life*, was sitting next to me on the float. All of the sudden, this girl came out of the crowd and ran right up to Kim.

"You're sitting next to my boyfriend," she said.

She punched Kim in the eye.

Kim started to cry. I'm sure it hurt a lot.

It only got crazier.

I went to Chicago to do the Bud Billiken Parade, which is held on the second Saturday in August every year as a way to celebrate African-American pride and unity. After the parade was over, my mom and I were getting into the limo when a bunch of female fans tried to pull me out of there. They had literally grabbed onto the upper half of my body and managed to drag me out of the car. My mom had to grab my foot and pull me back in, but even then, we almost couldn't get the door closed. The whole time, my heart was just hammering in my chest. I liked getting attention from girls, but that was scary.

When the limo finally got us out of there, we stopped at a restaurant on the way to the airport. The restaurant was empty except for this one little girl. Well, she must have seen me and run out to tell her friends. The restaurant was right near the Cabrini-Green housing project, and I guess a Todd Bridges sighting was big news. The next thing we knew, the waitress came over to warn us.

"You guys are not going to be able to get out of here," she said.

"Why?" my mom asked.

"Go look out the front," she said.

People were literally stacked on top of each other, and the glass at the front of the restaurant was covered from top to bottom.

"How are we going to get out?" my mom asked.

"We've got to call the police and get them to help us get you out," she said.

So they called the police and told them that Todd Bridges was visiting Chicago and needed to get to his limo so he could leave. The police came and locked arms with each other, forming a double line to keep the crowd back so we could reach the limo. My mom and I got between the cops and dashed out to the car. But it was total insanity. My adrenaline was racing even higher by this point. Even though I knew my fans were just showing their affection, it felt like we were being attacked. I couldn't believe what I was seeing. The police weren't able to keep order, and people kept breaking though and grabbing me.

Girls were shouting, "I love you, Todd."

"I love you, Todd."

"I love you, Todd."

When we finally got into the limousine, the car was completely stuck. The people were not only blocking the way, but they also had climbed onto the limousine, and they were covering the windows. They were waving and shouting, "Hi, Todd! Hi, Todd!"

"Hi, Todd!"

"I love you, Todd."

"Hi, Todd!"

The driver couldn't even see to drive. Finally, the police pulled everyone off. Even then, we had to inch along, making sure the driver didn't run anybody over. Those fans did not care. They were ready to risk life and limb.

We finally made it to the airport, and by this point we were really ready to get out of there. My mom and I were walking to the airplane when we heard this sound behind us. It was low and rumbling, like thunder. I'm not exaggerating. When we turned around, we saw all these girls just charging right at us. They actually knocked my mom down onto the ground. She had a soda in her hand, which went all over her. I had on this silver lamé jacket, which was the look everyone was into back then, and they tore that thing to shreds. I was wearing a gold necklace, and somebody tore that off of my neck, too. I was starting to get freaked out. Luckily, we were near the gate, and some people from the airline were able to hurry us onto the plane. By the time we settled into our seats, I had to sit and catch my breath.

"Wow, Mom, those people tried to kill you," I said.

"They love you, Todd," she said. "That's why they're acting crazy like that."

My mom always traveled with me when I made out-of-town appearances. But she had other clients, too, who kept her busy, plus my brother and sister, and so sometimes she wasn't available to take me places. And because I had been too afraid to tell my parents what Ronald had done to me, he was still my publicist.

When I had to do appearances in the Los Angeles area, Ronald often drove me. He started this ritual where, after the event was over, he would take me back to his house to hang out and have some Kool-Aid before he took me home.

Even though I was always nervous around him, most of the time he was just like he had been in the beginning. He was actually just as caring and supportive as he had ever been. It was really confusing for me because he acted like my friend, but I knew there was this other side of him that was bad. I was never sure which side of his personality to expect when we were hanging out together.

One day when we got to his house, Ronald sat down on the couch next to me and pulled out some magazines. He turned the pages until he came to a picture of a naked woman, and he showed it to me.

"Do you like her?" he asked, holding it out for me to see.

"I guess," I said. I was embarrassed, but I did like looking at the picture. I had never seen anything like it before, and it made me feel excited.

"Remember how I can make you feel just like a woman can make you feel?" he said. "But it has to be our secret."

Ronald unzipped my pants and did the same thing with his mouth that he had done before. I was even more confused this time. I knew that it was wrong, and I didn't like that he was doing it to me. But I also knew how good it felt to come, and I wanted to have that feeling again. All of these scrambled thoughts and emotions were too much for me to make sense of, so I just let him do what he wanted.

When it happened the second time, I thought it meant that I was gay. I was very confused. I really believed that I wasn't normal, and that made me feel even worse about myself than I had before. I might have been famous, but it wasn't like my life was easy. I had a father who was nuts, I lived in a world where people didn't like me because I was black, and now I was afraid that I was gay. Worst of all, I had to make sure no one ever found out any of this while I was going in front of the cameras every week on *Diff'rent Strokes*. My career meant more to me than anything else, and I didn't want to lose it.

It happened two more times at Ronald's house in the next few months.

Not that long after the fourth time, we were in Ronald's car, and he reached over to unzip my pants. Something had changed inside of me. I don't know what it was. Maybe I was just tired of feeling that bad about myself. But I had had enough.

"No," I said. "I don't want you to do this anymore. Take me home."

"Come on, Todd," Ronald said.

"No." I had made up my mind.

He got mad at me then. I could tell by the way he looked at me. That scared me. I wasn't worried that he would hurt me any more than he already had. No. As angry as I was, I had wanted him to like and care about me for so long it was hard for me to feel like I was disappointing him. That was how successfully he had gotten inside my brain. Obviously he was a total predator. But he didn't say anything more about it just then. He drove me home and dropped me off.

I tried to act normal after that. But my mom knew me too well. She could see that something was wrong. About a week later, I was sitting on the couch watching TV with Jimmy and Verda when my mom came into the living room and told us that Ronald was coming over. I did not want to see him ever again. I kept thinking about what he had done to me, and how ashamed and scared he had made me feel. By the time he got to the house, I couldn't contain my rage. It was like when a kid had pushed me too far on the playground at school. Once I hit my breaking point, all of the anger and fear and pain that were always swirling around inside me came pouring out. There was no stopping me until it had all been released.

Ronald walked into the room, looking just as relaxed and carefree as ever. As soon as he came in the door, I jumped up and attacked him. No one could believe it.

"What are you doing, Todd?" Jimmy asked.

I kept hitting him and hitting him, fueled by all my shame and fury.

"You freak!" I shouted. "You dirty freak."

"Mom!" my sister shouted. "Mom! Come here!"

My mom ran into the living room and saw me hitting Ronald, who was shielding his face with his arms.

"Have you lost your mind?" she shouted at me.

But I think she knew right away. My mom had been molested as a child herself, so she knew what it did to an otherwise sweet, happy kid.

"He touched me," I said. I was so scared to say the words out loud.

It didn't take more than that. My mom ran out of the room and came back with a butcher knife. I felt such a sense of relief when I saw that knife. She wasn't mad at me. She was going to help me to break free of Ronald. He would never be able to touch me again.

"Don't you ever come to this house again," she said. "If you do, I will stick a knife in your chest."

Ronald stood frozen. Just then, my dad walked in. For once, I was glad to see him. Surely he would stand up for me and protect me against Ronald.

"What are you doing, woman?" he asked, already sure it was my mom's fault.

"That son of a bitch molested our son," she said. "I'm calling the police."

"You ain't calling nobody," my dad said.

"What are you talking about?" my mom said. "He molested our son."

My dad looked at Ronald and then at my mom.

"Todd is lying," my dad said. "Ronald already told me that Todd was going to do this."

I couldn't believe what he was saying. My own father didn't believe me, and he was taking Ronald's side. It was almost worse than what had happened to me.

My mom looked Ronald right in the eye, knife raised.

"I don't care what James says. You come over here again, I will kill you."

My dad got Ronald out of there as quick as he could. I'm sure he was apologizing the whole time, and saying all sorts of crazy stuff about my mom and me. My dad always thought he had the angle on everything. And for him, business came before all else, even his family.

Ronald never set foot in our house again, but my dad remained friends with him. My dad wanted to use Ronald to make money off other people, and he wasn't about to lose the chance to do so just because of something that had to do with me. That was my dad's whole thing, making money, and doing anything he could to be considered a high roller. He was determined to get what he wanted in this world, even at the expense of his youngest child.

It was bad enough that my dad didn't spend time with me, that he slapped me when he was mad, and that no matter how successful I became, or how many other people seemed to love me, I could never make him proud.

But when he didn't believe me, and instead sided with the man who had molested me, it was the worst possible betrayal. I was already so full of shame and self-hatred, and so worried that I had done something to deserve being molested. And then, just like that, I lost my dad. It broke my heart.

I never, ever got over it.

Of all the many really terrible things that have happened to me in my life, having my dad call me a liar is my worst memory of all. In that moment, something changed in me. After that, I literally didn't care what happened to me. I knew I would do whatever it took to make my dad pay for not believing me, even if I had to destroy myself to do it.

I was only thirteen years old, and I didn't know how to deal with what had happened to me. It was a very difficult time for me. I was mad at Ronald for molesting me, I was mad at my dad for taking Ronald's side over mine, and I was even mad at God for letting me go through such a painful experience. I had been taught that my father and God were supposed to protect me. But neither of them had been there for me when I really needed them. The betrayal just wrecked me.

My mom knew personally how devastating it was to be molested. She called the police on Ronald because she was afraid he would do it to other children. But it was a different time back then, and people didn't understand sexual predators as well as they do today, especially not those who preyed on children. And Ronald was a smooth talker. I don't know exactly what he told them, but the police believed his word over mine.

After he was banned from our house, Ronald started stalking me. We had moved to Canoga Park, a suburban neighborhood in the San Fernando Valley, on the other side of the mountains from Hollywood. He would park his Cadillac on the corner near our house and just sit there for hours. Sometime he'd get out of his car and come toward my friends and me when we were playing outside.

I would get this sick, nervous feeling in my stomach when I saw him and run inside, shouting, "Mom, Mom, he's here!"

My mom would come racing out, determined to settle things once and for all, just like she'd warned him she would do if he ever dared come to our house again. But as soon as he saw her heading toward him, he'd jump in his car and take off.

One time he even sent some guy up to the house to ring the doorbell.

"Yes?" my mom said when she came to the door.

"Is Todd here?" the guy asked.

My mom looked hard at this young man, but she'd never seen him before.

"Who are you?" she asked.

"Well, Todd doesn't know me," he said. "But I want to talk to him."

"Oh, no, you will not talk to my son," she said. "I will ask you to leave. Otherwise I'm going to call the police."

Ronald went to the police department and told them my mom was holding me captive in my house. The police actually came over and asked my mom about it. She was like, "Have you lost your mind?"

Ronald got away with what he had done to me. I had no choice but to do my best to get over it. I really should have gone to a therapist so I could have had a safe place to talk about what had happened to me without worrying about being judged or blamed. But therapy wasn't as common back then as it is now. We thought of it as something only crazy people did. I certainly didn't want to seem crazy on top of everything else. I just wanted to forget, even though that was impossible to do.

6

THERE'S ONLY STARS
IN THE SKY

THERE WAS NO TIME to really stop and deal with what had happened to me. Even though Ronald had made me fear otherwise, I didn't need him as a publicist to keep me in the spotlight. My career had already taken off.

I was only a kid, but my job was very important to me. I wasn't about to let any of this affect my work. My mom had taught me to always be very professional, so I made sure no one could tell what was going on inside me. I pushed my secret down deep, so no one would ever find out what had happened.

The second season of *Diff'rent Strokes* was even better than the first. We were a top-rated show, and that brought a lot of great opportunities my way. I did a cameo on an episode of *CHiPs* called *CHiPs Goes to the Roller Disco*, where I got to play myself. I also landed a role on *The Return of the Mod Squad*, which was a sequel to the popular television show from the '60s.

Diff'rent Strokes launched a spin-off, *The Facts of Life*. It started as an episode of *Diff'rent Strokes* called "The Girls School," which ran on May 4, 1979. The premise of the show was that Edna Garrett, who had been our housekeeper on *Diff'rent Strokes*, left the Drummond household to open a girls' school. After *The Facts of Life* became a hit, too, we always used to do guest appearances on each other's shows, which was cool. I played Willis on an episode of their show that August.

We got to bring in some amazing guest stars that year, too. That fall, we shot my favorite episode in the show's entire eight-season run. Muhammad Ali played himself, and it aired on October 24, 1979. He was my idol, so I was really excited to meet him. Even better, he ended up being a great guy and so much fun to have on the set. He played around a lot. He would do this little thing with his hand. I'd be sitting there between scenes, and he'd sneak up on me, and then all of the sudden he'd grab me on the shoulder with his hand. It always made me laugh. It was amazing just to have him sit down and talk with me. He was Muhammad Ali, you know? What more can I say? It was an honor to spend time with him and especially to have the chance to work with him.

I never knew who I might run into on the set either. With all of the shows that were filmed on the same lot, it was like a who's who of TV stars passing by pretty much every day. Of course, no one could impress me as much as the man who first inspired me to be a TV actor in the first place. Because they filmed *Sanford and Son* right there, too, I saw Redd Foxx around a lot. It was always a thrill.

One day, I was sitting in the hallway of the area where we filmed *Diff'rent Strokes* and I had this motorcycle helmet in my hand. Don't ask me why, but the production company had bought it for me as a gift. The thing was, I didn't have a motorcycle, or a dirt bike, or even an ATV. I was so excited, thinking that if they'd bought me a helmet, they must be planning to get me a motorcycle or a four-wheeler, but nothing ever showed up. I couldn't figure it out, and neither could my mom or anyone else. To this day, I still don't know why they gave me such a weird gift.

Anyhow, Redd Foxx walked by and saw me.

"Nice motorcycle helmet," he said. "What are you going to do with that?"

"I don't know," I said. "They bought it for me for Christmas."

"Who bought it for you for Christmas?"

"You know, the people in the production office."

"They must have bought you something else, too," he said.

"No, they didn't, they just bought me this motorcycle helmet," I said.

"That's stupid," he said.

Redd Foxx was like that. He did not ever hold back when he had something he wanted to say about someone.

We talked a little longer, and then he had to go. A week later, he came into the studio pushing this little gas-operated three-wheeler.

"I bought you something," he said.

I couldn't believe it. I mean, how great is that? Not only did I get to meet my hero, but also he bought me a present. And I finally had something to go with my helmet.

I really was living my dream.

In a lot of ways, I was just a normal teenage boy who liked things like three-wheelers, and bikes, and roller skates. But I was dealing with a lot of emotions that most kids my age never had to think about. I was still haunted by what Ronald had done to me. I spent the next year trying to figure out my sexuality. I felt a pull toward girls. But I thought that because of what had happened to me, I must be gay. That was a lot to handle. I was very unhappy about the idea of being gay, especially because I associated it with Ronald. It was a different time, and people were much less tolerant than they are now. And at the age of twelve, I didn't have the capacity to understand what it meant to be gay. I thought I wasn't normal, and that made me feel even worse about myself. I had an abusive father. I had to deal with being harassed by people who didn't like me because of my skin color. And I didn't want to be a gay twelve-year-old boy on top of all that, too.

And then one day I was at the special school I had started attending with Gary and Dana, and we were all taking a nap. I woke up when I felt my pants being unzipped. After what Ronald had done to me, this made me feel nervous right away. I looked at the teacher, and he was sleeping. I looked at Gary, and he was sleeping, too. I looked at Dana, and I didn't see Dana. I looked under the covers, and Dana was down there. She was about a year older than I was, and much more advanced. She looked up at me and smiled.

"Shhh," she said.

And then she went back to what she was doing. That was the first time I got a blow job from a girl. It felt so good. I didn't get that sick feeling in my stomach that I had when Ronald did it to me. I was sure that this was the right way for me. I was so happy to know, once and for all, that I liked girls. I'll always have Dana to thank for that. We had a lot of fun together on the set over the next few years. We used to sneak off and fool around in our dressing rooms. We spent a lot of time together outside of the show, too, and Dana became a good friend. But we never dated seriously. I mean, she *was* my sister. On TV.

So I was not exactly living the life of the average kid my age. I was making $30,000 a week, there were people on the set whose job it was to make sure I had everything I wanted at all times, and whenever I walked down the street, cute girls screamed out my name and tried to rip my clothes off. I had it made. It would have been easy for me to become a spoiled brat, but my mother wasn't about to let me forget who I was or where I came from.

I was a guest on this talk show that Regis Philbin hosted called *A.M. Los Angeles*. He started asking me what it was like to be a famous teen.

"So," he said, "since you're a celebrity now, I guess you don't have to do any housework."

I laughed when I heard that one. He clearly didn't know my mom. "No, I have to take the trash out. I have to clean my room."

"You still do that?" he asked.

"Of course," I said.

My brother and sister and I all had chores we were expected to do, and the fact that I was on a hit TV show certainly didn't make me special. My mom made sure we all stayed grounded. I remember people used to meet me and say that I didn't seem like a big celebrity. "He's not," my mom would say. "He's Todd Bridges."

And if I ever started to get confused about how things really were, my mom would set me straight. "That's a job," she said. "You go do the job. You come home."

My mom had this one saying that pretty much summed up her feelings on the whole thing: "There aren't any stars in our house. There's only stars in the sky."

While my mom was trying to make sure I never thought of myself as better than regular kids because I was famous, I was finding out that a lot of people didn't think I was as good as other kids because I was black. I had experienced racism when we first moved to Los Angeles, but it wasn't until I started spending time in the San Fernando Valley that I really learned what racism was. I soon fully understood that the way I had grown up in San Francisco, and the feeling of equality I experienced on the set of *Diff'rent Strokes*, were far from the norm in America.

One time, I was visiting a friend who had moved to the valley, and we were out riding our bikes together with some of his friends. This little kid came up, and he was all upset and saying that I had run him over with my bike the day before. I tried to tell him that I'd never been to that neighborhood before in my life.

He went and got his mom. She wouldn't listen to me either. I had been taught to always obey adults, and so I tried to be as polite as I could be while also explaining that she was wrong. She dragged me off of my bicycle and started hitting me on my head. I was terrified. I couldn't believe that a grown-up—and someone's mom, no less— would do that to me. I fought her off and ran back to the apartment where my friend lived. The kid's mom called the police. They came and took my bike away and arrested me. That was even scarier. The officers put handcuffs on me and put me in the back of the police cruiser and everything.

"I wasn't even here yesterday," I kept trying to tell them.

They didn't care.

"We know you ran this kid over," they said to me. "You're not allowed to get your bike back until your mother can come pick it up."

They took me down to the police station and called my mom. I knew that I hadn't done anything wrong, but I was worried that she was going to be mad at me, too. Well, when she came in and saw the knots on my head from that kid's mom, she was furious. The police officers tried to tell her what I had done, but she stopped them right there. I was so relieved.

"Do you see my son's face?" she said, pointing to where I'd been hit.

"Well, she says he ran her son over," the police officer said.

It was a white woman's word against a black boy's, and that was all they needed to assume I had done it. But they didn't have any proof. My mom finally got them to believe I hadn't been there the day before. They released me and returned my bike. But the experience shook me up. That's what it meant to be black in the valley at that time. My mom wanted to sue the woman who hit me, but the police wouldn't give out any information about her.

After we moved to Canoga Park, police harassment became a regular part of my life. The first time it happened, I was riding the three-wheeler Redd Foxx had given me. I was with a friend of mine who was riding his own three-wheeler. There was an area near my house that hadn't been developed yet, and it was all covered in rocks. We were just racing around, having a great time. This police car pulled over, and the cops got out and came over to us. I didn't think I'd broken any rules, but I knew by now that it didn't necessarily matter if I had or not. I felt this sick, worried feeling in my stomach. They told me that I wasn't allowed to ride my three-wheeler there, and they gave me a ticket. The friend I was with happened to be white, and they didn't give him a ticket.

"Wait a minute," my friend said. "If you're giving him a ticket, how come you're not giving me a ticket?"

"Shut up and go stand over there," they said to him.

I was so mad, but I knew better than to say anything. I just stood there, feeling humiliated.

Some other kids saw all of this happen, and one of them ran and got my mother. She hurried over there and got between the cop and me. I immediately felt so relieved when I saw her.

"What's the problem?" she asked.

"Well, this property is private property," he said.

Now, there were no signs anywhere. Clearly, that wasn't the issue anyhow, because my friend never got a ticket for riding his three-wheeler there.

So when we went to court, my mom told the judge just what had happened. She brought my friend along with us so he could tell the judge his story.

"Is this what happened?" the judge asked my friend.

"Yes," my friend said. "I told the police officer, 'If you're giving him a ticket, why aren't you giving me one?' He told me to shut up."

The judge dismissed the ticket, and he turned and looked at the police officer and accused him of committing a racist act. But that didn't change anything. For years, the cops always singled me out. I know that celebrities are often said to get special treatment, but in my case I think my celebrity actually made it worse for me. Since then, a lot of stories have come out about police brutality against black people in Los Angeles, so I have no doubt that I would have experienced my share of racial profiling if I'd been any other black man. But I'm convinced that my fame made a group of already racist cops hate me even more, and go out of their way to hassle me. I really think they couldn't stand the thought that a young black kid had all of this money, and adoration, and success that they would never have. Whatever their motivation, they sure did succeed in their goal of making my life hell.

That same year, when I was thirteen, I was riding my bike with a group of my friends, who all happened to be white. This cop car pulled up behind us. Right away, I felt that same rush of adrenaline—part anger and part nerves—come over me.

"Pull over," an officer said. "We want to talk to you."

So we all pulled over. But really, they only wanted to talk to me. One of the two officers came up and grabbed me. He was a lot bigger than I was, and I focused on trying not to do anything that would make him any angrier.

"You, get off your bike," he said.

He yanked my bike away from me and took it over to his car. If he had been a bully at school, this would have been the point when I snapped, but I had to be cool.

"Why are you taking my bike over to the car?" I said. "What did I do?"

"This bike is stolen," he said.

My friends couldn't believe that. They all started talking at once.

"No, it's not."

"He's on *Diff'rent Strokes*. He can buy himself a bike. Why would he steal this bike?"

"You guys, shut up," the cop said.

The cop made us all wait there while he got on the radio and called in my bike to headquarters. Of course it wasn't stolen. But I think they both knew that all along. The officer walked back over to me and threw my bike down on the ground. I was furious then. It was embarrassing to be singled out like that in front of my friends, and I couldn't stand that they could do that to me and then drive off. But as with so much that was bad in my life, I had no choice but to stand there and take it.

When the police first started harassing me, I was scared every time it happened. But pretty soon it became another regular part of my existence. I knew what to expect every time I went somewhere in the valley. The cops pulled me over for no reason and gave me tickets even when I hadn't done anything wrong. They called me a nigger in front of my friends. In some instances they grabbed me and pushed me down onto the ground, even though I wasn't resisting them. No matter how well behaved I was, or how adored I was by my fans elsewhere in the city, the cops in the valley always found a reason to make trouble for me. After it happened enough times, my anger started to overpower me. Even at thirteen, I knew they shouldn't be treating me like that. And I knew that the only reason I was getting treated like that, when none of my friends were getting in trouble, was because I was the only person of color. Even worse, I was a successful person of color.

It wasn't just the cops who were racist, either. One day, I rode my bike to the store near my house, and when I came out of the store, I was suddenly surrounded by this pack of kids. I was by myself, and there were seven or eight of them, all white except for one kid, who was Latino. They started in on me right away.

"We're going to kick your ass, nigger," one kid said.

They kept up like that, calling me a nigger and telling me what they were going to do to me. I guess they didn't recognize me from TV, or if they did, they were like my dad and the cops, and that gave them even more reason to want to teach me a lesson. What they didn't know, though, was that I wasn't just the usual kid they could beat up. I had always been a fighter, and now I had some real anger inside me. I couldn't fight the adults who had hurt me, but I could fight them.

They all came at me at once, swinging from every which way. All of my rage went off, and I just started punching, just going nuts, until I finally got out of the circle. As I was pedaling away, I turned around and pointed at them.

"I will never forget this," I said. "I will get each and every one of you back."

And I did. It took me years, but I found each and every one of those kids and forced him to face off against me one on one, so we could have a fair fight.

I had the added pressure of dealing with all of this in the public eye. Every Friday, I stood in front of a live audience while the cameras rolled, and I put everything aside to be the Willis Jackson that America knew and loved.

But there was one thing I couldn't hide from the cameras: puberty. It came on strong when I was about fourteen, during the show's third season. My voice started cracking like crazy. I'm sure the producers loved it because it seemed so authentic. But I hated it. I'd be delivering a line and, all of the sudden, my voice would go all Scooby-Doo on me. That wasn't even the worst of it. I got clumsy. The main set was the Drummond family's apartment, and it featured a real staircase. I must have fallen down those stairs a million times that year. I had this scene where I was supposed to come downstairs, looking all cool. I ruined that effect when I fell down the stairs, all the way to the bottom. But I got up and kept right on going. I was embarrassed, but everyone thought it was the most hilarious thing in the world. The director and producers left it in the show because the audience was roaring.

Like a lot of teenagers, I started experimenting with drugs at about the age of fourteen or fifteen. The first thing I ever tried was pot, and Dana made that first time possible, too. She lived down the street from me in Canoga Park, and her mom was almost never around, so we used to always hang out at her house. I had my first drinks with Dana, too. I don't know who she was getting to buy for her, but we always had beers when we wanted them. We wouldn't get too out of control, but we used to have a great time. She was so vibrant and fun to be around. We'd hang out, drink a little, smoke some pot, maybe watch TV or listen to music, and make out.

I liked drinking more than getting high, because pot made me fall asleep. But both alcohol and drugs were great because they allowed me to forget about all of the things in my life I didn't want to think about. I had found three escapes that made me feel better: acting, sex, and drugs. Luckily for me, acting was still the one I cared about the most. As long as the show was doing well and I was keeping busy, the other two were just something I did for fun. The show always came first, and I didn't ever want to do anything that would screw up my ability to do a good job.

Dana wasn't quite as good at drawing those boundaries between work and socializing, but I was pretty naive at that point, so I didn't really know what was going on with her. We'd be rehearsing an episode of the show, and it'd be Dana's turn to deliver a line, and there'd be nothing but silence. We'd look around, and she would have wandered off right in the middle of the scene. Sometimes it even happened during tapings. I always thought it was just Dana being Dana—you know, scatterbrained and all of that. I didn't realize until later that she was smoking pot on the set and that it made her really flaky. We got used to it.

There were a lot of forces in my life pushing me toward dark feelings and unhealthy ways of repressing my pain, but at about that time, a positive influence came into my life in an unlikely package. His name was Ernest Johnson, and he was around my age. He was this real thin kid, and he always used to wear suits, even though he was only a teenager. I met Ernie while I was filming *Diff'rent Strokes*, but he wasn't an actor. He was a preacher. Even though he had no business being on the set, somehow he always managed to find a way to get to where I was. That wasn't exactly an easy thing to do. Sure, we taped in front of a live audience, but security was tight, and they didn't let just anyone wander back and bother the stars of a hit television show. But Ernie had a mission: He said God had told him to find me. He was delivering the messages he had been told to give to me.

"If you don't have Jesus, you don't have nothing," he said. "You need to be born again."

Well, of course I thought he was totally nuts. We all called him Weird Ernie, and we would have security remove him. But he always seemed to get back in. And eventually I got used to having him around.

I got my first girlfriend at about this time, too. I went to Hollywood Professional, which was a special school for actors and entertainers. We'd have class in the morning, and then go to the set to rehearse and tape that week's episode. Mackenzie Phillips and Dorothy Hamill both went there at the same time as I did. And that's where I met Janet Jackson. She was acting on *Good Times* at that point. Of course, I knew who she and was and who her family was. But then I saw her in the hallways, and I thought she was hot. It took me a while, but I finally got up the nerve to talk to her, and I asked for her number.

At about the same time, *Good Times* got canceled. They were talking about giving Willis a girlfriend on *Diff'rent Strokes*. I told them I already knew who I wanted to play the part: Janet Jackson. They told me they were going to interview other actresses, too, but I was adamant about it. I wanted Janet. They ended up casting her as my girlfriend, Charlene DuPrey, and a couple of months after that, we started dating in real life, too.

It was a really sweet relationship. We used to talk on the phone for hours and hours, until our parents finally told us to hang up and go to bed. It was great to have someone to talk to who understood what it had been like to grow up in the public eye and to live a life that was so unusual compared to most people our age. I always knew Janet would do really well. She did a great job on *Diff'rent Strokes*, and she had this vibrant personality, which was clearly going to make her a huge success.

Even though we were acting together on a hit TV show, we were regular kids. When I got my license, I would drive to her house and pick her up for dates. Her parents made her have a chaperone, so my mom or her older sister LaToya rode in the backseat. We used to do normal things like go see a movie, or play pinball at the arcade, or when we were old enough to go out without a chaperone, park in my car and make out. As Janet has told people, I was her first kiss.

After we had been dating for a little while, Janet told me that her brother Michael wanted to meet me. I was excited to be introduced to him. Like everyone else, I had grown up listening to the Jackson 5, so I was a fan. Also, Michael and I were pretty much the only black teen idols at that point, and I was curious to see what he was like and if his experience of fame was the same as mine.

I went to pick Janet up at the house her family was building then. They were in the middle of construction, and there were all of these exposed pipes everywhere. This was before Michael's album *Thriller* had come out, and Michael was going around the house singing "Thriller" into all of these little pipes.

"This is Thriller," he sang into one pipe.

And then he ran over to another pipe.

"Thriller," he sang into that pipe.

He had this high-pitched giggle, and he was laughing like crazy about how the pipes made his voice sound all weird and distorted. He was basically this big kid, always finding the fun in everything.

I didn't ever really get to know the rest of the family that well, but Janet, Michael, LaToya, and I spent a lot of time together that year. Michael was always just silly and a lot of fun. Not that he ever really had the chance to be himself. We were both struggling with the challenges of growing up in the public eye, and that meant putting on a smile even when things were far from fine. He never got a break. I think, eventually, it was too much for him. Now that he's gone from us, I hope he's found some peace. I'll always have a tremendous amount of admiration for him.

I really cared about Janet, and I always did my best to treat her with respect. It was hard, though, because I was getting a lot of attention from other girls at that point. Plus I had Dana in my life, and she was all about teaching me about sex and getting me to experiment in all these different ways. I ended up wanting to be free to be with other girls, and I didn't want to hurt Janet by doing so. We broke up after about a year, but she still played my girlfriend on the show until 1980. That would have been really hard for most teenagers, but by that point we were such good friends that we were able to still be close without getting jealous or upset with each other. We remained friends for years after that. I heard a rumor that she wrote a song for me, but I've never had the chance to ask her about it.

It was a lot of fun having Janet join the cast during the third season, but it was around that time that the mood on the set changed for the worse. Not only was the show a big hit, but also Gary Coleman was a huge star, and that changed things. Everyone loved his catchphrase "Whatchu talkin' about?" I couldn't go anywhere for years without having someone run up to me and say, "Whatchu talkin' about, Willis?"

Gary was always a great kid, and I wouldn't say the fame went to his head so much as it went to his parents' heads. They were being fed this line about how Gary was the star and nobody else was any good for him. They went from having no people to suddenly having all these lawyers, and managers, and agents, and they really did a number on Gary. His agent wanted to keep everybody away from Gary, too, because he didn't want anybody influencing him or telling him what was going on. Soon they wanted everything their way or else there would be trouble, but I don't think they ever really asked Gary what he wanted. He always seemed really unhappy and exhausted during that time.

Gary's parents got so full of themselves that they were impossible to be around. My mom got so tired of hearing Sue Coleman go on and on that she stopped attending rehearsals and only came to the set for tapings on Friday nights. My sister, Verda, turned eighteen at about that point, so she was old enough to be my setsitter until I turned eighteen.

The real problems started when Gary's dad, Willie Coleman, started hanging around the set a lot during the third season. I knew things had really changed when Willie walked in one day with some giant white guy who was carrying Gary on his shoulders. So now Gary had a bodyguard on the set. It didn't make any sense. Who was going to attack Gary on the set? One of us? You would have thought so, given how they acted after that. Willie didn't want Gary socializing with anybody. They absolutely did not want Gary hanging out with me anymore. We had been good friends until then, but Willie completely ruined our relationship.

I honestly think that Willie didn't want Gary hanging out with black people once he became a star. They didn't seem to have any black people in their life anymore at that point. It's sad, but a lot of black people were like that back then. They had been treated like they were lesser for so long that they had come to believe that blacks weren't as good as whites, so one of the most important parts of becoming successful was moving into the white world and being accepted there. My dad was definitely like that.

I honestly think that Gary was the victim in all of this, but the pressure from his parents affected his attitude, too. He started acting like he was better than everybody. It didn't take much for him to get nasty.

Finally I got sick of it. We were all there on the set, trying to do our jobs, and it seemed like he had an obnoxious comeback for everyone. This was the place I loved more than anywhere else in the world, and he was ruining it.

"Come on, Gary," I said.

"Shut up," he said.

"You're not going to talk to me that way anymore," I said.

He didn't have a comeback for that, so he slapped me.

My cheek stung where he had hit me.

I slapped him back.

If it had been anyone else, I would have done a lot worse. I clenched and unclenched my fists and walked away before I completely lost my cool.

I always thought Willie wanted me fired from the show. But they must have told him they couldn't fire me. The show was about two brothers, Arnold and Willis, and it wouldn't work without me. But they took me out of something like four shows that season to punish me.

I was fed up with Gary's behavior, but I still felt bad for him. Everyone eventually turned against the Colemans, and the sad part was that Gary was left all alone with his parents. It made me feel bad for Gary because he was really sick. Even with the operations, his health wasn't great, and they were working him to death. Gary was so sick after one of his operations that he was throwing up everywhere on the set. Willie was right there, but he wasn't comforting Gary.

"You need to go back to work, because people are depending on you," Willie said.

My mom never would have done that. She believed in the importance of a good work ethic, too, but she also knew that kids needed to be protected. I'm really lucky that I had her to make sure I got to be a kid, too. I did commercials and other work during the breaks between seasons of *Diff'rent Strokes*, but I always got to go on vacations and have time to play with my friends, too. Not Gary. When we would go on hiatus, Gary would go right from the set to some movie or other job. He never got to stop and rest, and I think that's why he ended up being such an angry person.

It might have seemed like there would have been competition between Gary and me. But I never minded that Gary was the star, and here's why: Gary was making more money, but I got the girls. Ask any fifteen-year-old boy which one he would prefer, and he'll say, "I'll take the girls."

I know that I, for one, was definitely all about the girls. One of the best things about being a teen idol was that there were lots and lots of girls. When I was sixteen, I got to be a guest on the sixth season of *Circus of the Stars*, which was a hugely popular show that was sort of like an early version of *Dancing with the Stars*. The only difference was that the show featured young actors who were at the heights of their careers. So I got to appear with the hot young stars of the day, like my good friend Scott Baio, and one of the most beautiful girls at the time, Brooke Shields.

My event was trapeze, and that was the best, because I got to work with a bunch of sexy women in leotards. I had always been very athletic growing up, so I was good at the tumbling they wanted me to do, and that was fun, too.

Well, we were shooting one day, and I looked over and Brooke Shields was on the trampoline. For once, her mom wasn't anywhere to be seen. Brooke's mom used to run off anyone who tried to get too close to her. I saw my chance. So I rolled up on her, and I tried to be all smooth.

Dana was on *Circus of the Stars* that season, too, and she came up right then and pulled me aside.

"My friend wants you to go to my house with us," she said.

"Can't you see I'm talking to Brooke?" I said. "I'm trying to get her number."

"But my friend wants you to go to my house with us," she said again.

Obviously I wasn't getting her meaning, so she broke it down for me.

"My friend wants to have sex with you and me at the same time," she said.

That was all it took. I was out of there. I mean Brooke was cute, but the idea of having sex with two girls was even hotter. We went to Dana's house when we were done with the show for the day, and I had my first threesome that night.

It might seem like Dana was a bad influence on me, but believe me, I was ready to try pretty much anything, especially when it came to girls. As long as it didn't jeopardize my ability to do a good job on the show, which was always my number one priority, I was game. Besides, Dana and I were so close that everything we tried together had sort of an innocent quality to it; we were two good friends eager to have crazy new experiences. Dana may have been partying harder than I was, but it didn't get really dark for either of us until after the show was canceled.

7

WHAT'S AN OFFICER LIKE YOU DOING IN A UNIFORM LIKE THAT?

IN MANY WAYS, those were the best years of my life. I had everything that any teenage boy could want, and there were a lot of great people in my life—my mom, my brother and sister, Conrad Bain, and Gerren Keith, who directed most of the episodes of *Diff'rent Strokes*. All of them were always there for me, supporting me and helping me become even more successful in my career. But it seemed like the older I got, the more pressure I started to feel from the forces in my life that didn't necessarily have my best interests at heart.

My dad got more and more jealous of me, and he tried to get back at me in whatever way he could. When I turned seventeen, I bought myself a brand-new BMW 320i. I used my own money to pay for it, but I was still just a kid, so my dad was the one who actually purchased it for me. Well, I didn't see that car for two months. My mom kept asking him about it, and he kept telling her that the car hadn't come in yet. When I finally got it from him, there were all of these miles on the odometer. The car had come in all right, but he'd been driving it without telling me.

When I finally got that car, it caused me to have a run-in with Willie Coleman. My parking place was right next to his, and I guess I parked my car too close to his. He stormed up to me on the set. I was used to Willie being unpleasant. But this was different. He got really close to me, and he grabbed me by the collar with both his hands. He held me there so I couldn't even squirm. His breath was hot on my face.

"You scratched my car!" he yelled at me.

I could take care of myself in a fight, but my parents had taught me to always respect adults and go to them first if an adult ever caused any trouble for me. My heart was hammering in my chest. But I couldn't do anything.

"I'm going to call my dad," I said.

"I don't care," he said. "Call your dad."

Willie let go of me, and I called my father. Even though my dad had disappointed me at pretty much every moment I ever needed him, he was still my dad. And he was my agent at that point, too, so even when we weren't getting along, we had to talk a lot.

My dad came down to the set. And let me just say this, if I had personally learned that anger makes a person fearless in a fight, my dad had the makings of one tough-ass son of a bitch. I don't know what he did to Willie, but I do know that Willie never, ever said anything to me again after that. It was the one time my dad actually stood up for me. It didn't matter as much as the fact that he had let me down when I really needed him to stand up to Ronald, but it still meant a lot to me. Unfortunately, it was just one small, good moment in a whole lifetime of bad experiences I had lived through with my dad, so it didn't do anything to fix our relationship. But at least it fixed Willie.

When I started driving, the police harassment got even worse, too. The same two officers were constantly pulling me over, either going to work or coming home from work. I must have spent $9,000 in tickets alone, and my car insurance went sky high. I even got an early car phone to call my mom when they pulled me over, so she could come find me and set them straight.

I clearly remember one officer who pulled me over while I was driving my BMW because he so eloquently summed up the feelings of all of the racist cops who had ever harassed me. After stopping me for no reason, he strolled up to my car.

"What's a nigger like you doing in a car like this?" he asked.

Now, they'd been calling me a nigger since I was a twelve-year-old kid on a bike. It wasn't any surprise to hear the "n" word come out of his mouth.

But finally I was sick of it. I snapped.

"I don't know. What's an officer like you doing in a uniform like that?" I said.

They had pushed me so hard, and for so long, that they made me defiant. That, right there, was the beginning of the fall of Todd Bridges, even if it took a few years to play itself out. All of the anger that I had held bottled up inside me for so long was starting to leak out. I struggled to hold it together because I didn't want to mess up the show and all of the perks that came with it. But sometimes I lost it. Only for a second. And then I pulled it back together. But as I was beginning to learn, there were consequences for losing control, especially for a young black man living in America in the 1970s. Being a TV star could do only so much to help.

I got pulled over by this cop. I hadn't been doing anything wrong, but as should be obvious by now, that didn't really matter. Getting stopped for no reason still made me angry. By this point I absolutely hated the police. He walked up to my car, took his hat off, and set it on my car. To me, that was just more disrespect.

"Don't put your hat on my car," I said. "If you're going to write me a ticket, keep your hat in your hand. Don't just set something down on my car."

"I'll do whatever I want," he said.

"No, you won't," I said. "I don't care if you're an officer. Keep your hat in your hand."

I took his hat off and threw it on the ground. This happened several times.

"If I put my hat on there, and you throw it down one more time, I'm going to take you to jail," he said.

I could tell he meant it, but I had a point to prove, too.

"Do you think I care?"

He put his hat on my car. I threw it down on the ground. He took me to jail.

In the end, the case got thrown out because the judge went to college with my mom. That might sound like favoritism, but I'd have to argue that I simply got a lucky break that gave me access to the same kind of privilege that most white people experienced every day. Even if I had gotten in trouble for it, I wouldn't have cared. All I cared about was that I had made my point to that cop. It felt good, pushing back on the people who had pushed on me, no matter what the consequences were.

Things finally came to a head with my dad around then, too. In 1982 it came out that my dad was having an affair. It wasn't like it was a total surprise. This same woman had come on to me once while driving me home when I was fifteen or sixteen. We were in the car, and she pulled up her skirt, and she wasn't wearing any underwear. I guess she was trying to bust two birds with one stone. That was before I knew they were having an affair, but it still made me feel weird. Soon after that, my sister caught my dad and this woman coming out of the bathroom together at my dad's office. My dad was zipping his fly, and she was straightening her skirt. Verda knew what was up, and soon my mom did, too.

My dad insisted on staying at the house in Canoga Park. One day around then, I heard him fighting with my mom. She was in really rough shape. Even though my dad was still drinking and being abusive, they had been married for twenty-four years. When their marriage fell apart, she fell apart. They came downstairs to where I was sitting in the living room, and they stood fighting by the front door.

"I'm staying here," my dad said.

"No, you're not," my mom said. "You have another woman, go with her."

As I watched my dad yell at my mom, the rage inside me grew. He was such a jerk, and I was so sick of bullies.

I wasn't afraid of him anymore, so I could see what a pathetic little man he was and how he needed to keep his family in fear to make himself feel big. By this point he was going wild, yelling and waving his arms. I had seen him hit my mom too many times to let it get that far again. I snapped.

I knew exactly what I had to do as I got up off the couch and ran into the kitchen, which opened off the living room. It was what I should have done a long time ago. I grabbed the biggest knife I could find. The handle felt good in my hand. My adrenaline was racing, but I felt strangely calm. I knew that I was ready for whatever happened next. I ran up close to my dad and held the knife on him. Everything stopped for a split second. We were all breathing heavily, watching each other. My mom looked scared, but she didn't say anything or try to stop me. My dad watched me closely.

"If you don't leave this house, I'm going to stab you," I said.

He looked at me for a long moment. I stood there, holding the knife up, and my hand didn't tremble at all. He realized that I was serious, and he went upstairs to their bedroom. I stayed there at the bottom of the stairs with the knife in my hand until he had gotten his stuff and left.

He was right to be afraid. I really would have stabbed him, especially if that's what it took to protect my mom. I couldn't ever stand to see her cry, and he had made her cry so many times over the years. That final fight was the last straw for me. If it seems unfeeling that I was willing to stab my own dad, remember that he was more like an outsider than a dad anyhow. If we had had a relationship, there's no way I could have even thought about hurting him.

He couldn't physically hurt us after that. But he had already done a lot of damage. My mom was devastated. She cried and cried. It tore me up to see her be so sad. But it was also hard for me to watch her getting that upset about losing a man I hated as much as I hated my father. When I woke up the morning after I stood up to my dad, I was ready to move out of the house. I didn't want anything more to do with anything that reminded me of him. And I needed to get away from all the bad memories and the pain that filled the house. A couple of weeks later, I turned eighteen and immediately moved out. I didn't go far, just down the street, but I finally had my own place. It felt great to be out on my own.

I couldn't really understand what my mom was going through. I was only eighteen, and I had no clue about all the complicated emotions that went into a marriage. All I could see was that she was wrecked over losing a man who I knew we were better off without, so I wasn't very sympathetic to her feelings. I found it easier to keep my distance after I moved out. Looking back, I feel bad about this. Since getting older and going through rehab, I've gotten a lot more in touch with my feelings. But right then, after everything I'd been through, I was kind of shut down.

My mom lost it for the next few years. She had tried to hold everything together for so long, and when it all fell apart, she gave up. I was really grateful for everything she had done for me, and I knew she deserved a break after everything she had been through, but I didn't know what to make of her new way of being. She went out dancing every night, which was a side of her I'd never seen before.

Even when my mom's emotional state was in shambles, she still cared so much about my well-being and my career. And she was able to see that she wasn't in a good place to watch out for me in the same way she once had. She told me that I was going to have to watch out for my own money for a while because she just couldn't do it right then. I was okay with that. It felt good to be independent.

I had the same accountants my parents had hired a few years before to take care of my family's finances and my parents' clients, so I let them worry about the details. All I wanted to focus on was being a successful eighteen-year-old who was starring on a hit television show and could get pretty much any girl he wanted.

But it wasn't quite that simple. In addition to dealing with my complicated relationship with my father, I was still struggling with the repercussions of the abuse I had received from Ronald. I might think I had it together, but then something would happen to bring it all back up again. *Diff'rent Strokes* was known for tackling big issues, not just race. In 1985, during season five, we did an episode called "Bicycle Man," in which a sexual predator stalks Arnold and his friend. We had already done an antidrug episode with guest star Nancy Reagan, who had recently launched her famous "Just Say No" campaign against drugs that was ironic, since I'm sure Dana and I went off together and just said "Yes" to getting high as soon as we had finished filming the show with her. Of course, the audience didn't know that. They thought we were the most wholesome role models there could be. It made sense for us to tackle sex abuse, too, and we got a lot of positive feedback for that episode. But any kind of attention around sexual molestation was the last thing I wanted. I didn't let on that the material in the script upset me. That was a very hard week for me, and I pushed my feelings down, hard.

On the outside, I continued to be one of the most successful young actors in Hollywood. That year I did a movie called *High School U.S.A.*, which featured a who's who of the day's teen stars. My character, Otto, was the nerdy sidekick to the hero, Jay-Jay, played by Michael J. Fox, who ended up being a good friend of mine for many years. His love interest was played by Nancy McKeon, who was a huge star from having played Jo on *The Facts of Life*. It also starred Crispin Glover, Anthony Edwards, and Crystal Bernard, who played K. C. Cunningham on *Happy Days*, and then went on to do the hit show *Wings* in the '90s. Dana was in it, too, but we didn't have any scenes together. It was a lot of fun working with all those people, but I had just turned eighteen, and I had never worked as an adult before. I was used to working maybe six hours a day as a child actor. Now they expected me to be there sixteen hours a day. They nearly killed me on that one. The other difference I noticed now that I was older was that my race seemed to be a bigger issue on the set than it had been before. Once again, I was the only black actor involved with the production, and I felt like some of the actresses weren't as comfortable around me as they were around the white actors. It was almost like it had been fine to hang around me or have a crush on me when I was a cute little boy, but as soon as I grew up into a black man, I was intimidating. No one ever actively discriminated against me, but I got a weird feeling when I was around some of the women on that movie. Obviously, by that point I was sensitive to even the smallest racial slights.

At about the same time, I almost got a part in another teen movie that would have been even bigger. I was on a plane, and I happened to sit next to John Hughes. He had just had a big hit in 1984 with *Sixteen Candles*, so I was well aware of who he was. We got to talking, and we immediately hit it off.

"I love you," he said. "You have so much personality. I want to work with you."

Of course I wanted to work with him, too.

"I'm doing a movie called *The Breakfast Club*," he said. "And I want you to be in this movie. I'm going to set up a meeting for you in LA."

I was so excited about the movie, and I figured that from what he had said, it was a sure thing. When I got back to LA, I had a meeting with one of his associates. I went into his office, and I sat down across from the guy.

"Hmmm," he said.

He looked at me for a long time. I had no idea what was coming next.

"I just don't see how to put a black character in this film," he said.

"You write for blacks the same way you write for whites," I said.

I was stunned. Even with as much racism as I experienced over the years, it still shocked me when I was faced with it, especially from a person who otherwise seemed intelligent and open-minded. I got out of there as quickly as I could. Obviously, I wasn't in *The Breakfast Club*.

I should have been in *The Breakfast Club*. How are you going to have kids in detention, and there aren't any black kids in detention? I mean, come on. I'm over it now, but I was bitter about that for a long time. It was the perfect moment in my career for me to land a part like that, and if I had been in *The Breakfast Club*, it would have made me into a major movie star, like it did for so many of the other actors in that film. But I wasn't like the other actors in that film. I was black. It was really frustrating to be denied the chance to show off my talents and work ethic and dedication to my craft simply because of the color of my skin.

My skin color was continuing to be a problem for the police department as well. Their abuse seemed to get worse and worse. By that point, everyone we knew was calling them the Gestapo Division, and many of my black friends had stopped coming to visit me in the San Fernando Valley because they knew they'd get hassled if they did.

By the time I was living in my own place in Canoga Park, I had gotten a Porsche with the license plate Todd B1. My mom thought I was crazy to get my name on my license plate, since I couldn't go anywhere without getting mobbed as it was. But I was young, it was my first Porsche, and that was what I wanted.

One day, I went to get into my Porsche, which I had parked on the street near my house, and the battery was dead. I started pushing the car with help from my brother, Jimmy, and this friend of ours, who happened to be white. When we got it started up, I turned it around and drove it back to my driveway. Well, the police had seen two black guys pushing a Porsche down the street, and they pulled up behind me with their lights flashing. I got that familiar, queasy feeling in my stomach.

"Get out of the car!" one of the officers said. "It's stolen!"

"Stolen?" I said, trying to keep the anger out of my voice. "This is my car."

"We had a report that someone was pushing a Porsche," he said.

"Yeah, I was pushing it," I said. "It's my car. My name's on the license plate. Todd B1. Would you like to see my registration and insurance?"

"No," he said. "Shut up. Get out of the car."

This had to be the most ridiculous stunt they had ever pulled. How could I steal my own car? I almost wanted to laugh, but I couldn't because I was too furious. He took me out of the car, handcuffed me, and put me in the back of his police car. I couldn't believe I was going through this yet again, but there was nothing I could do. My brother couldn't believe what he was seeing.

"What are you guys doing to him?" he asked.

That was enough for them to handcuff him and put him in the back of the car.

Our white friend spoke up next.

"Well, if they're in trouble, obviously I'm in trouble," he said. "I was pushing the car, too."

"Just shut up and get over there," the cop said. He wasn't in trouble, maybe because he was white. It was exactly like my friend with the three-wheeler when I was thirteen. I know these stories start to sound alike after a while, but it really was the same bullshit each and every time. By this point, all cops had become one hateful, racist cop in my mind.

All of my neighbors had gathered around to see what was going on. Obviously they knew it was my car.

"What are you doing?" they said.

"Why do you have him in the back of the car?"

"It's his car."

I craned my neck to see what was going on from where I was handcuffed next to my brother in the back of the cop car. My neighbors were yelling by this point, so the officers called for more police to back them up. They were afraid it was going to get out of control. It probably would have, and rightfully so. What did they expect when they tried to arrest a guy for stealing his own car? All of these police cars showed up, and someone ran to get my mom, who lived a couple of blocks away. She was still my protector, and I appreciated it. My mom came over in such a hurry that she wasn't even wearing any shoes.

"Have you guys lost your minds?" she said. "What do you think this is, South Africa? This is not South Africa. This is America. And he has every right to push his car down the street to get it started."

When she saw Jimmy in the back of the car, she really lost it. I don't think my brother ever caused a single moment of trouble for anyone in his whole life.

"Get my son out of that car right now," she said.

So they pulled Jimmy out and let him go.

My mom finally convinced them to release me, too. They pulled me out of the car and took off the cuffs. And then one of the officers thunked me in my chest with his fingers. That riled me, but I knew that if I said anything, I'd be cuffed and back in the car in an instant. I forced my anger down.

"Don't you ever, so long as you live, touch my child," my mom said. "I don't know what you think you're doing, but you're messing with the wrong children."

They finally drove away without charging us with anything. But we were fed up. My mom hired Johnnie Cochran to file a lawsuit against the LAPD for police harassment. They hated me more after that, and two black officers actually came to our house to warn us that a note had been passed around the precinct instructing them to get whatever they could on me. That's okay, though; I hated most police officers, too.

By that point, I really hated everyone in authority. Every male authority figure I'd ever had—my father, Ronald, the police—had abused their powers. At about this same time, I found another powerful way to deal with my fear and anger. When I got overwhelmed, I used pot to take it away. I still wasn't smoking that much or that often, and never when I had to work, but sometimes I really needed that escape.

Because I was a TV star, I could get in to any club in Los Angeles. I had money, I was famous, and I had the choice of just about any girl I wanted. Those next three years were the best of my life. My brother and my friends and I had so many fun nights. When I was eighteen, we used to always go to this place called Flippers, which was a roller skating rink with a liquor license—well, we found out when it got shut down later that they didn't really have a liquor license, but they served booze. We used to skate around, have some drinks, and pick up girls. Sometimes we didn't even make it home with our dates, and I had sex in my car a lot of nights outside Flippers, too.

It was great being able to get in anywhere, do anything, and not have most girls say no. Well, some girls said no, but then I'd usually have sex with one of their friends instead. That's how it was.

Once, I was dating this really cute girl. We had gone out a couple of times, but she always wanted to wait for everything. I was not into waiting for anything at that point. One night we went out with her friend, and I ended up leaving with her friend instead of her. The girl's friend and I didn't leave the bedroom for four days. We ordered food in and everything. And then I never talked to her again, or to her friend who I'd originally been dating. That wasn't a big deal back then. Everyone was very casual about sex, and both the guys and the girls were into having a good time. I had female friends, like Dana. And I did stay friends with a few of the girls I dated, but I was dating a lot back then, so it would have been impossible to keep in touch with everyone. I didn't really care to anyhow. I'd go out to a club and wake up the next morning at some girl's house and have no idea where I was, or who she was, and I was fine with that as long as I could get out of there fast. There was always another girl to be had the next night. Or, sometimes, two.

I'll be completely honest. That was one of my favorite things about being famous: There were so many girls to choose from. I never dated actresses, though. I don't want to be mean, but they weren't cute enough. It's not like it is today, with all of these beautiful girls who are on shows like *Gossip Girl* and the new *Beverly Hills 90210*. Back then, the child actresses were all meant to look like somebody's awkward little sister. I preferred Playmates and Raiderette cheerleaders.

When we went out, there were these different groups—the actors, the football players, the basketball players, and the singers—and the girls kind of went around from group to group. So we all ended up sharing the same girls. That's why, when Magic Johnson got sick, all of us guys who used to hang out back then were really worried. We all knew that we had definitely had encounters with the same girls as he had. So when we heard that he tested positive for HIV, all of us guys were on the phone, going, "Hey, man, I'm going to the doctor right now." There were about eight of us guys who all got tested. None of us had anything, but it was scary.

I was definitely more into sex than anything else when I was young. I was never a hard-core drinker, even when I was clubbing a lot. I drank a few beers when I went out, or maybe had some tequila—to-kill-ya, as I liked to call it. And I smoked some pot, too, but I never got too out of control. I always knew that I had to be ready to go back to work on Monday. None of my friends from that time were into drugs either. It wasn't like we needed drugs to have fun anyhow. I always went out with my brother, Jimmy, and three of our good friends, one of whom owned the Lakers. I got to go to all of their games. We'd have steak and lobster at Down Below and then be courtside for the game. We always had our choice of the Lakers' Girls and pretty much any other women who were hanging around. After the games, we'd grab some girls and go to a club, or we'd go back to his house. My friend who owned the Lakers lived at Pickford Mansion at the time, which was an amazing place for parties. We had some great times at that house.

Most nights started at my house. We'd have a bunch of guys over, have a few drinks, decide on what club we wanted to hit, and then what party we wanted to do afterward. We clubbed a lot. I loved to dance, and it was always a lot of fun to be out, looking sharp, and surrounded by this great, loud music and all of these beautiful women. The anger that had started building inside me as a kid was never far from the surface, though. We had some big brawls during those years. Many times we actually shut clubs down because we were fighting with everybody in the place. Just like back in elementary school, I never started trouble, but I also never backed down if somebody started with me.

The fights did get out of control a few times, but luckily nothing ever came of it. When I was young, the press and the public didn't scrutinize stars the way they do now, and the studios were able to do a lot to take care of us. If something happened to an actor, the studios could buy it up before it hit the press, and the story never got out. They did that for me once in 1983. I got pulled over in my car, and I was fined for carrying a concealed weapon without a permit. I had bought a gun that year because I didn't feel safe with the police always harassing me, and people starting fights with me when I went out. But getting in trouble that first time was an isolated incident. The studio bought up the story, and no one ever heard anything about it.

That protection was great while it lasted, but it was clear that there was trouble brewing behind the scenes at *Diff'rent Strokes*. I'm not sure exactly what happened, because we still had a top-rated show going into the second-to-last season. But NBC dropped us in 1984. That was hard to take after we'd been on the network for seven seasons. We were fortunate that ABC picked us up right away, which is a relatively rare thing to happen. Still, it wasn't hard to tell that the show's final days were approaching.

I really think the biggest problem was that Gary Coleman's people were making such crazy financial demands and being such a nightmare. I don't think he wanted to do the show anymore anyhow. He seemed totally miserable. I don't know for sure, though, because all of the tensions between us had escalated to the point where we weren't speaking any longer. It had been bad enough when he was avoiding me and refusing to talk to me because his parents didn't want him to, but when it started to seem like he was jeopardizing the job I loved, I totally lost patience with him and his attitude. I didn't ever really blame him, because it was clear how much pressure he was under and how miserable he was, but I didn't want any part of it. We did our scenes together like nothing was wrong, because we were both professionals, but beyond that, we tried to stay out of each other's way.

In fact, when the final episode aired on March 7, 1986, I wasn't on it. Who knows exactly why? Maybe I wasn't concealing the effects of everything I'd been through as well as I thought I was, but I do know that nothing was more important to me than that show, and I was still giving it my all. I really think Gary and his agent and manager were behind the decision to take me out of the last two episodes. Again, I don't really blame Gary because I think it was his parents and his people pulling the strings, but his whole thing was, "I'm not working with Todd Bridges." There are a lot of projects I'm sure he got me blackballed from, and not just during *Diff'rent Strokes*, either. A few years later, he and Conrad did a cameo on *The Fresh Prince of Bel Air*. I was under the impression that I was supposed to make an appearance, too, but learned that I was cut out of the script at the last minute.

It was hard to walk away from *Diff'rent Strokes*. That show was a huge part of my life. And to this day, so many people I worked with on it are still like family to me. But things had definitely changed in the final years. And it wasn't just the Colemans. Dana's drug use had gotten progressively worse, and it had started to affect her behavior on the set. Sometimes she was just kind of out of it, and it would take us longer to get through a rehearsal than it would have otherwise. Sometimes she did really crazy stuff. In the show's final years, we started filming at Universal Studios. It had this spinning tunnel that was used once on an episode of *The Six Million Dollar Man*. If you've ever toured the Universal lot, you know what I'm talking about. Well, one time, Dana was all messed up on the set, and she decided to drive her car through that tunnel. I guess she didn't realize that there was a special mechanism that pulled the trams through. Once she got her car into the tunnel, she ended up getting stuck. She couldn't get her car to move and, I guess because of the spinning sensation, she started throwing up all over the place. It was a mess. They had to stop the tours for the day and figure out a way to pull her car out.

No matter what Dana was going through personally, we remained close and we always had fun when we worked together. But her drug problems definitely created tensions on the show. When she got pregnant in 1985, that was not a story line they thought would be appropriate for Kimberly's character, so they fired her. Dana only appeared on a few episodes after that.

With all of these tensions going on behind the scenes, it didn't feel as good to go to the set as it had in the beginning. I was still very committed to being a professional actor, but it was getting harder for me to hold it together, too. By the time the show ended in 1986, as sad as I was to say good-bye, I really needed a break.

8

LIFE AFTER WILLIS

AT ABOUT THE TIME that *Diff'rent Strokes* was ending, I bought a big house in Northridge. It had belonged to a drug dealer, and one of the rooms was covered in the same wallpaper that Tony Montana had in his house in *Scarface*, which everyone had been crazy for since it came out in 1983. That was one of the main reasons I bought the house, actually. I could relate to that movie. It had nothing to do with the drugs. I got the character of Tony because I understood the feeling of having something to prove to those who thought I was lesser because of my race. No matter how successful I was, it never seemed to be enough for them.

When I first moved into the house, I replaced the carpet. I decided to rip up the old carpet myself in order to save some money. I was tearing the carpet out of one of the closets and I found a big, fat plastic bag full of white powder. At that point I drank a little and smoked some pot, but I was really pretty innocent. Obviously I had seen coke before, but not so much all at once, and not right there in my hands. Some friends of mine were over at the house, and they started laughing when they saw the perplexed look on my face.

"Man, that's cocaine," one of my friends said. "Try it."

"I don't want to try it," I said.

"You sniff it," he said.

"I know that," I said.

Well, I wasn't afraid to try new things. And I liked how getting high on pot made me forget the things I didn't want to think about. I sniffed it. And I got seriously high. That was some real cocaine.

I wasn't sure about cocaine in the beginning. I didn't really enjoy the way it made me feel, and I still liked drinking more than anything else. But I soon came to realize that I loved what happened when I went out to clubs and parties with cocaine on me. I got even more girls than I had gotten just for being a teen idol. There were always plenty of gorgeous girls who wanted to do drugs, so the two went hand in hand, as I soon learned. This was a very happy discovery for me because I loved the ladies more than just about anything else in the world. It also meant that I was willing to give cocaine another try. If I had coke, and the girl I wanted to sleep with was interested in doing some with me, then I certainly wasn't going to say no. Doing drugs with a sexy girl was very hot, especially when she started to feel good and wanted to show her appreciation in all sorts of naughty ways. Once we were high, I loved that cocaine made me able to drink more without getting wasted and, even better, have sex for hours and hours at a time.

When I first started doing coke, it was a good time. The '80s were the era of cocaine, and as soon as I knew to look for it, I realized it was everywhere. Everyone was high and having the best time ever. I'd go to a party and see mounds of cocaine just sitting there, all spread out on the table for anyone who walked by. Quaaludes were big back then, too. We called them 714 lemonheads. We'd go to a party and have a few drinks. The girls took quaaludes. We'd all do some coke. I'd find the prettiest girl I could, and we'd be up all night having sex.

It seemed like there was always an adventure to be had. I got a bunch of my boys together, and we decided to go skiing. We had two cases of beer and a bunch of coke and weed. We were drinking and doing coke while we were driving up to the ski resort at Mammoth, which is about 350 miles north of Los Angeles. I was driving, and everyone else fell asleep. I was flying along, and the next thing I knew, I had made it all the way to Twin Lakes without realizing that I had driven right past Mammoth. I had to turn around and drive back. When we finally got there, we went to see a movie. We were all passing one of those grinders of coke back and forth, sniffing lines right in the theater. To this day I can't begin to tell you what that movie was.

I had also made friends with most of the other child stars working in Hollywood. We knew each other's work, of course, and it was cool to meet someone else who could relate to what it was like to have all the privileges and pressures that went along with being famous at such a young age. There was always a party at someone's house, and drugs were very much out in the open, so there was always coke and booze, and we all had a good time. Unfortunately, a lot of us ended up in serious trouble because of that, and several of those friends ended up dead from drug overdoses. But just like with all of the unprotected sex we were having before anyone knew anything about AIDS, there weren't any consequences yet.

I befriended a young actor, right as he was becoming a huge star with a nice-guy reputation he'd earned from playing the dorky kid next door. Well, he liked coke even more than I did, and we had some wild nights together. Once, on the Sunset Strip, we were partying at Carlos n' Charlie's, which was one of the places everyone went around then. By the time we were ready to leave and we walked out of the club, he was so loaded that he wasn't really walking, more like staggering and weaving. He started to fall, grabbed my suit as he went down, and ripped it. I pulled him up and looked him over. He had white powder all over his nose.

"You've got stuff all over your face," I said. "Wipe your face off."

I knew his fans would have been shocked if they saw him like that, and I was trying to keep him from making a scene and drawing attention to himself. But it wasn't anything like it would have been today. There weren't swarms of paparazzi waiting to swoop down and capture us at our worst. We got home, slept it off, and probably went out again the next night. Drugs didn't seem like that big a big deal to us, and we were able to get away with a lot.

Well, that's true and it's not true. Drugs were still a big deal for me as long as I was doing *Diff'rent Strokes*. I may have been smoking pot and doing a little coke on the weekends during the last two seasons, but when Sunday came around, I knew it was time to shape up and get myself ready to get back to work on Monday. And I always did. It was never a problem for me. That's how much I loved to work.

But I had been working for sixteen years straight, and I was worn out. By the time the show ended, I wanted to stop and be normal for a while and take a long break and travel the world. My plan was to go from Los Angeles to New York, and then take the Concorde to London. From London, I was going to travel all around Europe by myself. I called my accountants and told them I needed the money to buy the plane tickets. It took them a few days to get back to me, but I didn't think much about it. They had been handling my family's money for years, plus all of the money my parents managed for their acting clients. I figured they were busy. I was busy, too, making plans for my trip. I called back to check in about the money for the tickets. We got it worked out, and I bought my ticket for the Concorde.

Right before I was scheduled to leave, I got a call from my mom. She had just realized that several checks she had given to our accountants had never been deposited. When the money hadn't shown up a week later, she called the accountants to check on it. One of the accountants assured my mom that the money had gone through. But when my mom got our accountant on the phone and asked her to look up the account again, my mom said it sounded like the woman was only pretending to hit the keys of her computer while actually tapping her fingers on her desk.

My mom started shaking. Something was really wrong.

As my mother, and my longtime manager, she had always handled all of the deposits herself. But when my dad had left her for another woman a few years earlier, she totally lost it. At least she had the good sense to know she wasn't in any condition to take care of her money or mine. That's when she started relying on our accountants more, and then I agreed to take over my own finances.

What she didn't realize, and what I don't think I fully realized either, was that I was nearly as much of a mess over the divorce as she was. I had wanted my dad gone from our house because I was tired of being abused and watching him abuse my mom. I knew she deserved better. But at the same time, it was really hard for me to accept my dad's decision to leave. When I was growing up, most of the other mothers were raising their kids alone. It was a big deal that I had both parents at home. And it was hard for me to let go of that. When he left, it also ended any hope I might have had that he would someday become the loving dad I had always wanted.

And so I was a little bit crazy after the divorce, too. I had told my mom that I would take over my own finances, but I wasn't really together enough to do so. Any person with any sense would have been paying better attention. But it seemed like all the money was in my account, and I didn't look any closer than that. Our accountants had become close to our family. They knew about the divorce, of course, and they also knew about the emotional fallout it had caused.

By the time we realized all of this, the IRS was coming after me for more than $200,000 that I owed in back taxes. This was news to me.

In the end, my accountants not only caused me to lose a substantial amount of money, but my mom and I were responsible for these huge tax bills we owed.

Now I understood why there had been a delay when I was trying to buy my ticket for the Concorde. My accountants had been stalling me. By that point, nearly everything I had ever earned was gone. I had to cash in my ticket and stay in Los Angeles to try and salvage what little I had left.

I was pretty shaky at that point, and I couldn't handle it by myself. It took my mom six months just to go through all of the records and find out everything they had done. But the worst part was discovering that my dad should have known our accountants couldn't be trusted because of what they had done to him. He could have stopped it from happening to us if he had told us what happened to him. He chose not to tell us. I guess that was his way of getting back at my mom during their divorce, but it ended up hurting me more than it did her. When we confronted him, he said he thought we had known. And he never apologized.

When I was totally broke and trying to get back on my feet, he betrayed me again. I had put my car in my dad's name so the IRS couldn't get it. I know this wasn't the right thing to do, but I was trying to hold on to what little I had left, and it seemed like my only option. It didn't matter anyhow, because my dad ratted me out to the IRS. Maybe he was getting revenge on me, too, punishing me for all of those years when he had hated me for making more money than he did. This latest betrayal broke my heart all over again.

I was still very much in the public eye at this time, and *Jet* magazine reported the story of how my mom and I filed a lawsuit against our accountants, charging them with embezzling more than $400,000. We settled, but they never really paid me back. I was forced to sell my house in Northridge because I couldn't afford it anymore. As part of the settlement, I was given a house in Sun Valley. This was small comfort, since they continued to live in a nice house that I'm sure I paid for. My mom ran into one of our former accountants a few years back, and the woman said she was buying lottery tickets so she could win the lottery and give me my money. Yeah, right.

I think the worst part of all was that I still owed money to the IRS, and when I couldn't come up with it, they came after me. That's what finally broke me, the fact that, on top of everything else, I was getting in trouble for something I hadn't knowingly done wrong.

I needed money, so I had to go back to work. But I had been feeling like I needed a break before all of this happened. By the time the truth had come out, I was in no condition to work.

Now that there was no *Diff'rent Strokes* set to report to on Monday mornings, for the first time in eight years, and no commercials or TV movies lined up, for the first time in more than a decade, everything caught up with me. It was all too much: my dad's abuse, the child molestation, the racism, losing the money I'd earned. I started having these dark thoughts that I couldn't shake, that I must be a loser for so many bad things to happen to me, that I must be a loser because I didn't have any money, that I must be a loser simply because of who I was. I wanted it all to go away. I could make that happen as long as I had enough drugs, and enough of the sexually adventurous girls who came along with the drugs. I started using drugs every day. I started going out every single night. I was just going out, going out, going out, clubbing, doing drugs, doing more drugs, having sex with women, and then more drugs, and women, and drugs, over and over, until I went under.

I should have been working because I needed money to pay the IRS and get back on my feet. I could have been working. I wasn't one of those child stars who hits puberty and never works again. I was twenty when *Diff'rent Strokes* ended, and by that point I had already made the transition to playing older characters. I didn't stop working because nobody wanted me. I stopped working because I got into hard-core drugs, and I wasn't there to be employed. I was gone.

I wasn't about to line up work and then blow it off. Even though I was a total mess in every other area, I still cared about my professional reputation. But there was one time that I got a job and I didn't show up. It wasn't even because I was doing drugs. My dad was still my agent, and he had gotten me a job on a Roger Corman film. But I didn't want to do anything for my dad at that point, so I bailed on the job. Of course, looking back, I can see that my decision was probably a huge mistake and the beginning of my downfall. But I wasn't able to think things through at all right then. I didn't work as an actor again for a very long time.

I was becoming more and more self-destructive in all areas of my life in late '85 and early '86. I used to ride motorcycles, and I was hit by a car on each one of my bikes. My most serious accident happened while I was driving to a party at my friend's house. I had been drinking, so I shouldn't have been driving anyhow. I came around the corner, and there was a construction sign in the street. I hit the construction sign, flew up in the air about ten feet, and came crashing down. I was knocked out for about twenty minutes. My friends came driving along and saw me lying there on the side of the road. They picked me up, put me in the car, and brought me to my house. I had amnesia for about eight hours. I had no idea who I was. I had also cracked my twelfth vertebra, and I ended up spending a couple of weeks in the hospital. My helmet was completely demolished. I'm lucky I lived. But I didn't feel lucky, and I went on to risk my life again and again in the years to come.

I started getting into trouble around then, too. In 1986 I hired this guy named Miles Gryber to make some small alterations to my Porsche by painting the outside and fixing some things up on the inside. But instead of doing a good job, he jerry-rigged everything in it, and the whole car started driving really weird. I would go to turn on the lights, and the windshield wipers would turn on instead. I had already paid him $4,000 for the work, so I was pissed, especially when he told my mom she owed him even more money. Like an idiot, I opened my big mouth.

"If you don't take care of this, I'll come back and blow your shop up," I said.

A couple of weeks later, someone really did blow up one of his cars. I know that probably sounds like way too much of a coincidence to be true, but I guess someone else must have been after him. I swear, though, it wasn't me. I've come clean about doing some crazy things in my life, but this wasn't one of them. Of course, no one was going to believe that. So the police came to my house and arrested me on suspicion of threatening this guy. They found some old fireworks lying around, and they decided that must be what I used to blow up the car. I couldn't believe it. I ended up beating the charges, but it was all over the news. I had to hold a press conference at my mom's house to deny that I'd even made the threat in the first place. I mean, how was I going to explain something like that? Especially when the papers were getting their first taste of me as the source of one of their favorite stories: the former child star who's all grown up and having a run of trouble with the law. They milked my problems for all they were worth.

During that time, I met and started dating Becky, the woman who would become my first wife. We had both grown up in the San Fernando Valley, and I met her at the end of *Diff'rent Strokes* through a friend of a friend. I liked her because she was cute and fun, and she had this great, sassy attitude. After all of the Playmates and Raiderettes I had been with, I was into being with a nice, normal girl from a middle-class family for a change. The only problem was that her dad and I never got along so even though I liked her mom, I never really felt comfortable around her family. There was another problem, too. Becky and I fought a lot. And we hung out and did drugs together at my place in Sun Valley. I was in pretty bad shape.

I had another run-in with my dad at a family party. He was mouthing off about me in front of everyone, and I couldn't take the disrespect and abuse anymore. I told him off and then stormed out of the party, and that was the last time I saw him for many years. I was glad to finally have him out of my life.

I was using coke to numb my feelings, and with nothing else to do all day, and a lot of pain to numb, I was soon doing a lot of coke. I still didn't like snorting it that much, though, and when I started doing enough of it, I started getting nosebleeds, which hurt and were disgusting. I'd be coming down, and that was the last thing I wanted, because if my head cleared, my feelings might break through.

When I'd been in the Hollywood party scene, there were always drugs around, and it was easy to buy as much as I needed. But once I started using more, I had to start buying my drugs from dealers I didn't know, and that was a problem, too. People were shady, and I didn't have a clue how to handle myself. Sometimes I'd give someone money, and he'd take off with it and never come back, or he wouldn't come back for an hour, and by then he'd already have done half of my drugs. There wasn't much I could do about it, no matter how pissed off I was. It wasn't like I could call the cops, and I needed the drugs.

I was introduced to a solution by someone I had been friends with in Canoga Park as a kid. He was a Russian guy, Vlad, so he was part of the little gang of foreigners and outsiders we had gotten together to stand off against the prejudice we all faced at the time. I had known him for years at that point. We were hanging out one day, and we decided to do some coke.

"You've got to try it this way," he said.

He brought the coke into the kitchen and put it in a glass with some water, which he then put into a pot filled with water on the stove. He added some baking soda and cooked it up into crack. He showed me how to cut off a rock with a razor blade and smoke it in a little glass pipe. I leaned against the counter and watched him warily, my arms crossed over my chest. Now, at this point, coke was everywhere, but nobody I knew smoked crack. It was considered very ghetto. That's the funny thing about drug addicts. They're snobs, just like everybody else. They always think whatever they're doing is better than whatever everyone else is doing, and that everyone should stop using but them. Drugs don't do anything for the IQ.

"Why are you messing with that stuff?" I asked him.

"Just try it, my friend," he said. "It's the best high ever."

I watched carefully as he balanced a piece of rock on a crack pipe, put it to his lips, lit it, and then inhaled deeply. I could tell it was good by the way his face went all blank and happy. Maybe I'd try it just this once. He handed me the pipe and I copied what he had done. When I inhaled, it burned my throat, my eyes watered, and I coughed. I was high, but I felt weird.

At first I didn't like how crack made me feel. A coke high was light and fun, but this was more intense. I could feel it completely take over every cell in my body. But the thing about crack is it's possible to smoke a lot of it, which meant I could stay high all the time. I definitely wanted to be high all the time. Once I got used to how crack consumed me, I switched over. And I stayed high all the time.

My friend lived near South Central, which definitely deserved its reputation for gangs and drugs. We would hang out at his house and then go to a drug house he knew of, where we'd buy coke to cook up into crack. The first time he took me into a crack house, I was disgusted. There were torn, dirty sheets draped over the windows to block the daylight. And it smelled bad, stale and rotten, with the chemical stink of crack hanging thick over everything. As my eyes adjusted to the dim light, I registered total filth: bare, stained mattresses strewn about on the floor, ratty couches and chairs with the stuffing torn out, broken-down figures, skinny and feral, more monster than human, except for their wide-eyed, wired faces, sprawled about wherever, garbage crumpled and scattered on the floor around them.

Soon all of this became normal to me. I couldn't wait to go back to Vlad's house to cook up the drugs myself, so I started buying the crack rock and smoking it right where we had gone to score. Once I started getting high in South Central, I couldn't always make the twenty-minute drive back to my house. I was still new to crack, and driving on the freeway when I was high made me too paranoid, especially with the way the cops loved to torment me. I started renting myself a motel room in South Central. Becky and I fought about it. But I didn't care. Soon I was spending all my time in South Central, with or without Vlad, and smoking half an ounce a day.

When I first started scoring crack alone, I was seriously green. I had no clue about all of the stunts crackheads pulled to scam rock out of people who didn't know any better. I was an easy mark, especially because people recognized me from TV and figured I must be rich and soft. They were half right. And they took full advantage.

I sprawled back on the couch, having just smoked some of the rock I had bought, my eyes fluttering in my skull. The old guy who ran the place started shaking his head and complaining under his breath.

"Damn, that's cold," he said.

"What?" I said, trying to focus.

"I let you get high in my house," he said. "That I bought back in '72, and you ain't even gonna break me off a piece? You gonna have to raise on out of here."

I reached into my pocket and felt around for a rock. Maybe there was some etiquette I didn't know about. I handed him a small piece of crack. He snatched it out of my hand and hurried off to a corner to smoke, still muttering as he went.

I took another hit. I was flying.

A younger guy moved in on me then, skinny, twitchy, dirty, like a thousand crack addicts I would see over the years. But you would have thought he was the master of ceremonies.

"Todd, my man," he said, moving up on me real smooth. "I know who you is, man. You don't need to be slumming it here. I don't even like to come around here myself. I know a better place. You come with me. I'll show you."

"Really?" I asked. "Better than this?"

"Hell of a lot better," he said. "Nobody be hassling you. And this other spot? They got pretty girls there. I'll hook you up, just cuz you a friend of mine. Just give me a few rocks first, and I'll take you."

I reached into my pocket and handed him a rock.

Before I knew it, they had played me all the way out of pocket in that crack house. Of course, once I'd heard those stories a few hundred times, along with the sob stories about lost jobs, homes, kids, I knew better than to believe. Or even to listen.

There are twenty-eight grams in an ounce. That's a lot of crack. It would have been hard as hell to snort fourteen grams of coke a day without my nose falling off. But I could smoke fourteen grams easy. A crack high was a nasty high, at least for me, because it was euphoric, but it made me evil. It drained the life out of me. I was not the same person anymore when I was high on crack. Anything could happen under the influence of crack, but only bad things, nothing good.

Some people who cross the line from powder cocaine to more hard-core use are into freebase, which is made by mixing a pure form of cocaine with ether. It's an intense high. But the stuff itself is incredibly flammable, especially when it first comes out of the ether. You've probably heard about how Richard Pryor set himself on fire back in the '80s while he was lighting freebase cocaine, and he used to do a bit about it in his stand-up routine.

I was into crack, which most people rocked up like my friend had taught me, by heating it up in a glass of water sitting in a pan of water. Most coke that gets sold on the street in LA has been cut with something, like baby laxative, to stretch the quantity more, but when it's cooked up, all of the filler evaporates, and only the pure drug is left. Crack is basically the pure form of coke, which is what makes the high so intense. Once it was cooked, it formed what looked like a tan bubble in the water. And then I added baking soda to make it form a rock, cooled it off with water, and waited for it to get hard before using a razor blade to cut it up.

Crack is sold by the size of the rock. A $20 rock is a dub, and larger quantities are bought in multiple dubs, as in, "Give me two dubs of rock, dog." All experienced dealers and addicts know exactly what size a rock should be and how much money it's worth. The problem with rocking it up that way, though, was that the glass was always getting too hot and breaking. When it broke, it was a hassle to fish out the crack. I'd throw some more baking soda in there and try to get it sorted out, working around the glass and chipping the crack off, but it was a hassle. I always lost a bunch of my stuff in the water, which pissed me off, especially when I really needed to get high. One day I was in the kitchen getting ready to rock up some coke and I happened to look at the microwave and realize it would do the same thing as a pan of water. I found an unbreakable glass, and it worked. If I got the coke hot enough, it melted down, and I'd swirl it around, throw in the baking soda, and I had crack. It was easy, and whatever I put in was what I got out.

Once I had my crack, I smoked it using a pipe. I was still into taking things apart and Macgyvering them back together, just like when I was a kid, but now, instead of building model airplanes, I built my own crack pipes. At home I used a crack pipe bottle, which looked like a bong. But when I was on the road, I always had a stem in my pocket, which was basically a glass pipe with a screen in it. Stems were good because they were easy to carry, but they could break. Or if they were too small they'd heat up like crazy. That's why a lot of crack addicts have burn marks around their mouth. Like I said, crack isn't exactly brain food. For actually smoking the crack, lighters were no good because they got too hot and left a nasty aftertaste, and matches burned too quickly. The best burn for coke was a nice blue flame. So a blowtorch was common, or alcohol on a cotton swab gripped with forceps.

These were the details that consumed my life. I didn't care about anything else anymore. Well, that's not exactly true. I cared about weird things. I didn't care about my career or my health, but I cared about the best way to rock up crack. And I cared about how I smelled. I was always taking showers. When I was high, I had to be naked. For some reason, I couldn't tolerate having clothes on me. If I was at a crack house, or hanging out with Vlad, I kept my clothes on, of course. But if I was getting high with a woman I was sleeping with, which was what I preferred anyhow, I pretty much always got naked and stayed naked until the crack ran out and it was time to go get more. I liked the women who were involved in the drug world, and I liked the things I could do with them, which was anything and everything, especially when I had drugs and they didn't. I really think that the women kept me hooked on drugs as much as the actual high did. They definitely helped me to forget.

I had a few nice things left after losing my money, but once I got into crack, I started getting rid of them. I sold my Porsche back to the dealer because it just didn't make sense to be driving a Porsche down to South Central LA to buy crack. Sure, I missed the things that went along with being a TV star when they were gone. I had earned good money for most of my life, and I was used to being able to buy whatever I wanted. It was hard, at first, to get used to going without these luxuries. But that was part of being an addict, too, and I was definitely an addict by this point. I didn't feel like I deserved nice things. I deserved nothing. Everything from my past had caught up with me, and I felt so bad about myself that I really believed I deserved to be a drug addict, and I deserved to live this dangerous, busted-up lifestyle. I had given up on acting completely. I didn't even think about it anymore. I had given up on myself. I didn't care how my life ended up. I just wanted it to be over. I wanted to be dead. Being high all the time was the next best thing.

I didn't care about anybody else in my life, either. I started avoiding Becky and my family and spending all my time in South Central. I think my sister, Verda, was the first person to figure out that I was using drugs. She and my brother, Jimmy, told my mom that she needed to talk to me about it. My mom couldn't believe it. Everybody thought I was the least likely person to get into drugs because there were so many years when drugs were all around me and I wasn't even tempted. When it later came out in public that I was using crack, my mom was approached by many young actors who told her how surprised they were, because I had actually stopped them from using drugs when we were friends as teenagers.

Of course, when my mom first confronted me, I denied it and said I wasn't using drugs. It was harder for me to hide what was going on from my brother, Jimmy. He was my best friend, and even though he never even drank, let alone did drugs, he was always up for hitting the town with me during my Hollywood years. And when I first moved out of our mom's house, Jimmy lived with me in the house I bought in Northridge. But by the time I was using heavily, he got fed up with the sketchy people I was bringing around and how out of it I always was, and he moved out. Becky took off, too. This was before interventions became so popular. There wasn't much they could do beyond trying to talk to me. When that didn't work, they just worried, and prayed, and tried to keep an eye on me as best they could.

But I didn't make this easy for them. When I started using, I would go underground for six months at a time. During that whole period, they wouldn't hear from me, and they wouldn't be able to find me, no matter how much they tried. Even if they did see me, it wasn't really me. Jimmy saw me on the street once during this period, and he didn't even recognize me. I wasn't his brother. I was just this person he had never seen before in his life. It freaked him out because I was so far gone.

I avoided my family when I was using because I couldn't stand to see how upset my mom was. I hated to cause her pain. But I also didn't want to stop getting high, and that was exactly what she was determined to make me do. She did convince me to go to rehab twice in the early years. The first time, I went to the Betty Ford Center, which was awful. Don't get me wrong, it was a beautiful place, and the pools were pretty, and the ducks on the grounds were cute. But it wasn't the right environment for me. I didn't learn anything while I was there. Not that I was ready to hear what they had to say anyhow. I used to fall asleep a lot during the workshops because I thought they was boring, and I hated being lectured. As soon I got let out, I started using again. After that, I went to St. Joseph's Medical Center. The first day I was there, they let me go on a walk. That was a bad move. I was walking with the group, and then, all of a sudden, they went right and I went left. I kept on walking, right back to the dope man. I wasn't ready for rehab at that point because I wasn't going for myself. I was going for everybody else. That never works.

My whole world soon revolved around crack. Every day was spent getting my daily fix and then smoking it, and usually having sex with whatever woman I was using drugs to keep near me at the time. I still had enough money left over from my acting career to cover my basic needs, which at that point were crack and a motel room where I could smoke it.

9

BILLY THE KID

I WAS A CRACK ADDICT, plain and simple. I had gotten rid of almost everything and everyone from my old life. I didn't want to be reminded of the days when I had lived my dreams. So I was killing Willis, cutting all ties to the people who remembered how full of possibility that time had been, when I was launching my career and helping to expand the idea of what black people could do on TV and in our culture. I wasn't that person anymore. I didn't want to run the risk of coming into contact with anyone who might remember him or remind me of how far I had fallen. That was the good thing about addicts. They had all fallen, too. They couldn't care less about who I was or where I'd been before. All they cared about was crack.

It was right before Christmas. Even in South Central LA, where I was holed up at this real low-rent place, the Star Motel, there were signs of the season. One house had "peace and joy" scrawled on the window in white spray paint. Another had multicolored Christmas lights strung up in the eaves. This used to be my favorite season. It was the only time of the year when everyone was nice to each other. Even my dad didn't seem so mean around the holidays. I had always loved it as a kid when we would get together with my mom's big family, all of those aunts and uncles and cousins crowded into the house, laughing and singing and eating good food. I wouldn't be going home for Christmas this year. I hadn't spoken to my mom or Jimmy and Verda in I didn't even know how long.

As a matter of fact, I wasn't going anywhere just then. I had locked myself out of my motel room again. But I was too far gone to do anything about it. I had lost my shoes, or maybe they were in my motel room. I didn't know. Either way, I was barefoot. That was an all-night binge for you. I was dirty. The T-shirt I was wearing was torn up. I didn't care. I sat there outside, smoking a cigarette and thinking.

"Hey, Todd, my man, what's happening?"

I looked up. It was Lewis and his girlfriend Melody. He was a postal worker, or a UPS deliveryman, or something. He was wearing some kind of a uniform. I didn't care enough to ask what kind. Crack addicts were all the same to me.

"Hey, I want to introduce you to this guy," he said, his voice excited, hustling me, as all addicts were always trying to get something out of someone.

I shrugged him off. I was not exactly feeling social.

"Billy's the man," he said. "They call him Billy the Kid. He'll hook you up. He runs all of these places around here."

That meant a connection to crack. Now I was interested. Lewis took me over to another room at the same motel where I was staying, which was ghetto fabulous all the way. The light blue paint was peeling, and the walls were scarred with bullet holes. He was excited for me to meet Billy, so he hurried us along like a master of ceremonies.

When we entered the room, the warm air smelled of stale to-bacco smoke and the sour odor of dried vomit. The shag green carpet was full of cigarette burns. Unlike my room, there was a long hall-way we had to walk down before we came into the main bedroom, where I was able to see the person I was there to meet. He was a good-looking, light-skinned black guy. He was sitting on a bed that was covered with a yellow and green paisley comforter, and he had these two beautiful girls sitting next to him. When we came in, the three of them looked away from a bolted-down Zenith television, which was playing a CNN newscast. The dude smiled at me. Right away, I liked his style. I could tell he was a real hustla. He was older than I was, in his forties, maybe, slim and handsome in a movie villain way. His hair was gray and black, and slicked back in a ponytail that extended halfway down his back. It was tied back with four rubber bands, in true pimp sophisticate style.

He had a motel pillow on his lap, which seemed odd to me, but I didn't give it much thought. I was too busy checking out the girls sitting next to him, who I learned later were called Dita and Tracy. They were sexy girls in their early twenties. Both of them wore denim miniskirts and tank tops tied up in a navel-revealing knot. One of Dita's tank straps draped off her shoulder, revealing that she was going braless.

Lewis made the introductions. "Billy, I want you to meet Todd Bridges," he said. "And Todd, this is my main man, Billy. Todd likes the no-tell motels, too, because when he falls asleep in a crack house, someone always boosts his shit."

I glared at Lewis. I did not need him introducing me around as the crackhead who gets so strung out he can't handle his own.

"Nice to meet you, Billy," I said politely.

Billy moved the pillow off his lap, revealing a Ruger 9mm. He stood up, nonchalantly stuffed the gun down the back of his pants, and gave me a big hug.

"What's up, baby?" Billy said. "It's an honor. Believe me. Did Lewis tell you that I remember you when you were on that show *Fish* with Abe Vigoda?"

"Yeah, Lewis told me," I said. "Thanks, man."

"I always thought of you as this smart, tough kid," he said. "I can tell your parents are good people."

That almost rocked me back on my heels.

Lewis let out a short, sarcastic laugh, but then caught himself.

I smiled at Billy and nodded in acknowledgment of what he'd said. I couldn't believe how kind and genuine he was being. Most people who spotted me around here said, "What the fuck happened?" or "What's a guy like you doing here?"

But Billy was different. Right from the start, I liked and respected him. Even more than that, I admired him. There was something civilized about him. And he didn't want anything from me. All he wanted was to be able to say that he'd met Todd Bridges. Nice as he was, I was happy to oblige him.

Lewis was well aware of how much Billy wanted to meet me, and like all addicts, he was working the angles, hoping to get something out of it.

"Billy, since I brought Todd to meet you, I was wondering if we could discuss that piece I owed you," he said. "You know, so I could get some la-la on—"

Billy interrupted him before Lewis could say the word "credit."

"We'll talk about that later, dog," Billy said.

He stepped forward and motioned for me to come all the way into the room. Lewis was about to follow, but Billy blocked his way.

"This is grown folks' business," he said.

Lewis shook off his embarrassment and fear and tried to look cool.

"Sure, Billy, I'm a run downstairs to the machine and get me a pack of bigarettes," he said, taking off with his Melody.

Billy fake-smiled at him. "You do that," he said.

Billy motioned for me to have a seat.

"Did you hear that nigga set tripping with me?" Billy asked.

"I don't get it," I said. With Billy, I felt like I didn't have to be on my guard.

"He was talking about getting him a pack of 'bigarettes,'" Billy said. "Some Bloods won't say the letter 'c' when they want to call out their colors. Thinks he's gonna run game on me. I'd like to see him try."

I sat on the bed while Billy squatted down and reached under the bed for a small metal lockbox. Sitting down next to me, he removed two pipes and a small plastic bag filled with jumbo pieces. Most crack rock is about the size of gravel, if that. But these were some rocks. They were a little larger than those big, black jumbo grapes with the seeds in them. Billy watched my face.

"You like the jumbos, huh?" he said.

"I like," I replied.

I watched Billy carefully as he removed one of the glass pipes from his box. He blew into the primary chamber of the resin-stained device, trying to remove some of the buildup from his previous smoke-outs. It was no use. The glass was permanently colored an opaque, yellowish-brown.

He retrieved an off-white crack rock from the Baggie, perched the la-la on top of the pipe, and placed it in front of my face. I grinned as he handed me a Zippo.

Click.

I smelled butane from the lighter and then the sweet-sour crack smell. Just as I started to inhale, I thought, "I love this stuff." Another thought quickly followed. "Maybe too much." But then everything was swept away by an orgasmic numbness that moved like a wave through my body. It started in my lungs and worked its way outward. The pleasurable movement seemed to take minutes to ease its way throughout my entire body. But, in reality, it was no more than a second before my eyes had rolled back and I was smiling blissfully.

Billy let out a happy chuckle that seemed to say, "I've got the shit."

I returned the pipe to Billy.

Click.

The sound of Billy taking his hit echoed in my head gently, as if it were a million miles away. The cocaine surged through my veins, and my heart beat like a hummingbird's wings. Like the kid I had been on Christmas morning, I didn't have a care in the world. I leaned back and enjoyed the only good feeling I had in my life right then. The euphoria slowly receded, and I sat back up.

As I focused on the room again, Billy passed the pipe to the two girls. Dita put the pipe between her full lips and examined the half-smoked rock sitting at the end of the chamber. Before lighting it, she changed her focus to make eye contact with me. Still very much on my high, I got horny, like I always did. I gave her a subtle nod, and she smiled at me. Billy noticed this go-down and smirked at me, gesturing toward the bathroom.

"Go on and handle your scandal, Todd," he said. "She plays a mean trumpet."

Still dazed from my hit, I didn't understand at first. Then I got it, and I laughed. Billy, Tracy, and Dita all laughed along with me.

After sucking down her hit of the candy, Dita stood and headed to the bathroom. I followed behind her and closed the door. Billy had not lied. She was a regular Dizzy Gillespie.

When we came out of the bathroom, I saw that Lewis and Melody were back and standing just inside the door. They were each smoking a cigarette. Billy sat on the floor with his back against the bed. His sleeve was rolled up, and he was watching the news broadcast that still played on the TV. Tracy tied off his arm and prepared his hit of coke.

Best friends forever: Me, already loving the camera at an early age, with my brother Jimmy and my sister Verda. We've always been best friends, and there was never any competition in our house.
Courtesy of Todd Bridges

Happy days: A rare happy moment with my dad, James Bridges. From left to right: my dad, my sister Verda, and me, hamming it up for the camera.
Courtesy of Todd Bridges

Little devil: I insisted my mom let me be the devil for Halloween. From left to right: my brother Jimmy, me, my mom, and my sister Verda.
Courtesy of Todd Bridges

My TV family: The cast of *Diff'rent Strokes*—me as Willis Jackson, Charlotte Rae as Edna Garrett, Gary Coleman as Arnold Jackson, Conrad Bain as Philip Drummond, and Dana Plato as Kimberly Drummond—in the early, innocent days, before tension—and romance—blossomed on the set. *Everett Collection, Inc.*

A big brother at last: The youngest of three children, I always wanted to be an older brother. I finally got my chance, playing Willis Jackson with Gary Coleman as my little brother, Arnold Jackson. And for the first two seasons, we were as close as brothers. *Everett Collection, Inc.*

Art imitates life and life imitates art: With my *Diff'rent Strokes* girlfriend, Charlene DuPrey, played by my real-life girlfriend, Janet Jackson.
Everett Collection, Inc.

Meet and greet: One of the many perks of being a child star was getting to meet my heroes. This picture is of the football player Ricky Bell, my mom and manager Betty Bridges, and me.
Courtesy of Todd Bridges

Don't blame me for the '80s. Here I am making one of many public appearances I did during the height of my *Diff'rent Strokes* fame. This was a cool look back then, I swear. *Courtesy of Todd Bridges*

You can see where I get my smile. This family reunion includes (left to right): my sister Verda, my cousin Vickie Pryor, my grandmother Catherine Lawrence, my great grandmother Alice Pounds, my brother Jimmy, my mom Betty, and, of course, me. *Courtesy of Todd Bridges*

MUNICIPAL COURT OF BURBANK JUDICIAL DISTRICT

COUNTY OF LOS ANGELES, STATE OF CALIFORNIA

THE PEOPLE OF THE STATE OF CALIFORNIA,

                           Plaintiff | Case No. GA013909

         v.

01 TODD ANTHONY BRIDGES, | FELONY COMPLAINT
   aka MICHAEL WAYNE WINSTON

                     Defendant

FILED
LOS ANGELES SUPERIOR COURT

MAR - 2 1993

JAMES H. DEMPSEY, CLERK
BY R. MALDONADO, DEPUTY

The undersigned is informed and believes that:

                COUNT 1

    On or about December 29, 1992, in the County of Los Angeles, the crime of
SALE OF A CONTROLLED SUBSTANCE, in violation of HEALTH AND SAFETY CODE SECTION
11379(a), a Felony, was committed by TODD ANTHONY BRIDGES, who did willfully
and unlawfully transport, import into the State of California, sell, furnish,
administer, and give away, and offer to transport, import into the State of
California, sell, furnish, administer, and give away, and attempt to import
into the State of California and transport a controlled substance, to wit,
methamphetamine.

    "NOTICE: If convicted of this offense the court must suspend your driving
privileges if you are under the age of 21 years. Vehicle Code section
13202.5".

FILED
'93 JUN 11 AM 28
MUNICIPAL COURT
DEPUTY

            Page 1 of Case No. GA013909

MEDICAL ORDER

_____ COURT OF CALIFORNIA, COUNTY OF LOS ANGELES

___ OF CALIFORNIA,) CASE NO. GA013909
) BKG # FISH
       PLAINTIFF,)
) LOCATION MCJ/IRC1
___ ANTHONY) DIV/DEPT NEC
       DEFENDANT,)

___ COUNTY OF LOS ANGELES, AND MEDICAL SERVICES, LOS ANGELES

___ndant has moved this court for an order requiring a medical examination or specific medical

___med defendant appears to need the following:

    Medical Examination ☐   Dental Examination

KOTE 1250 Mg - Daily
ARE 1600 mg - Daily
___PEUTIC EXERCISE - DAILY

___ant to 1202.1, 1202.6 P.C., 199.96, 199.97, 199.99 H&S)

___ass to be completed on or before _____ (date)

___h to be advised of the results on or before _____ (date)

☐   The Court does not wish to be advised of the results.

DEFENDANT ORDERED TO RETURN TO COURT: _____ (date)

___RING THEREFORE, IT IS ORDERED.
51-93   JUDICIAL OFFICER: _____ SIGNATURE/STAMP

        COURT ADDRESS:
                County Clerk
                300 East Walnut
                Pasadena, California 91101

___IFF'S DEPARTMENT, MEDICAL RECORDS FACSIMILE #: (213) 620-1308 or 620-0225

9-1-93 AM 10:00 AM

FILED
LOS ANGELES SUPERIOR COURT

NOV 29 1993

EDWARD M. KRITZMAN

M.B. JIMENEZ, DEPUTY

    SUPERIOR COURT OF THE STATE OF CALIFORNIA

      FOR THE COUNTY OF LOS ANGELES

DEPARTMENT NORTHEAST C   HON. THOMAS W. STOEVER, JUDGE

THE PEOPLE OF THE STATE OF CALIFORNIA,)
                PLAINTIFF,)
)
         VS.   ) NO. GA 013909-01
)   PLEA
TODD ANTHONY BRIDGES,)
                DEFENDANT.)

    PASADENA, CALIFORNIA; THURSDAY, JULY 29, 1993

            11:45 A.M.

    UPON THE ABOVE DATE, THE DEFENDANT BEING PRESENT
IN COURT AND REPRESENTED BY COUNSEL, JOHN COCHRANE,
ESQUIRE, OF LOS ANGELES COUNTY; THE PEOPLE BEING
REPRESENTED BY CAROL RASH, DEPUTY DISTRICT
ATTORNEY OF LOS ANGELES COUNTY, THE FOLLOWING
PROCEEDINGS WERE HELD:

ORIGINAL

Documents from my 1993 court case,
in which I was charged with sale of a
controlled substance and possession of a
controlled substance with a firearm.

3 P & S

SUPERIOR COURT OF CALIFORNIA, COUNTY OF LOS ANGELES

HONORABLE THOMAS W STOEVER   S VAN LEEUWEN   JUDGE   Deputy Sheriff

DEPT.   NE C

K KALLMAN   Deputy Clerk
M REID   Reporter

CASE NO.   GA013909-01

(Parties and counsel checked if present)

PEOPLE OF THE STATE OF CALIFORNIA

VS

01 BRIDGES TODD ANTHONY (X)

CHARGE   AKA   WINSTON MICHAEL WAYNE

H11370.A 01CT., H11379.A 01CT.

Counsel for People:
DEPUTY DISTRICT ATTY: C RASH (X)

Counsel for Defendant: J L COCHRAN, PVT. (X)

X _____ (BOX CHECKED IF ORDER APPLICABLE)

NATURE OF PROCEEDINGS 1203.03 REVIEW/P & S   REM   3-12-93

71 ☐   _____, IS SWORN AS THE ENGLISH/ _____ INTERPRETER. ☐ OATH FILED PER 68560 G.C.
☐ DUE TO CONFLICT OF INTERESTS, PUBLIC DEFENDER RELIEVED. PURSUANT TO **PENAL CODE SECTION 987.2**/**GOVERNMENT CODE SECTION 31000** ALTERNATE DEFENSE COUNSEL _____ IS APPOINTED.

72 ☒   CRIMINAL PROCEEDINGS ~~XXXXXXXXXXXXXXXXXXXXXXX~~/ARE RESUMED.
73 ☐   DEFENDANT ORDERED DELIVERED TO DEPARTMENT OF CORRECTIONS PURSUANT TO PENAL CODE SECTION 1203.03.
☐ DEFENDANT ORDERED DELIVERED TO CALIFORNIA YOUTH AUTHORITY PURSUANT TO WELFARE AND INSTITUTIONS CODE SECTION 707.2.

74 ☐   ON _____ MOTION, PROBATION AND SENTENCE HEARING/FURTHER PROCEEDINGS CONTINUED TO _____
AT _____ A.M. IN DEPT. _____ ☐ NON-APPEARANCE CALENDAR ☐ DEFENDANT ORDERED TO RETURN
75 ☐   ☐ DEFENDANT PERSONALLY AND ALL COUNSEL WAIVE TIME FOR SENTENCING.
☐ SUPPLEMENTAL PROBATION REPORT/PROGRESS REPORT ORDERED RE: _____

76 ☒   PROBATION DENIED/SENTENCE IMPOSED AS FOLLOWS:
☒ IMPRISONED IN STATE PRISON FOR ■ TERM PRESCRIBED BY LAW _____ ☒ TOTAL OF __6__ YEARS __0__ MONTHS
☒ COURT SELECTS THE _MID_ TERM OF __3__ YEARS/~~MONTHS~~ FOR THE BASE TERM AS TO COUNT __1__
☒ PLUS __X 3__ YEARS/~~MONTHS~~ PURSUANT TO SECTION _12022.C_ OF THE _PENAL_ CODE
☒ PLUS _MID TERM OF 3 YEARS PURSUANT TO SECTION 11370.1A OF THE PENAL_ ~~XXXXXXXXXXXXX~~ ◆
☐ TO BE HOUSED AT CALIFORNIA YOUTH AUTHORITY PURSUANT TO SECTION 1731.5(C) W.I.C.
☐ COMMITTED TO CALIFORNIA YOUTH AUTHORITY. THE TERM OF IMPRISONMENT TO WHICH THE DEFENDANT WOULD HAVE BEEN SENTENCED _CODE_
PURSUANT TO SECTION 1170 PENAL CODE IS _____ YEARS _____ MONTHS.
☐ IMPRISONED IN LOS ANGELES COUNTY JAIL FOR TERM OF _____ AS TO COUNT(S) _____
☐ PAY $ _____ FINE TO SUPERIOR COURT, PLUS PENALTY AND SURCHARGE.
☐ PAY $ _____ RESTITUTION FINE TO STATE VICTIMS RESTITUTION FUND PURSUANT TO SECTION 13967(A) G.C.

77 ☐   SENTENCE IS SUSPENDED.
78 ☒   IMPOSITION OF SENTENCE SUSPENDED. **PROBATION** GRANTED FOR __5__ YEAR(S). ☐ PROBATION TO BE WITHOUT FORMAL SUPERVISION.
79 ☐   DIVERSION GRANTED FOR PERIOD OF _____ YEARS/MONTHS PER SECTION 1000.2 P.C.
☐ DEFENDANT PERSONALLY AND ALL COUNSEL WAIVE TIME FOR TRIAL.

1 ☒   SPEND FIRST __153__ DAYS/~~MONTHS~~ IN COUNTY JAIL. ☐ NOT TO BE ELIGIBLE FOR COUNTY PAROLE
☐ WORK FURLOUGH PROGRAM RECOMMENDED
2 ☐   PAY A FINE OF $ _____ PLUS PENALTY ASSESSMENT (1484 P.C. & 76000 G.C.) THROUGH PROBATION OFFICER.
☒ PAY $ _50.00_ LAB FEE PURSUANT TO 11372.5 H&S CODE ($50 FOR EACH H&S VIOLATION) THROUGH PROBATION OFFICER.
3 ☐   PAY RESTITUTION TO THE VICTIM(S)/VICTIM RESTITUTION FUND PURSUANT TO 1203.04 P.C. **IN AMOUNT OF $** _____
IN AMOUNT AND MANNER AS INSTRUCTED BY PROBATION OFFICER, INCLUDING SERVICE CHARGE PER 1203.1 P.C.
☐ MINIMUM PAYMENT OF RESTITUTION TO BE _____
4 ☒   PAY $ _200.00_ RESTITUTION FINE PURSUANT TO SECTION 13967 (A) G.C. THROUGH PROBATION OFFICER. ☐ TOTAL AMOUNT
TO INCLUDE A SERVICE CHARGE IN THE AMOUNT OF $ _____ PURSUANT TO SECTION 13967(d) G.C. ☐ STAYED WHILE
DEFENDENT PAYS RESTITUTION AND IF RESTITUTION IS PAID IN FULL, STAY SHALL BE PERMANENT.
5 ☒   NOT DRINK OR POSSESS ANY ALCOHOLIC BEVERAGE AND STAY OUT OF PLACES WHERE THEY ARE THE CHIEF ITEM OF SALE.
6 ☒   NOT USE OR POSSESS ANY NARCOTICS, DANGEROUS OR RESTRICTED DRUGS OR ASSOCIATED PARAPHERNALIA EXCEPT WITH VAILD
PRESCRIPTION, AND STAY AWAY FROM PLACES WHERE USERS, BUYERS OR SELLERS CONGREGATE.
7 ☒   NOT ASSOCIATE WITH PERSONS KNOWN BY YOU TO BE NARCOTIC OR DRUG USERS OR SELLERS.
8 ☒   SUBMIT TO PERIODIC **ANTI-NARCOTIC TESTS**/~~XXXXXXXXXXXX~~ AS DIRECTED BY THE PROBATION OFFICER OR OTHER PEACE OFFICER.   SEE BOX 90
9 ☐   HAVE NO BLANK CHECKS IN POSSESSION; NOT WRITE ANY PORTION OF ANY CHECKS; AND NOT HAVE BANK ACCOUNT UPON WHICH
YOU MAY DRAW CHECKS. NOT USE OR POSSESS OR APPLY FOR ANY CREDIT OR ATM CARD.
10 ☐   **NOT ASSOCIATE WITH**/STAY AWAY FROM _____
11 ☒   COOPERATE WITH PROBATION OFFICER IN A PLAN FOR _PSYCHOLOGICAL AND SUBSTANCE ABUSE COUNSELING_
12 ☐   SUPPORT DEPENDENTS AS DIRECTED BY PROBATION OFFICER.
13 ☒   SEEK AND MAINTAIN TRAINING, SCHOOLING, OR EMPLOYMENT AS APPROVED BY PROBATION OFFICER.
14 ☒   KEEP PROBATION OFFICER ADVISED OF YOUR RESIDENCE AT ALL TIMES.
15 ☐   SURRENDER DRIVER'S LICENSE TO CLERK OF COURT TO BE RETURNED TO DEPARTMENT OF MOTOR VEHICLES.
16 ☐   NOT DRIVE A MOTOR VEHICLE UNLESS LAWFULLY LICENSED AND INSURED.
17 ☒   NOT OWN, USE OR POSSESS ANY DANGEROUS OR DEADLY WEAPONS.
18 ☒   SUBMIT YOUR PERSON AND PROPERTY UNDER YOUR CONTROL TO SEARCH OR SEIZURE AT ANY TIME OF THE DAY OR NIGHT BY
ANY PROBATION OFFICER OR OTHER PEACE OFFICER, WITH OR WITHOUT A WARRANT OR PROBABLE CAUSE. _WITH OR WITHOUT_
19 ☒   OBEY ALL LAWS. OBEY ALL ORDERS, RULES AND REGULATIONS OF THE PROBATION DEPARTMENT AND OF THE COURT. _REASONABLE_
20 ☐   USE ONLY YOUR TRUE NAME, STATED TO BE _____ ~~SUSPENSION~~
21 ☐   REPORT TO PROBATION OFFICER UPON RELEASE FROM CUSTODY/WITHIN _____
22 ☐   IF YOU LEAVE THE COUNTRY, DO NOT REENTER THE UNITED STATES ILLEGALLY. IF YOU DO RETURN, REPORT TO THE PROBATION
OFFICER WITHIN _____ AND PRESENT DOCUMENTATION WHICH PROVES YOU ARE IN THE UNITED STATES LEGALLY.

80 ☒   DEFENDANT GIVEN TOTAL CREDIT FOR __153__ DAYS IN CUSTODY (__102__ DAYS ACTUAL CUSTODY AND __51__ DAYS GOOD TIME/WORK TIME).
81 ☒   ~~XXXXXX~~/COUNTS TO RUN ~~XXXXXXXXXXXX~~ CONCURRENTLY WITH _EACH OTHER, ALLEGATION TO RUN CONSECUTIVE_
82 ☐   STAY OF EXECUTION OF _____ GRANTED TO _TO COUNT 1_
83 ☐   ON MOTION OF PEOPLE, **COUNTS/ENHANCEMENTS** REMAINING ARE DISMISSED IN FURTHERANCE OF JUSTICE/PER CASE SETTLEMENT
AGREEMENT.
84 ☐   COURT ADVISES DEFENDANT OF HIS APPEAL/PAROLE RIGHTS. ☐ NOTICE OF APPEAL IS RECEIVED.
85 ☐   "NOTICE RE CERTIFICATE OF REHABILITATION AND PARDON" GIVEN TO DEFENDANT.
86 ☐   DEFENDANT TO PAY COSTS OF PROBATION SERVICES IN AMOUNT OF $ _____ /AMOUNT TO BE DETERMINED BY PROBATION
OFFICER.
87 ☐   COURT FINDS DEFENDANT DOES NOT HAVE PRESENT ABILITY TO PAY COSTS OF INCARCERATION/LEGAL SERVICES/PROBATION SERVICES.
88 ☐   DEFENDANT IS REFERRED TO THE TREASURER/TAX COLLECTOR FOR FINANCIAL EVALUATION.
89 ☐   PROBATION OFFICER TO REGISTER THE DEFENDANT WITH C.I.I. AND REPORT ANY NEW ARREST TO THE COURT.
90 ☒   ~~XXXXXXXXXXXXXXXXXXXXX~~ ADDITIONAL CONDITIONS OF PROBATION _IN LIEU OF ADDITIONAL JAIL TIME AND IN_
ADDITION TO CONDITION #8, DEFENDANT TO ATTEND PSYCHOLOGICAL AND SUBSTANCE ABUSE COUNSELING
AS OUTLINED IN BROTMAN MEDICAL CENTER REPORT. UPON RELEASE FROM CUSTODY DEFENDANT IS
TO ENROLL IN RESIDENTIAL DRUG TREATMENT PROGRAM FOR A PERIOD OF NOT LESS THAN 1 YEAR.
91 ☐   SHERIFF IS ORDERED TO ALLOW DEFENDANT _____ PHONE CALLS AT DEFENDANT'S OWN EXPENSE
92 ☐   DEFENDANT FAILS TO APPEAR WITH/WITHOUT SUFFICIENT CAUSE _ALL VIOLATIONS TO BE HEARD IN FRONT OF JUDGE_
93 ☐   BAIL, IF POSTED, FORFEITED/O.R. REVOKED. BENCH WARRANT ORDERED ISSUED/REISSUED/AND HELD UNTIL _THOMAS STOEVER_
☐ NO BAIL ☐ BAIL FIXED AT $ _____
94 ☐   DEFENDANT APPEARING, BENCH ORDERED RECALLED/QUASHED. ☐ RECALL NO. _____ ISSUED. ☐ ABSTRACT FILED.

☒ REMANDED   ☐ BAIL   ☐ BAIL EXON.   ☒ ON PROBATION   PAGE ____ OF ____
☒ RELEASED   ☐ O.R.   ☐ BOND NO. _____   ☐ IN CUSTODY OTHER MATTER
#334471   ☐ BENCH WARRANT   ☐ O.R. DISCHARGED   ☐ ON DIVERSION
MINUTES ENTERED
12-9-93

76C778 (R 2-93)   **3** P & S

Documents from my 1993 court case. Thanks to my mom's intervention, I was
able to go to an inpatient rehab facility and serve time on probation, rather
than face a trial and potential prison sentence.

Like father, like son: Me with my son Spencir, who has already
entered the family business, landing roles in several films.
Courtesy of Todd Bridges

Proud papa: Me with my daughter Bo.
Courtesy of Todd Bridges

Looks like we made it . . . I could not have survived
the hard times without the support of my family.
From left to right: my sister Verda, my mom Betty,
me, and my brother Jimmy.
Courtesy of Todd Bridges

"You know what?" he said. "Reagan is sleeping on that nigga Saddam Hussein. He's gonna be a problem. And the thing is, we're the ones a gave him all the weapons, back when we needed him as an ally."

He could have been a political analyst, the way he was talking. I was liking Billy more and more.

"So, Billy the Kid, you wanted to meet Todd Bridges, and my homeboy is sitting right over there, so . . . about that money I owe you? Can we forget that, dog?"

Billy slid a syringe into a bulging vein in the upper part of his forearm. I quickly looked away. Even though I smoked crack, needles still tripped me out as much as they did when I'd had to get a shot as a little kid. Here he was, taking the needle voluntarily. Ugh. Billy's head drifted back against the bed. Looking like some kind of perverse medical assistant, Tracy removed the needle that now dangled from his arm.

As soon as the tip of the hypodermic needle exited his body, Billy clenched his fists. His head whipped forward. Holy shit. Something was going down. The veins in his neck and on his forehead surged, his muscles tensed. His narcotic haze was gone, replaced with rage. I had never seen anyone change so drastically or so quickly. He jumped up and yanked his gun out of his waistband. Just like that, he ran over and smacked Lewis in the face with the butt of his semiautomatic weapon.

Lewis's head whipped to the side. He screamed and cuffed his mouth, which now dripped blood.

The girls and I looked at each other uncertainly. His anger peaking, Billy turned his gun on everybody in the room. We were all high and paranoid to begin with, and now we were wondering what he would do next.

"EVERYBODY! GET AGAINST THAT WALL! NOW!" Billy barked like a drill sergeant while waving his gun at us.

I moved slowly, unable to believe what was happening, trying to fight off the haze of my high.

"Billy?" I said. "What's going on, man?"

"Shut the fuck up and get against the wall!" he yelled. "All y'alls been stealing from me! Every last one of you bitches!"

"Stealing from you?" I said, my voice quivering, even though I tried hard to control it. "I just met you. I would never steal from you, or anybody else."

"Didn't I say shut the fuck up?" Billy yelled. He was even more agitated now.

I kept quiet after that. Billy really believed everyone in that room was running a mad game on him. Even me, who'd just met him for the first time.

Billy stood right in front of Lewis, who had tears in his eyes and was shaking from head to toe.

"You're gonna unass the money you owe me, Lewis," he yelled. "I ain't running no charity organization!"

"But Billy," Lewis whimpered.

Billy smacked him in the face again with the gun butt. Lewis's knees gave out and he screamed as he hit the ground with a thud. Like a bloodied boxer desperately climbing the ringside ropes, he leaned on the wall to get back up.

"Unass my money, bitch," Billy ordered again. He cocked his gun, reached into the bedroom closet, and pulled out an aluminum Little League bat.

"Y'all take off all your clothes," he said.

Lewis's girlfriend, Melody, had been watching all of this, her eyes huge.

"Billy, he made me skim some rocks off you," Melody said quickly. "But it was only four at the most."

"Youse a lie, you bitch!" Lewis said, shaking his bloody head in disgust.

"Quiet, both of you!" Billy demanded, pointing his Ruger at them.

"I knew it was Mr. Lewis Bigarettes, stealing from me," he said. "Mr. Lewis, peep this, if you want your debt forgiven, take this bat and stick it up in you."

Lewis's eyes got so wide, they looked like they might pop. They traveled between the bat and Billy, a pleading expression on his face.

"Now!" he said, pointing his gun at Lewis's head.

"And for your thieving, fat-ass girlfriend, I want her to eat out Dita and Tracy."

Both Lewis and Melody stood frozen in place while the rest of us watched in horror. Billy gestured at them with his gun.

Lewis took a deep breath and bent over with the baseball bat in his trembling right hand. He looked around the room. None of us moved. And then he proceeded.

When Melody saw this, she kneeled down in front of Tracy, who was lifting her skirt.

Lewis had the bat partly in when, oddly, he made a joke. "Hey, dude, got any lube?"

Billy actually loosened up and laughed. I couldn't believe it.

I tried not to look, but it was like a car accident, I couldn't help myself, and I watched from the corner of my eye as Lewis and Melody took their punishment. I was starting to panic. I was afraid I was going to be next, and I did not want any part of that action.

"Hey, Billy, man, please," I said. "I didn't steal nothing. Let me get my clothes on. I'll take you to my house, and you'll see that I have no reason to steal from you."

Everyone was silent for what seemed like the longest moment of my life as Billy considered my offer. He looked over at Lewis and Melody.

"Y'all get your clothes on and get your nasty, criminal asses away from me," he said. "Dita and Tracy, you're going with me and Todd."

Lewis and Melody ran out of the room half naked, still pulling their clothes on as they went. I watched them go, hoping I would get out of this one alive and unscathed.

Luckily, when we reached my five-bedroom house in Sun Valley, Billy was clearly impressed by what he saw. No matter how strung out I was during that time, I always kept my house nice, and it was clean and well furnished.

"Make yourselves at home," I said as Tracy and Dita walked around, admiring things. Billy came over and patted me on the back. I started to relax.

"This is nice," Billy said. "You're right, Todd. You don't need to steal from me."

I was relieved, but I kept like I'd been cool all along. We decided to hang out and do some coke. I offered drinks to everyone, and we ordered some pizza.

We were all getting comfortable, sitting at my Ethan Allen dining room table eating pepperoni pizza and drinking beers, when Dita let out a huge, manly belch and smacked her glass back down on the table.

Billy got up and backhanded her across the face.

"What the hell is wrong with your ignorant ass?" Billy said. "Say 'Excuse me' when you belch. And put a coaster underneath your glass."

"Sorry," she said, fighting back tears.

"You're going to tear this man's table up," he said. "You know how much a table like this costs?"

Not knowing what to do, I gave Billy a quick half nod and smile. After what I'd just seen, I certainly wasn't going to get between Billy and whatever justice he thought someone deserved.

"I'm sorry about her," he said. "She has no home training."

I couldn't get over Billy. The same guy who made two people

strip and sexually exploit themselves corrected a girl for her poor table etiquette? On the one hand, he definitely had a dark side. But he was almost refined, too. It depended on who he was with and what was going down. South Central isn't exactly a finishing school, and I was impressed that he had any kind of manners. I also liked that he was the one person I had met during that time who didn't need anything from me. He had his own drugs, his own money, his own girls. I knew he wasn't going to try to get anything over on me. That was rare in the drug world. When he saw my house, he relaxed around me, too. We ended up having a good time that night.

Billy and I hung out every day after that. We would do coke all day and all night, and then for the whole next day and night. And then we'd pass out two days later in a motel somewhere, sleep for a day and a half, wake up, and start all over again. That was about all of the living I could handle right about then.

Soon Billy started mentoring me, and that felt great. I'd always longed for the guidance I would have gotten from a real father figure. Finally I had one, no matter how misguided. I was too consumed by crack to grasp how dangerous Billy's influence was. But in many ways, Billy raised and matured me more than my own dad ever did. He definitely liked and respected me more, too. Even though Billy was far from a positive role model, and he definitely fed my addiction, he helped me to stay alive. He even built me up in some ways, too. That's how far gone I was; even the friendship of a violent, coke-addicted drug dealer made me feel better about myself than I had before.

Billy had two drug houses in South Central, and much of our daily routine involved bringing them drugs and then going back to collect money. To get the drugs, we did business with everyone who was dealing in South Central at the time—the Jamaicans, the Crips, and the Bloods—and there were things to know about each group to avoid getting ripped off or hurt. They were all pretty brutal, but the Jamaicans were the scariest. If a guy crossed them, they didn't just go after him. They took down his whole family. But as long as I was with Billy, I felt safe, no matter where we went. Billy was a relatively small player in the city at that time, but he had his neighborhood locked down, and he was respected by the right people, and that meant we could do business across different affiliations without trouble. Beyond that, I was too far gone to know or care that the DEA had officially labeled crack a national epidemic by 1989. I was clueless that it was becoming a serious plague in that neighborhood during the mid-'80s, or that in that neighborhood, a serious cook house produced crack in huge steel vats that were stirred with canoe paddles and could take in as much as $2 million or $3 million dollars a day.

Even though he was operating on a much smaller scale than that, there was a lot to know about dealing drugs to turn a profit and stay alive. Pretty much everything Billy and I did together was a lesson in some aspect of running a drug business. The first rule was never to sleep at a drug house. It was too dangerous. The drug addicts who came to score drugs would do anything it took to get the drugs they needed. If somebody came to rob the place, we didn't want to be there when it happened. In the world of drugs, people were totally expendable. Billy's lesson to me was: Sleep in a drug house and wake up dead. That's why we always took care of business and then went off to a motel somewhere to get high and then sleep, eventually, whenever we came down.

When we traveled between the houses, or transported drugs, we always made sure the drugs were stashed somewhere in the car where the police couldn't find them. Billy taught me how to create secret drug compartments. I made them in the Bronco I was driving then, and for years after that, all my cars were rigged. My trunks had secret trunks, and I had hiding spots everywhere.

As we drove around doing business, Billy explained things to me. Pretty much everything Billy and I did together was a lesson in some aspect of running a drug business. "Peep this, dog," he said. "I got every crack house within ten blocks of here hemmed up. Dita counts the money and keeps it right. My man Hank is my strong arm. Hank fucks with everybody. But Hank don't fuck with me. Kids don't fuck with grown folk, and Hank knows it."

Usually, the crack houses were close to each other, in case one needed to get shut down quickly, and because it was easier for them to supply each other. If one ran out of drugs, the people who worked there would page Billy, and we'd supply them. If we didn't have any drugs handy, we'd run to the other house, grab some, and bring them to the house that needed to be replenished. There was a secret knock, so the people inside would know it was us. They'd let us in, and we'd hook them up. Billy taught me how many rocks to give people, how much they would sell them for, and how much to expect back. The way it worked was, we'd give them a certain amount of rock—say, $100 worth—and tell them how much we wanted back for it—say, $300. It didn't matter what they did to get that $300, but they'd better have it when we went back. After I started helping Billy, I could make something like $10,000 to $20,000 a week, and I usually had anywhere between $1,000 and $2,000 on me at any given time. But it was fluid. The money came in and went out. We used pretty much everything that came in to buy drugs—for ourselves, and for the operation. We didn't exactly have a 401(k) plan.

One of the things Billy taught me was how to open a new drug house.

"You ever seen a house takeover?" he asked me while we were driving near one of his drug houses.

"No, man, what's that?" I asked. That was the great thing about

Billy. I didn't have to put on a front of knowing more than I did. He loved to teach me, and I loved to sit there and soak up his lessons.

"Watch and learn," he said, pulling up in front of a house that looked pretty much like every other place in South Central: small, dirty, and run-down.

Billy knew everything that was happening in the neighborhood where he ran his drug houses. He especially knew who was using, what, and how much.

When we went to the front door of the house, we could hear someone moving around inside. This wasn't exactly a neighborhood where people threw open the door for whoever rang the bell. Finally the door was opened, just a little. The black guy on the other side looked like everyone else I was used to seeing then: skinny, and more than a little worse for wear. When he saw Billy, he made a big show of opening the door wide and welcoming us in, like Billy was the king or something. As I was learning, in those few blocks, he pretty much was.

"Billy, my man," he said. "Come in, come in."

Billy did the introductions as we walked in.

"Roger, this here's Todd," he said. "He's my right-hand man."

The man, Roger, led us into the living room, and we all sat down. It wasn't long before Billy broke out some crack, and we all passed around a pipe and smoked it. While Roger was taking his hit, Billy watched him closely.

"That's the shit," Roger said when he was done, sinking back into the couch, his face awash in the euphoric blank of a crack high.

This was the first step in a house takeover, finding a person who had a house and who liked to get loaded.

"The next thing is to get him sprung," Billy later told me.

That meant hooked. It was not hard to do.

"Peep this, we make him think, if we sell out of his house, he's got the hookup," Billy said. "Only ain't nothing free, dog."

When we got up to leave, Billy left Roger with some rock. Not much. But it was enough to make Roger a very happy man.

"You cool, baby," Billy said as we walked out.

Roger wasn't about to try to give Billy money for rock if Billy wasn't asking. Roger was looking real pleased as he followed us to the door. I could tell he was feeling lucky and thinking about what he could do to keep the free rock coming.

"A couple people I know are gonna stop by and get some rock from you," Billy said.

"Whatever you need, Billy, I'm your man," Roger said, his voice eager.

Now he was thinking he was in, and we would look after him from then on out. Only we wouldn't.

"You just give him enough to keep him wanting more," Billy said. That way, they'd always let us keep selling out of their houses. Basically, we punked them into letting us have total use of their place. All it cost us was a few free rocks.

A drug house was a tore-down place. Usually, the only thing that was turned on was the power. The water was turned off and the toilets didn't work, so we'd get water from someplace else, and then when we had to go to the bathroom, we'd pour it into the toilet to make it flush. Of course, crack addicts don't eat much, so we definitely weren't going to the bathroom a lot. Other than that, it was a place to hang out and do drugs while selling drugs to whoever came by. There was usually a couch and chairs, ratty stuff we found on the street, or even just a few lawn chairs, a TV, a VCR, and that was about it. The most important feature was the king's chair. The person who ran the house, which was Billy at that point, was the only person who could sit in that chair. Nobody fucked with the king or his chair.

Each house had a set stable of workers, usually two girls and a guy. During my time with Billy, Dita and Tracy ran one of the houses, with Hank as their protection. There was another trio running the other house. We controlled them with drugs, and they did whatever we told them to do, so we didn't cut off their supply. That's why it was good to have girls working at the drug houses, because they were easier to manipulate. Plus, we could have sex with them if we felt like it. Billy hung out with Dita, so she was his. But I hooked up with Tracy plenty of times, and pretty much every other girl who worked for us. If we needed a new girl, we'd get her sprung, and then she would work in the house to stay high. There was always a house lady, like Dita, who kept the other girls in line, and if anyone acted up, she kicked their ass.

Each house had an enforcer, too, so this was usually the guy's job. He was somebody who could be trusted with a gun, like Billy's strong arm, Hank. If anything went wrong, he had to defend the place. But as soon as Billy got inside, he took the gun from the guy. I was the only person Billy allowed to carry a gun inside a house when he was there.

People who came to buy drugs weren't allowed into the house. There was a gate over the door, and they would hand the money through. We put the drugs on this big spoon, which we stuck through the door, and then we turned the drugs into their hands. We also took food stamps for crack. That was back when they had food stamp booklets instead of a card, and that was common currency in that neighborhood. It wasn't a dollar-for-dollar deal, though—$50 in food stamps would usually buy a dub, or about $20 in crack. Once we had collected some food stamps, we'd find a crackhead and give them to him with special instructions.

"Hey, go to the store and get me some food," we said. "Bring my food back to me, and I'll give you a dub."

Believe me, he'd go and come right back. He wanted that crack.

Not that we ate very much. But when we did, that's how it happened. It was easy to get people to do things in exchange for crack. If we wanted to watch TV, and we didn't have a TV, we would send somebody to go get a TV set for us. And they would. If we didn't know what time it was, we'd ask for a watch. They'd go get us a watch. I'm sure it was a stolen watch, but we didn't care about a little detail like that.

The only time people usually came inside the drug house was if they owed Billy money, and they needed to plead their case. As they walked inside, I'd get behind them with my gun ready, in case they tried anything.

The main thing Billy taught me was how to survive in the world of drugs. It was a brutal world. It really was. It was a world that was uncaring and unforgiving. The whole point was to make money, and to do that, it was perfectly fine to take money from anybody, take advantage of anybody, and misuse anybody who was around. Girls were easy targets, so they made out the worst.

To survive, I had to be careful not to get misused, while at the same time misusing everybody else I could. I also had to learn how to spot the games that drug addicts and drug dealers played, and most importantly, know how not to get killed. I consider myself pretty blessed that I didn't end up dead, actually. I was a kid from the suburbs who'd mostly grown up on a television set. Sure, I knew how to fight, but this was South Central. There were gangs and drugs everywhere, people were desperate, and human life didn't have much value. It was really scary at times.

I always had a gun on me, but that was actually more dangerous than being unarmed if it wasn't handled properly. Billy taught me that I always had to make the other person think I'd go the extra mile. Luckily, because I was an actor, this wasn't hard for me to do. But the thing was, if the time came to go that extra mile, Billy let me know that I would have to be prepared to do it. I couldn't just let it go. Otherwise no one would have respect for me, and if there happened to be a dispute, or someone wanted to take my drugs or money from me, they wouldn't think twice about killing me to do so.

Those were some pretty heavy lessons, but I wasn't in my right frame of mind, and very little fazed me at that point. I was high all of the time, and while I was loaded, my life was like a movie. I had been acting since I was a kid, onscreen and off, and this was just another new part to play. It was a character I knew well, too, from the gangster movies I loved, such as *Scarface* and *The Godfather*. I threw myself into the role, and pretty soon everyone in that world was convinced that I would do what it took to protect what was mine and keep myself alive. I started to believe that, if threatened, I was capable of pretty much anything, too.

Billy controlled everything that happened in his world, which meant that in the beginning I didn't do anything without his permission. One of the three girls who sold drugs for him was this really beautiful, light-skinned black girl, Kiara. We were all hanging out together in his motel room one night, getting high and watching TV. Kiara and I were sitting on the edge of the bed, a little away from the rest of the group, talking and laughing.

Billy was up at the head of the bed, keeping an eye on everything, as he always did. He nodded me over. I moved around the side of the bed and sat down next to him so we could talk, but I was still watching Kiara. She smiled at me, real flirty, and I smiled back. She was something else.

"You feeling that, baby?" Billy asked.

"You know it," I said.

"You go on ahead then," he said, giving me a knowing look.

I didn't have to be told twice. She and I went into the bathroom and had sex against the sink. I had wanted her since I first met her, but I knew enough to wait until I got the okay from Billy.

Within a couple of months, I had become Billy's right-hand man. After that, I didn't need his approval anymore. If I wanted something, I could have it. But if anything went down, I was expected to be by his side, with my gun drawn.

10

LIFE IN THE HOOD

AS I'VE ALREADY SAID, Billy was like a father to me, so I was honored to earn his trust and have him depend on me. The only problem was that Billy already had a right-hand man, Henry "Hank" Jackson, who was not happy when Billy started bringing me around. Hank was this bald, light-skinned black guy from Texas. He was tall but not particularly big. He smoked his share of crack, just like everyone else who worked at the drug houses, and crack isn't exactly known for bulking up a person's physique. Hank was Billy's bodyguard, so he was used to being close to Billy. He did not like it when I suddenly took his place, especially because I was doing things that no one else was allowed to do. He was always giving me attitude. He'd glare at me and make snide comments, even threaten me in little ways when he thought he could get away with it. None of that bothered me, though, because I knew I had Billy's protection. And when Hank tried to say anything against me to Billy, Billy put him in his place right away.

"Todd's my right-hand man," Billy said. "You'd better watch yourself."

What really turned Hank against me was that I taught Billy to cook crack in the microwave. No, we weren't fighting over who had the best recipe for crack. Before that, Billy would just bring raw coke to Hank and Kiara, who ran his other drug house, and they would cook it into rock themselves. Once we started cooking up the crack in the microwave, Billy realized exactly how much rock he could get from a certain amount of coke, and it added up to a lot more rock—and therefore a lot more money—than Hank had been giving him for the same amount of coke. Billy realized that Hank had been stealing from him, and when Billy called Hank out, Hank was pissed. Hank was not at all happy that he wasn't able to steal from Billy anymore, and he was not happy with me for causing him to get found out.

Billy didn't trust Hank after that, and he basically demoted him. He wouldn't let him carry a gun in the drug house anymore, and he watched him all the time. Hank gave me even more attitude after that, but he couldn't do anything to me, especially since Billy was already pissed at him. Well, Hank still managed to find little ways to keep skimming the money he was giving to Billy. He finally got kicked out of the drug house. He's lucky he didn't get a lot worse than that.

Hank really had it out for me after that. I mostly drove my Bronco when I was in South Central, but I still had my BMW, and one night around that time, Hank stole it from where it was parked outside of the motel where Billy and I were staying. He drove it around until we tracked him down. Billy confronted him, and he was still scared enough of Billy that he gave it back to me. He had burned out the clutch, so Billy made him take it to the shop to get it fixed.

That may sound fairly civilized for a bunch of crack dealers. But just wait. While my car was getting fixed, Hank went to the shop and stole it at gunpoint from the guy who was fixing it. The cops tried to charge me with the crime.

As all this played out, Billy was starting to realize just how much Hank had been getting away with behind his back, and he was starting to trust me more. When he thought I had proven my loyalty, he invited me even deeper into his world.

"I think it's time for you to meet some people," Billy said.

"Really?" I said. I was excited because I knew this meant Billy trusted me.

"I'm going to take you to this place where all of the big ballers go to have breakfast," he said.

This sounded like something right out of *Scarface*, and I couldn't wait to see what it was like. Late that night we went to this little place in the neighborhood that I had never noticed before. When we walked in, it seemed like a regular restaurant. The air smelled like grease and old coffee. But I could tell right away that it was a trip place. It was packed with people. All the tables were full. I knew better than to be caught staring at anyone, but I sized up the scene as casually as I could, and it was easy to tell that pretty much everyone had a gun. I couldn't believe it. Where were the police? I guess they knew better than to come around, or maybe they were getting paid to stay away.

People nodded at Billy and reached out to slap his hand as we walked back to our table.

"Billy, baby, wha's up?"

"How you been, dog?"

It felt good to walk into that room with him. He was respected, and maybe even a little feared, and that made me feel powerful, too. I kept close to Billy and nodded at the people who greeted us.

We sat down at a table and picked up our menus. Even though it was the middle of the night, we had breakfast. While we ate, Billy pointed out other players from across the room.

"You need to know these people in case you start running things around here," he said. "These bitches may talk loud and wear the deadface, but they all full of *mucho* shit. The play is the thing, player. We all actors just like you. Survival ain't nothing more than making everyone believe you'll go the extra mile. However you get there. Let's peel out."

Before we got up to leave, he took me around and introduced me to the people he thought I needed to meet.

"This here's Todd," he said as we stopped at a table. That's all it took for people to know I was Billy's right-hand man.

That felt good, knowing he respected me that much. But I never had a moment where I found myself wanting the kind of power Billy had. No matter how well I could play the game, I was just a user who dealt to support my habit.

I did love the girls who went along with dealing, and what I could do with them—even beautiful girls would do whatever they were told to do to get their drugs. But as long as I had drugs and girls, I didn't need any more than that.

Billy loved the power. But Billy was much more brutal than I was. If someone didn't do what I told him to do, I'd just dump him and find someone else to do it. But with Billy, there'd be serious consequences. People never got killed for owing money. That would defeat the whole purpose of the threat. If they were dead, they wouldn't ever be able to pay back their debt. And it wasn't like the movies, where people got a finger cut off or something like that. Then they'd just have to go to the hospital and get bandaged up. Usually, the threat of a bat across the knee was enough to get the money out of them. Or they'd get beat up. Hitting people with a garden hose was a good way to go because it hurt a lot but didn't leave much of a visible mark. During the time I knew him, I saw Billy mess some people up. Or sometimes he'd humiliate them; make a girl lick another girl's asshole in front of everyone, that sort of thing. Even more common than that was for a girl to pay off her debt by having sex with Billy, or with me. The goal was to take whatever the person had in payment, or to make them never want to owe Billy money again. Of course, crack addicts weren't too good with logic, so there were always plenty of people who owed him.

Once the drugs took over, it was like my old life had never happened. I was in a new world that was about as far away from Hollywood as a person could get, and I was fine with that. I was nothing but a lowlife drug addict, and I didn't want anyone trying to tell me any differently. I didn't see anyone from *Diff'rent Strokes*, not even Dana, who was having her own problems with drugs after the show ended. And even though I had worked with plenty of actors and producers who had drug habits of their own, they weren't exactly buying their drugs in South Central. I did run into two very famous female singers buying drugs together one night. But they're both doing well now, and I certainly respect how hard it is to come back from that world, so I'd rather not say more. I have no problem saying that Ike Turner still owes me money, though. I guess I'll have to let that one go.

Even though I did my best to disappear from my family's life, too, my mom never gave up on me. She was used to the old days, when I would call her three or four times a day. And so when the drugs took over, and I stopped calling her and started hiding from her instead, she really worried. One time she heard that I had been spotted around Sixty-fifth Street in South Central, so she went down there.

She parked her car and went up to the first person she saw on the street.

"Do you know where the drug houses are?" she asked.

"Oh, yeah," the person said, pointing. "There's one here. There's one over there. There's another one farther down. Go around the corner, there's another one there."

She decided she was going to go to every one until she found me.

I can only imagine what people thought when my mom walked right into the first drug house, pushing everyone out of the way, yelling as loud as she could, or what my mom thought when she saw all those drugged-out people sitting around in what must have looked like a trash can to her. But she was determined.

"Todd!" she shouted. "Todd!"

I hadn't heard her calling me, but a guy I knew came running up to where I was sprawled out, getting high.

"You better peel out, homie," he said. "It's your mom. But peep this, let me have your crack and pipe. I don't want you to get busted."

That was an addict. Always working the angles. I handed him my pipe and rock. Of course it was my mom. No one else loved me like that. But I was not about to let her see me, not in the condition I was in. So I ran right out of there and went to the next house.

My mom pushed on the guy in the first house until he finally talked.

"He ain't in here," he said. "He's gone. He ran."

So my mom went back outside and started running down the street to the next house. When she got there, she did the exact same thing all over again. But I stayed just ahead of her. Even though she went to all four of the houses she'd been told about, she never did find me. I was not ready to be found.

I made sure the cops couldn't find me, either. Well, they were watching me, so they always knew where I was, but they never found anything on me that could be used against me. It wasn't for lack of trying, though. After my family and I hired Johnnie Cochran to file my lawsuit against the LAPD, the police officers in San Fernando Valley hated me even more than they had before. They would hover their helicopters real low over my house and really go out of their way to mess with me. It was scary because I knew they were capable of anything. One time during the lawsuit, I was on vacation in Jamaica with my mom, and these two officers busted into my house, saying I had fired a gun through someone's window. All they found was my bodyguard asleep in my bed. But as soon as we got back into town, they pulled my mom over and made it clear that they weren't playing anymore.

"We know you've been out of town," the officer said.

That was too much for me. I left town and went to Jamaica for two months.

Once I was working with Billy, they must have known that I was dealing drugs, too. I was being watched by CRASH, an antigang and drug unit, and they made it a point to know everyone who was anyone in that neighborhood. But we knew how to hide our stuff and how not to get caught. They knew where all the houses were, but they had to make a buy in order to bust into the house and arrest us. They sometimes tried to get us to sell to their buyer, who was an undercover cop, but we never fell for it. We could tell a mile away if a dude wasn't a crack addict, and we'd set him straight.

"We don't sell shit here," we'd say when he came to the door.

"You sure you ain't got nothing?" he'd say.

"Nothing, dude. Sorry, we don't sell here."

Finally he had no choice but to leave.

Those were the kind of street smarts I learned from Billy, which helped me to stay out of trouble for as long as I did. Sometimes I just got lucky. After I'd been working with Billy for a few months, he trusted me enough to send me to take care of errands by myself. While I was walking to a drug house to buy drugs for one of his houses, CRASH ran by me and kicked in the door. I kept right on walking. But if they had busted the place ten minutes later, I would have been inside there with a whole mess of drugs in my system and even more in my possession.

The police had harassed me without cause for so many years. I almost felt good to be breaking the law when they pulled me over, especially because they couldn't prove I was doing anything wrong, instead of just being singled out because I was black. By that point I certainly didn't respect their authority. They'd never treated me like a real American, so I had no use for their rules.

But, as they say, nothing lasts forever. Late one night at the end of '88, Billy and I were in my car, heading back to one of the drug houses from a motel where we'd been sleeping for a couple of days. As we pulled up to the house, we saw that CRASH was waiting for us. I didn't have anything on me, but Billy had a lot of drugs and a gun on him. The drugs were already hidden, but there was no time to get rid of the gun. Right before they pulled up on us, Billy turned to me and broke it down.

"We're about to get knocked," he said. "You're going to get out. I'm not. I'm going to be on a parole violation. I'm gone. I need you to take over my houses."

"But I'm no gangster, man."

"You don't need to be a gangster, baby," he said. "Just go the extra mile, however you need to get there. Use the drugs I stashed to get back in the game."

"No problem, Billy," I said. "You have my word."

I felt like I owed it to him. He had taught me so much. I probably would have been dead if it weren't for him.

CRASH jumped out of their car and ran up to us. They put a gun to Billy's head and then they put a gun to mine. They grabbed Billy out of the car and threw him up against it. When they frisked him, they found his gun, and they already knew about his parole violation, so they cuffed him. There was nothing to find on me, but they arrested me anyhow and took me to jail. Well, Billy was right. He didn't get out. He got hung up on that parole violation, and they held him on a no-bail warrant, which meant he couldn't get out and try to run away before his case could go to trial.

They set my bail low, along the lines of $10,000, because I was never seen as a flight risk. And with bail bonds, which allow the families of people in jail to buy what amounts to insurance guaranteeing the accused won't split before their trial, that meant paying something like $1,000. I was only in jail for about eight hours. My mom came down and got me out. She knew I was far gone, but I'd succeeded in hiding from her for several months and she hadn't seen the damage the drugs had done. When she caught sight of how thin and horrible I looked, she fainted. When she came to, she started crying because I was being so weird. I don't remember all this, but she told me later that I was so paranoid and out of my mind that I was hiding behind poles and saying all this strange stuff. She begged me to go home with her, but that was the last thing I wanted because I was nowhere near being ready to stop. She had a friend with her, and I told her friend that I'd be okay and that she should take care of my mom and get her home. I went outside, jumped in a cab, and left. I still had some credit cards, so I used one of them to pay for the cab. I knew where Billy had hid his drugs, and I went back to South Central to find them.

Sure enough, I found them right where he'd left them, in the secret hiding place in my Bronco, but it wasn't enough to get started again. I wasn't sure what to do because I didn't have any money, and I only knew a couple of people I had met through Billy. I had an idea. I knew where Billy's guns were hidden, so I went around the drug house, gathering them up. I decided I would go to the Jamaicans. I went to one of their houses, where Billy had brought me a bunch of times to buy drugs.

"Hey, brotha, what's up?" the head Jamaican asked as I was led into the living room. As I remembered from my experience of dealing with the Jamaicans before, their place was a lot nicer than most of the cribs where we went to buy drugs. It was clean and comfortable, with the kind of laid-back vibe that welcomed a long toke on a big spliff and the hours of relaxation that would bring. But I was far from relaxed. This was my first time doing business without Billy, and as I'd done back at my drug house, I needed to prove myself right from the start. I made a point to look relaxed but alert, so they'd know not to try anything on me.

"I'm here on business," I said.

"And what business is that, man?" he asked.

"I've got some guns," I said. "And I need some drugs. I'd be willing to trade. But I'd prefer the cash."

It went without saying that I could get the drugs cheaper if I bought them somewhere else. Anyone who knew what they were doing never wanted to get paid in product because they were sure to get cheated. Cash was always a lot better.

"What kind of guns?" he asked.

I had three or four MAC-10s, which are small, handheld machine guns. This one was a .45-caliber, so it could light some stuff up. I pulled it out.

The Jamaican looked me over. I was careful to keep my cool. I had a loaded gun in my hand. Even though I was holding it as part of a business transaction, I knew I had to choose my next move carefully.

"Well, brotha," he said, "how the hell do I know that works?"

I pointed it at the sky and fired off a round. My heart was beating from the noise of the gun and my nerves as I watched to see if he went for his gun.

He started to laugh.

"You're fucking crazy," he said. "Okay, okay."

He gave me $600 for the gun.

I bought about two ounces of coke and cooked it up. That could have probably earned me two or three grand, depending on how good the coke was and how I cut it. But the problem was, I could smoke that amount of crack in two or three days, easy. And that's pretty much what I did. So soon enough, I had run out of money again. That was always the issue. It was just like Tony Montana said in *Scarface*: "Don't get high on your own supply." I didn't listen to him, but I should have, because it's true; it can get to the point where a dealer is only paying for his own habit. The only good thing about how I operated was that I never owed anybody any money. No matter how bad I got, I could always take care of myself.

But right then, taking care of myself wasn't enough. I needed to do something else to make real money, so I could get myself up and running again. I took my credit card, and I went to Sears and bought twenty-five TVs.

The sales guy couldn't figure it out.

"Why are you buying all these TVs?" he asked.

"Christmas presents," I said.

Pretty clever, right? Well, it worked. The guys at the store even helped me load them into the back of my truck. I took those TVs right over to the Jamaicans.

"Hey, I've got TVs," I said.

They gave me a couple hundred dollars for each of those TVs. Then I was really ready to get moving again.

Soon after that, I went on a really big drug binge, and that's when the world got insane. My whole operation was keeping itself afloat, but I was smoking so much crack that I couldn't always support my own habit with the money I was making. There was a time when I needed money to buy more drugs. I started to think about how my mom still had some of the money I had asked her to take care of for me. If I just had that money for myself, then I could buy all the drugs I needed to stay high for as long as I could.

Only, I knew my mom. And once I had told her not to give me my money, she'd never go back on her word, no matter how much I begged and pleaded. I needed a plan. I called my mom and told her that a drug dealer was holding me hostage because I owed him $5,000, and if I didn't give it to him, he was going to kill me. My mom got scared and sent me the money. But it wasn't enough. I smoked it all up, and pretty soon I needed more money to buy more drugs.

So I called back and tried to use the same story on her again. It wasn't as believable the second time. And my mom had started going to Al-Anon, which is like AA for the friends and family members of addicts. After a few meetings, she had started finding out what not to do if she wanted to help me get sober. At the top of that list was to stop giving the addict money to support his habit.

"Mom, I need $4,000 of that money I gave you," I said. "I owe this drug dealer. And he's going to hurt me if I don't give it to him."

"You can't have it," she said.

"I need that money," I said. "You've got to give me that money."

"No, you told me not to give it to you," she said. "If you're going to kill yourself, go kill yourself. You don't need me to do it."

If I had been anywhere near my right mind, it would have devastated me to realize that my mom had finally given up on me until I was ready to get sober. I was on my own. But all I cared about was getting money for drugs. One of my friends got on the phone to try to convince her. He started cursing her out.

"If you don't give it to us, we're going to come get it anyways," he said.

"Come on out here if you want that money," she said. "Come try to get it."

When I hung up the receiver, my friend was all amped up and ready to go.

"Let's go," he said.

"You don't want to go," I said.

"What do you mean?" he asked.

"Trust me," I said. "As soon as you knock on that door, my mother will kill you. She will shoot you, and me, and whoever else is standing at that door."

He started laughing. He thought it was hilarious that I was scared of my mom.

"Believe me," I said. "I know my mom, man. She isn't scared of us. She'll kill every one of us."

I knew that my mom had all of my guns. She had nearly two dozen guns under her bed, and she had plenty of ammunition. And I knew that my mom was a crack shot because she used to tell us stories about how her grandfather taught her how to shoot when she was nine years old. I had seen it for myself, too. Once when I was really angry at my dad, my mom had come up with a solution.

"Come on," she said. "Let's go kill him."

"Kill him?" I said. I hated him, but I couldn't believe I had heard her right.

"Yeah, let's go kill him."

She took me to the rifle range, and she pointed at the target.

"That's your father," she said. "Now shoot him."

And we just shot those targets to pieces. My mom hit all of the vitals—the heart, the eyes, the head—one after the other.

"God, Mom," I said. "You really know how to shoot."

I felt a lot less angry when we came out of there, but I vowed never to find myself on the wrong end of a gun that my mom was holding.

My buddy didn't know my mom, though. He probably figured there was no way my mom could be as scary as the people we went up against daily. Well, he was wrong about that, and I wasn't having any part of his plan.

"You're crazy," I said. "You want to die, go ahead, man. Go ahead, knock on the door, be a dummy."

I found out later that I was right not to have gone over there. When my mom got off the phone with me that day, she and my sister, Verda, went right downstairs, took every one of my guns out, and loaded them up. Then she laid all of the rifles and handguns out on her living room set, and she sat and faced the door, just waiting for the doorbell to ring. She stayed like that for three days. She'd go and eat quickly in the kitchen, and then she would go back to her seat in front of the door and wait for us. She was ready, and willing, to shoot all of us.

That's how crazy my life was when I was dealing and using drugs. I did anything I had to do to get the money to buy drugs, so I could sell drugs, to get the money to buy more drugs, so I could use drugs and stay high.

In the first days I was in charge, I was scared. Like I said, this wasn't anything I'd dreamed of doing, and I knew the dangers that went along with being the boss. But then I started getting high, and there was no more fear. There was only doing what I had to do. I had more to think about when I was running things, but my main priorities hadn't changed at all. For me, the focus was always drugs and girls. I wanted to be high, and I wanted to have women around so I could have sex with them. That was one of the things I liked most about being in charge. I got to have the first pick of the women. And there were always plenty of girls who were around because they were using or wanted to use. If a girl was into drugs, it wasn't hard to get her clothes off. I would basically just get her sprung, and that was it. To get a girl sprung, I would just give her a major rock hit. That would spring her out in a few seconds because the withdrawal was so strong. She'd be begging me for another hit after that, but I wouldn't give it to her right away.

I was sitting on the bed in one of the motels where I always stayed. I held the crack pipe to my mouth and took a hit. A sexy but ravaged Latino woman watched me hungrily from a few feet away.

"Come on, Popi, I wanna play, too," she said.

"If you want to play, you've got to pay," I said.

The girl started swaying her hips, dancing provocatively in front of me as she rubbed her hands all over her body.

"Take your clothes off," I said.

She stripped down to her bra and panties and then danced over close to me. She sank to her knees, pulled down my zipper, and went to work on me. I leaned back and got into it. When she was done, I held up the crack pipe for her. She gave me a sexy look as she sucked on the pipe. I lit the bowl of the pipe for her. She smiled as the drug high rolled over her. I took the pipe back and took another hit.

After that, she would stay for as long as I let her, and she would do anything I told her to do. I definitely liked that. Sometimes I'd hang out with a girl for longer than one night, and we'd have whatever kind of relationship two people could have in that condition. But even then, I couldn't trust anybody, and I always had to hide my drugs. That's just how it was. I spent a lot of time with Tracy, who I'd known since the first night I met Billy. She had worked for him before he got sent away, and she was still running one of the houses for me. It wasn't all just getting high and having sex, and the fact that Billy had trusted her meant a lot to me. Because I knew she wasn't going to steal from me or rat me out, that was one less thing to worry about. There was plenty to worry about. When I took over for Billy, I definitely had to defend my right to be the new boss. The nature of that world was that if I showed any weakness, I'd be done. So I had to hold my ground and prove that I wasn't afraid. Billy's lessons really came in handy then. I knew never to pull my gun out of my waistband unless I was going to shoot somebody. I could use it as a threatening gesture, or I could just keep it in my hand while I talked to people. But I never actually aimed it at somebody unless I really meant to shoot him. It was more menacing if people knew I had a gun, and that if I pulled my gun out, I was going to use it. And soon I had reason to pull my gun out.

11

THE FALL

I KEPT MY PROMISE to Billy and ran his two drug houses for him after he was sent away. I had Tracy to help me, and I found another girl to work in the second drug house. I also met a neighborhood guy, Bradley Garcia, who seemed trustworthy. I brought him into the operation and asked him to take over as the enforcer at the drug house that Hank had run. Bradley and I were never as close as Billy and I had been, but we spent a lot of time together. He would go on drug runs with me, or we'd hang out at one of the houses together, and we always got along well. Until we didn't anymore. But I didn't know what was on the horizon.

Other than the new blood, everything was pretty much the same as it had been before, except I made the rounds by myself or with Bradley. Because I had taken Billy's place, I had to be aware of the potential threat I faced from the LAPD and any rivals who might be thinking about moving against me. As I soon found out, there was good reason to be on my guard.

I hadn't seen Hank since Billy ran him off after he stole my BMW, and then stole it from the people who were fixing the damage he had done to it. I was still pissed about that. And while I wasn't actively seeking him out, if he happened to cross my path, I was going to show him that he couldn't go around making trouble for me like that. What I didn't know was that Hank was ready to settle up, too. And he was looking for me.

On February 2, 1989, I was walking from my secondary drug house up to the back door of my main drug house. I was wearing a big coat, like I always did, so I could easily cover whatever I had on me that needed to be concealed. Even though this was my neighborhood now, I didn't like to be out on the street at night for any longer than I had to be, so I was moving fast, alert to any sound or movement around me. My daily crack habit had taken its toll, and I was breathing hard. I heard a noise off to my side, but before I could prepare myself, Hank came out of nowhere and grabbed me. He had a good grip on my chest and shoulders. I latched right onto him and started pushing pack. I was out to do some damage, and we wrestled hard, but he had surprised me and I wasn't at my best. He threw me over these ratty bushes that bordered the path behind the drug house and ran inside. I scrambled up off the ground, brushing myself off as I ran after him. I pounded up the steps and grabbed the knob, but the door was locked. I shook it hard, furious at him, but I couldn't get inside.

Thirty minutes later, CRASH busted me as I stepped out the front door of my secondary drug house, where I had gone to do what most drug addicts do in times of stress: get high. The cops were out in full force, fully armed. I put my hands up in the air and tried to be cool. A police helicopter hovered low overhead, a white search beam illuminating the scene around me, the sound of the propeller blades pounding the air. Their huge dogs barked and growled at me. I had just smoked a big rock, but this was sobering me up, fast. My adrenaline raced, and my brain went over what I had on me and whether they would be able to find it. I was instantly filled with relief. I never carried a gun when I was traveling between the two drug houses, unless I was moving drugs between them, and miraculously, I didn't have any drugs on me at the moment.

I knew they had been watching me for months—years, even—but I was totally bewildered as to why they were arresting me just then. I had been on a five- or six-day binge, and so I couldn't exactly say what I'd been up to before that night.

"You know what you did," one of the cops said.

"No, I don't," I said, really meaning it.

When they brought me in for questioning, it didn't do them much good. But they were able to tell me some things. They informed me that Hank had been shot eight times, and then been stabbed in the throat with a knife, at my main drug house. I wasn't the least bit surprised. Hank was a thief and a thug, and I wasn't the only one who hated him. He had plenty of enemies in that neighborhood. But I didn't know anything more than that about what had happened to him.

The LAPD and the district attorney's office thought they knew plenty about the events of that night, though. They had witnesses placing me outside of the main drug house at the time of the shooting, and I faced three charges: attempted murder, attempted voluntary manslaughter, and assault with a deadly weapon. When I got to jail, I kept hearing the same thing over and over again. I was put in a cell with another prisoner, and he started taunting me. "Oh, man, you shot somebody, you're going to prison," he said.

"What?" I said. "No, I didn't shoot anybody. I'm not going to prison."

"Oh, man, that's it for you," another prisoner said. "I can't believe you threw your whole life away."

They were just as bad as the drug addicts who used to tell me I should quit drugs while we were smoking crack together. Those idiots were in jail right along with me. I kept thinking, "If you're in here with me, you threw your life away too, dumb-ass."

Hearing those fools run their mouths was not helping my mood at all. I was in jail, the crack was wearing off, and I was miserable. When I was high, like I've said, my life felt like a movie. But after an arrest, that's when it all became real, just like that. After five or six days of being as high as a person could possibly be, I had to come down in jail, and I wanted to leave so badly. I kept thinking, "In the movie, I would just go home. But it doesn't happen that way in real life."

And my old friends the cops didn't make it any easier on me. When I first got taken to jail, this one officer brought me downstairs to process me.

"Take your clothes off," he said.

He made me strip down. I was standing there, totally naked, and the sergeant came in and gave me a funny look.

"Why are you naked, Todd?" he asked me.

"That officer made me take off my clothes," I said and pointed at the guy.

Well, that officer got bitched out. I had a red bracelet on, which meant that I was a high-profile prisoner. They weren't supposed to strip us down or do anything crazy to us, because it could make the jail look bad.

My real life had caught up with me, but it hadn't really sunk in yet. I still thought everything would be fine. I didn't know anything about the shooting, so what could they possibly do to me? I told everyone in earshot that I was going be heading home in no time. And then one of the officers laid it out for me.

"What are you talking about?" he said. "You're in jail, buddy. You're not going home. We've got you in here on a no-bail hold right now."

"Oh, God," I thought. "That's it."

As if I wasn't feeling low enough when I realized I had no chance of getting out, I had to detox. At that point I had been a daily user for about two years, and the withdrawal hit me full on and just rocked me. I had the shakes, and I was sweating and feverish. I kept throwing up and crapping myself. All I needed was one little hit of crack and it would all go away. But that wasn't going to happen. There was nothing to be done except to bear down and get through it.

The only good thing about detoxing from crack is that it's only really bad for three days, and then the physical symptoms go away. It's not like heroin, which clings to an addict's system for weeks and weeks. Crack is a short kick. But the memory of how good the high is gets most people back on the rock as soon as they get off. And so even though I had sobered up, all I could think about was how much I wanted to get back out and start using again. The jail didn't have any recovery programs to help me, and I certainly wasn't going to stop on my own.

It didn't help, either, that they put me in the worst area possible. Most of the other inmates facing charges like mine were on the 7000 floor. I was down on Palm Hall, which is floor 1750, and I didn't belong there at all. I was in there with the real hard-core killers—God knows who, or how many, people they killed. My neighbors were in for some of the most notorious crimes of that decade. Picture my sorry butt surrounded by Lyle Menendez, one of the celebrity murderers of the day; Eddie Nash, suspected of having masterminded the Wonderland killings, which involved four people butchered more brutally than anyone had seen since the Manson killings; Richard Ramirez, a serial rapist and killer known as the Night Stalker, who had fourteen alleged victims, plus those he raped and tortured and left for dead. And me.

I wasn't scared of being held on this literal "murderers' row." What upset me was that I was being treated like one of them. Even when I had been totally gone on drugs, I hadn't so much as stolen a single crack rock. And even at my craziest, and with all of the power I had when I was running things, I was no killer. I wasn't like these monsters. It really upset me to be labeled a killer. And because of my history with the LAPD, I was terrified that they were going to find a way to make the charges stick.

Those first few days were some of the worst I've ever been through. Detoxing was hell. And then, once I was sober, I had to come to terms with what a mess I had made of my life. It seemed impossible to imagine falling any farther than I had, given that only a few years earlier I had been a teen idol with $1 million in the bank and my whole life ahead of me. But I had fallen. And this was where I had landed. So I adapted. Thankfully, I had Johnnie Cochran as my lawyer, and he had this way about him that made me feel like someone was finally looking out for me. He only came to see me in jail a few times while he was getting my case together, and he never made a big show of acting like the charges against me weren't serious, but somehow that made me feel better. The way he asked me questions and gathered information was straightforward, and I felt like he was the best man for the job.

At first my family and I weren't sure whom we should get to be my lawyer. I appreciated that Johnnie Cochran had done great work representing my past legal needs and been like a father to me, too. But this was long before he successfully defended O. J. Simpson in his murder trial, and we weren't sure if he could handle this kind of a big case. My mom called around to a bunch of different lawyers. She had the idea that we needed to find a Jewish lawyer at a really good firm. So she talked to three different Jewish lawyers. But before she hired any of them, she asked them all the same question.

"If you had a child who was a celebrity, and this kid was having problems and needed a lawyer, who would you get for your child?" she asked.

Every single one of those lawyers said Johnnie Cochran. They were all doing the same job as Johnnie, but when the situation was put to them under the guise of their own children, they all thought of Johnnie right away. So that's exactly who we got. Of course, my dad didn't like that one bit.

"You're stupid to get a nigga lawyer," my dad said to my mom.

My mom couldn't believe she was hearing that, even from him.

"Well, listen," she said. "Everybody said that's who I should get, and so that's who I got."

My mom liked that all of the well-respected lawyers had said they would get Johnnie for their own kids, and she also liked how Johnnie handled himself when she went down to talk to him about taking my case.

"I read about Todd having some problems," Johnnie said. "And I saw it on the news. We'll help him. We'll help him."

That was what my mom wanted to hear more than anything else.

With the drugs out of my system and Johnnie on the job, I settled into a sort of routine in the jail. I even got used to my neighbors. I wouldn't say we exactly became friends. But it was lonely and boring in there, and we kept each other company. Eddie Nash was actually a really nice guy, but he was in his fifties, so we didn't have much in common. Lyle, he was a different kind of person. It was like he knew what he had done, and he felt no remorse for it. There was something dark about him. He didn't seem to care too much about being in jail because he thought he was going to go home. He didn't care much about himself or anything else. Except his hair. He was balding, and he wore a hairpiece in court, but he couldn't wear it in jail.

Richard Ramirez was a strange cat. The thing that was interesting about being in jail with him was that he had killed somebody in Northridge during the time I was living there, and I remember how scared we were after the murder. We made sure all of our windows were locked at all times, and we walked people to their cars with guns. My life had actually been touched by his crimes.

I never found it hard to believe that he had done all the terrible things they accused him of—raping and torturing little old ladies and carving pentagrams into their skin. First of all, he was a devil-worshipper. That's heavy. And then he never seemed sorry about killing all those people. That was who he really was.

He used to come by my cell and shake my door really hard. He always tried to freak me out by doing things like putting the devil sign up against the bars.

"I'm going to come in and get you," he said.

"Come on in here," I said. "You come on in here. I know if I take you out, I'm going to get acquitted. Just like that."

I remember, the day he found out he was going to the gas chamber, he came back to our cellblock, and he had this really somber look on his face. He looked different, but I knew that inside he was still the same monster he'd always been.

"Hey, Richard," I said.

He turned and looked at me.

"What?" he said.

"Get ready," I said, and I puffed my cheeks out real big, like I was holding my breath. "How long can you hold your breath? You're done."

"Fuck you, Bridges," he said. "You're done, too. You're going to go to prison."

"You know the unfortunate part for everyone here?" I said. "I'm the only guy who's going home. All the rest of you guys are going to prison. I'm only a drug addict. I got caught up in some crap, but I'll be out of here."

Little did I know, it wasn't going to be quite that easy.

While I was in jail, they tried to get me for the armed robbery that Hank had committed, too. Since he had stolen my car, which was registered in my name, and the mechanic who got robbed said it was a light-skinned black man who held him up, the police questioned me about it. I kept telling them it wasn't me, and that they should be looking for Hank instead of me, but they were sure I was the guy.

So they put me in this police lineup. The first thing I noticed was that I was in there with a bunch of dark-skinned black people.

"What a setup this is," I thought.

They brought in the mechanic, who was a Latino guy with a thick Mexican accent. The officer explained to him how it would go down, and then they started.

"Okay number one, step forward," the officer said.

Number one stepped forward.

"Number two, step forward."

Number two stepped forward.

I was number three.

"Number three, step forward."

I stepped forward.

"Turn to the side."

I turned to the side.

"Is that him?" the cop said.

"No, that's not him," the mechanic said.

"Are you sure that's not him?"

"No, that's not him."

"Are you sure that's not him?"

I couldn't believe it. The mechanic couldn't believe it, either. He was getting flustered.

"That's not him, señor," he said. "That's not him."

"Are you sure that's not him?"

"No, señor, that is not him," he said. "The guy is much bigger. Same color, but a lot bigger."

"Are you sure?"

Finally, I'd had it.

"Man, you heard the guy say it wasn't me," I said.

"Shut up, number three," the cop said. "Step back."

That made me really nervous about my trial. The media's coverage of my case didn't make me feel any better. The story was everywhere. The *Los Angeles Times* ran headlines that covered every new twist and turn as it happened:

"TV's Todd Bridges Held in Shooting"

"Actor Todd Bridges Held Without Bail"

"$2 Million Bail Set for Todd Bridges"

People loved being able to shake their heads in dismay at the idea of some adorable little kid they used to watch on TV ending up in a dumpy motel with a crack pipe in his mouth. I was the butt of jokes on the Oscars, on Jay Leno. Here's one I remember from that time: "I hear that the Lakers need a new shooting guard. And they've hired Todd Bridges from *Diff'rent Strokes*."

Wah-wah.

Over the years, Jay Leno made tons of jokes about all us kids from *Diff'rent Strokes*, but especially about me. In fact, he's still making jokes about me to this day. I ran into him a couple of years ago and called him out on it.

"Why do you always make jokes about me?" I said.

"Because you're famous," he said.

Well, he actually got a laugh out of me with that. It made sense. His job is making fun of people who are famous. He does it to everybody. Maybe I shouldn't complain. It's when he stops talking about me that I'll need to worry.

I couldn't laugh about any of it back then, though. My life was in a shambles, and they were making fun of me. It really hurt. I was used to being the adorable child star everyone loved. Even more than that, I was really upset by all the nasty, untrue things that were written and broadcast about me. Although my *Diff'rent Strokes* costars Gary Coleman and Dana Plato went on to have trouble with the law as well, this was before their personal problems hit the news, so I bore the brunt of the negative coverage myself. I had the chance to tell my side of things on an episode of *Entertainment Tonight* that aired on March 1, 1989. Other than that, the media just went wild with the story. The news made it seem like I was standing over Hank with a smoking gun in my hand. And there wasn't any proof of that. I was really upset that people thought those kinds of things about me.

Emotionally, it was a really rough time for me in general. For the years leading up to my arrest, the drugs had taken away my memories of everything I had gone through, and the hurt that went along with them. As soon as the drugs were out of my system, the pain just decimated me. Plus, I was faced with how far I had fallen from my old life as a TV star and teen idol. I didn't have any money. I didn't have a career. And I was in jail awaiting trial on charges that could very well put me away for the rest of my life. It was way too much for me to handle.

My mom, my brother, my sister, and my girlfriend Becky, who somehow hadn't given up on me, even after I'd disappeared as much as I had, did their best to help me through this difficult period. They all came to see me in jail as much as they were allowed, and my mom and Becky gave the guards money to give me, so I could buy things I needed. Not surprisingly, my dad never came to see me once in nine months, and I don't remember him ever being at my trial, either. My dad may have sneered at Johnnie and called him a nigga, but really, my dad didn't like Johnnie because he was a black man who was more successful than he was. And, of course, my dad always put his own prejudices and priorities ahead of his kids.

My mom was always there for me, but it was really hard for her. She was sad about what had happened to me, so she cried a lot. I had always hated to see my mom cry, and I felt awful about being the cause of her tears. But even though I was seeing her without drugs in my system for the first time in years, and realizing how much worry and heartache I had caused her, and how much she wanted me to stay sober, none of it really registered. I didn't want to hurt her, but I didn't care about anything she had to say because I was in too much pain. All I could think about was getting out, so I could get high and push my memories back down.

Amazingly, Weird Ernie, from my days on the set of *Diff'rent Strokes*, used to come by and see me a lot, too. He was known as Pastor Johnson by then, and he had his own congregation in Carson, which is a suburb of Los Angeles. Whenever he was there, he told me that he prayed for me, and all of this would work out. He'd said I'd be released and find my way back to God and get sober. I thought it was nice that he came to visit, but I didn't really hear him, either.

I couldn't hear what anybody was saying because I had only one thing on my mind, and that was getting my hands on some crack. I had reached the point where I was so far gone emotionally that I was really kind of heartless. I didn't want to stop using, and I didn't think I could stop, even if I tried. I mean, I had gone to rehab before, and it hadn't ever worked. I certainly wasn't getting what I needed to stay sober in jail. So no matter what anyone did for me, or said to support me, all I could think about was using again.

But I wasn't going anywhere. They had me on a no-bail warrant, which they really shouldn't have done, because I wasn't a flight risk. Where, exactly, was I going to go? And then, when they finally set bail, after I'd already been in jail for a month, they put it at $2 million, which was way more than I could ever afford, so I couldn't get out. Johnnie told me later that he probably could have gotten my bail reduced, but he was afraid I would get in more trouble if I was out on the street. He was probably right.

In jail, my life settled into a sort of routine. In the row where I was housed, there were about eight of us. We were never allowed to be out with other prisoners, but we knew everyone on the row. We'd get an hour or two of what was called freeway time every day. During that period, we were allowed to leave our cells, make phone calls, take a shower, and watch TV. Whoever was on the freeway would change the channels on the TV, and since there was only one TV, everyone had to watch whatever show he put on. We had certain shows we watched during the day. On Saturdays we watched *Soul Train* to see the girls dancing. Sometimes we'd see shows about our court cases, and that was always awful for me because they said such negative stuff about me in the media.

I learned how to do a lot of little things that made my life easier in jail. Like, if we wanted to get a message, or something else, to one of the guys in another cell, we would take string out of the blanket on our bed and use it to make what we called a kite. Then we could throw it from one end of the row all the way down to the other. Everyone helped out, tossing it along from cell to cell, until it reached its destination.

I found other ways to keep busy and make some money, too. After I had been inside for a little while, I learned that my mom had grown up with the jail's cook, so the cook sent me a lot of good food. The trustees brought it to me, and I was grateful for their kindness. But I had to recook the food because it was always cold by the time I got it. I had a metal chair in my cell, and I'd clean it off really good. Next, I'd take toilet paper and wrap it around and around my hand. And then, when I had a big, tightly rolled wad, I'd fold it up and put it under the chair. When I lit the middle of the paper, it would burn for twenty minutes and heat up the seat of the chair. There was a vent in my room, which I covered at night because it let in a draft, but when I opened it, it drew out the smoke. Once the chair's seat was hot, it worked just like a griddle. I'd put butter and salt and pepper on there and cook my food up, just like that.

I sold food to the different guys on the row. They were glad for the good eats because the deputies ate really well in jail, but the rest of us ate crap. One dish, we called shit on a shingle. It appeared to be some kind of beef dish, but it was so disgusting, I'm not even sure what it really was. And then we had something we used to call chicken surprise. If we found a real piece of chicken, we'd yell, "Surprise!" We had bologna and cheese sandwiches that were just horrible. Everything was bad. It was all full of the worst stuff—chicken that wasn't cooked well, cheese that would never melt, no matter how much they cooked it. I called it county cheese.

But that was living the high life compared to when they stuck me in the hole. The hole was what they called solitary confinement, and it was way down in the bottom of the old wing. I got put in there once because they said I was smarting up, even though I wasn't. They lost me down there for something like two months. Nobody knew where I was. Well, the guards knew where I was. They just couldn't be bothered to let me out because they wanted to teach me a lesson. My family and Johnnie were freaking out until they bugged the administration enough and someone finally pulled me out of there.

While I was in the hole, they fed me jute balls, which were disciplinary food that they made by taking all of my food, blending it together, and then baking it. It was absolutely horrible. I wouldn't eat the jute balls, so I ate apples, which was all they would give me, other than jute balls, the whole time I was down there. To this very day, I can't stand apples. They remind me of being in the hole.

Down in the hole, they kept me in a tiny cell that was something like four feet by seven feet. My acting experience really came in handy then. I passed the time by talking back and forth to myself in these different, weird voices I made up. I had to do something to keep myself from going too crazy, because I really believe that being locked up in there could have driven me mad. It was so hard being alone like that day after day. I was actually glad to finally go back to my regular cell.

This whole time, I was seeing a psychiatrist, and he couldn't figure out why they were still keeping me on the 7000 floor, even though I wasn't being held on anything close to the same kind of brutal charges that my neighbors faced.

"You should be on another floor," he said. "I don't know why they won't move you up to this floor where I'm at."

"They won't do it," I said. "For some reason, they keep me down here."

"Do me a favor," he said. "Tell them you want to kill yourself."

"Why would I do that?" I asked.

"That's the only way they're going to move you," he said. "Then I can get you upstairs to the hospital level."

So I went back to my cell, and I called for one of the guards.

"Hey, I'm going to kill myself," I said.

"You're going to do what?" the guard said.

"I'm going to kill myself," I said.

"Hold on a minute," he said.

He got some other guards together, and they opened my cell door right away. I was so relieved that they were finally going to get me out of there. Well, they took me upstairs, all right. They rushed in, grabbed me, slammed me down on the ground, and handcuffed me. When we got upstairs, they didn't take me to a cell. They took me to the crazy house, where they put me in a diaper and strapped me down in four points.

"This is not good," I thought.

As I would experience again in my life, unfortunately, they first released one hand. After the second day, they released the other hand. After three days, they released me completely. I was allowed to stand up, and walk around, and put my regular clothes back on. It felt good just to be able to move around again. I did get to leave the 7000 floor after that, but I think that must have been one of the most humbling experiences of my entire life. Even then, I couldn't imagine I'd end up in that kind of situation again, as I did later in rehab.

While I was waiting for my attempted murder trial to begin, I got some good news about the armed robbery charges I was also facing, thanks to Hank. Apparently Hank had been running his mouth about how he had stolen my car and gotten the whole thing pinned on me, and one of his family members had heard about it.

This family member went to Johnnie Cochran and told him that the same guy who was shot at the drug house was also the one behind the armed robbery the cops were pinning on me. So those armed robbery charges ended up being dismissed in early May. The thing that pisses me off, though, is that the charge is still on my record. I never robbed anybody in my entire life.

At least that was one less thing for me to worry about at the time. But the issue of the stolen car was still very much a part of my attempted murder trial. In fact, the prosecutors kept trying to say that I shot Hank because we were fighting over the use of my BMW, when in reality that scumbag did a lot worse than that.

Finally, in late October, they selected a jury and my trial began. The prosecution had a lot of witnesses lined up against me. All of the witnesses, including Bradley Garcia, said that I was the one who shot Hank. Well, of course they said that because they were all given deals by the prosecution. They were willing to rat me out in exchange for a plea bargain because they all had these big cases of their own that they were worrying about. Johnnie Cochran's slogan was "He who is in the mud wants to get somebody else dirty." And that's exactly what was going on during my trial. The witnesses were all dirty, and they wanted to get me dirty, too. The police had been after me for years, and this was their chance to finally get me. They wanted me so badly for the shooting that they didn't care about anything else.

But once they started calling the witnesses, it didn't work out quite as well as they had hoped. Because Hank's family member had come forward, and everything he had done to me was out in the open, he had to get up on the stand during the trial and tell the truth about the robbery. And then the mechanic pointed Hank out in the courtroom and said Hank was the guy who had held him up. So all of that came out in court. The prosecution and the police department were mortified. They couldn't believe it wasn't me who stole that car. It ruined their whole case. They had tried to make Hank out to be this innocent guy who happened to be a drug dealer. Now that he had admitted to stealing my car and pinning it on me, he didn't look so innocent anymore.

The prosecution had attempted to say that Hank got shot because I was trying to steal drugs from him. But I was a drug dealer at the time. I had plenty of my own drugs, and I didn't need to steal anything from him. He was the one who was coming to rob me, or to finally take me out for ruining the good thing he had had going when he was stealing from Billy. I'll never know what his intentions were, but I'm sure he would have killed me that night if he could have.

Only, after he assaulted me and ran into my drug house, whether to rob it or wait for me there so he could take me out, I'll never know, somebody shot him instead. That's not my fault. He had a lot of enemies because he did a lot of dirt to a lot of people in that area. I'm very lucky that it all went down the way it did. I could easily be in prison, or dead.

When it came time for Hank to describe what happened on the night of the shooting, he claimed during his testimony that he and I had had an argument that night, and then I had stood over him and shot him eight times at close range.

I testified, too. The angle Johnnie took for my defense was that I had been so screwed up the night of the shooting, I couldn't remember what had happened. And that, even if I had shot Hank, and then forgotten, because of how high I was, the very fact that I was so high at the time meant that there was no way I could have actually intended to kill Hank. I know that sounds like some wily legal maneuvering, and in a way it was. But it was true that I never had any intention of killing Hank that night. It also was true that I was not in my right mind because of the crack. I hadn't been in my right mind for years. So when the prosecutor questioned me, I kept saying that I had no memory of who shot Hank that night. He kept trying to trip me up by asking me the same questions again and again and again. But he couldn't get me to change my story, and at one point he got so frustrated that he had to take a break.

Then they finally called to the stand the only person involved in the situation who wasn't out of his mind on crack that night, this made him a pretty credible witness, especially compared to the rest of us. He was a regular guy who happened to live next door to the drug house where the shooting had gone down, and he had seen some interesting things that night. The District Attorney questioned him. As far as I can remember without the court documents, which we were not able to locate in the time that we had to prepare this book, the testimony went something like this.

"Okay, I need to know, did you see Todd Bridges running from the scene when the shots were fired?" the DA asked.

"No, I was having a conversation with Todd outside the house when the shots were fired," the man said. "Todd and I both turned around and looked, and then Todd ran."

"What do you mean, Todd wasn't in the house?" the DA asked.

"No, he wasn't in the house," the man said. "Todd was outside the house."

Now, the police had taken this man's statement and put it in with their report. I don't know how the district attorney could have not known what the guy was going to say, but the DA looked shocked, and it totally blew apart his case.

The way the neighbor described the night's events is also how I recall them. Johnnie may have known the best defense to use, given how high I was at the time, but here's what really happened, as I remember it. After Hank threw me into the bushes, I got up and went around to the front of the house. I'd composed myself and tried to figure out how I was going to handle the situation before I went inside to face him. Normally, I always had a gun on me, but that night I wasn't armed. I knew CRASH was in the area, so I wasn't about to carry a gun when I was going from house to house, in case they stopped me. I didn't have any drugs on me for the same reason. I had guns inside the house, but that's where Hank was, and I was sure he was armed. As high and out of it as I was, I still had the good sense to know I didn't want to get shot. For all I knew, he was in there robbing them at that very minute. I wasn't about to get caught up in all of that. If I wasn't there to defend the house, then it wasn't on me. If they couldn't defend themselves, that was their fault. They had protection, and they knew how to use it.

While I was standing there thinking, or doing my best to think, what with all of the crack I'd been smoking for the past six days, the neighbors in the house next door came to the window to see what had caused the commotion they had heard. It was a black couple, and they clearly recognized me from TV. They were being really nice to me, especially given that I was standing in front of a drug house that probably kept them up plenty of nights. It was like that in South Central; there would be a drug house, and then the houses all around it would belong to innocent people who were trying to live their lives the best they could in a neighborhood plagued by drugs and the people, like me, who sold them.

"What are you doing here?" the man said. "Why are you in this area, Todd?"

"What do you mean?" I asked.

"You know you shouldn't be here," he said.

"I know," I said. "But this is what I do now."

"You shouldn't be in this neighborhood doing drugs," his wife said. "You should stop using and take yourself home. Something is going to happen."

I knew they were right. But I wasn't ready to stop.

The sound of gunshots rang out from the drug house. We all stopped talking and listened, but it was quiet after that. I looked over at the door I had been about to walk through and thought, "Wow, I'm glad I didn't go in there."

The couple shut their blinds really quickly after that. I turned around and ran down the street to the other drug house I was dealing out of at the time.

The witness wasn't there to see what happened next, but I was. I went inside and got loaded. There was this girl in there that I had always thought was fine. We started talking, and then we started having sex. But I couldn't really get into it because I was too preoccupied with what was going on back at the other house. I figured I'd better go check it out and see if the police were over there. What I expected to do was stand in the back of the crowd and blend in with the neighbors. But I never made it. I found out later that CRASH knew I was somewhere in the area, but they weren't sure where, so they were on the streets looking for me. When I came out, they were ready and waiting, and that's when they arrested me.

There was one more witness in my trial who ended up helping my case a great deal: Billy. The prosecution was making me out to be this ruthless drug addict who would have done anything, even kill a man, to win my side of an argument and get my hands on his drugs. Billy wanted to explain to them that I wasn't like that at all, so he came down from prison and testified for me. He told them about the lost young man he had first met, who could have been an easy target in South Central if he hadn't taught me how the streets worked. He let them know that no amount of crack or street smarts could have turned me into a cold-blooded killer.

The only question was whether the jury would believe him and acquit me, or believe the DA and send me to prison.

12

JUSTICE AND ITS AFTERMATH

THE JURY FINALLY began deliberations on November 3, 1989. It took them a week to come back with a verdict. That was probably the longest week of my life, waiting to find out if I would be going away to prison, or if I would get to go back out on the streets and do the thing I had been longing to do most: get high. When they finally returned with their decision, they had come to a conclusion on only two of the three charges. They acquitted me on the big counts—attempted murder and attempted voluntary manslaughter—but they couldn't reach an agreement regarding the third charge, assault with a deadly weapon. At least I was relieved to know that I wouldn't be doing significant time in prison. But this final charge was still serious enough to make me worry plenty. Finally, a day later, the jurors announced that they were deadlocked, eight to four, with more jurors in favor of acquitting me. The judge declared a mistrial, and as soon as I was processed, I was free to go, at least for the time being. I would still have to face the third charge, but not right away.

There were several officers from the LAPD in court the day I was acquitted, and they were clearly furious when the verdict was read out loud. They had tried everything they could to get me over the years, and they were sure they had really cornered me this time. When they heard the verdict, they stormed out.

I was so relieved that I was going to be able to leave jail and get my life back, and it was great to see my mom and my family looking so happy. But my jubilation at the news of my acquittal was short-lived. The first thing that ruined my mood was the way my release was handled in the media. They had never said anything positive about me before, and even though I had been acquitted by a jury in a court of law, that didn't change how they talked about me now. The general reaction seemed to be, "How did he ever get acquitted?" No one ever seemed to report the facts of the case. They were basically saying that I was still guilty. The district attorney even got on the news and said that he knew I was guilty, and he was determined to get a retrial. Now I had to worry about that, too. But for the moment, I was just glad to go home.

By the time I was released from jail, I didn't feel up for doing much more than trying to get my bearings in the real world. I was still pretty raw from the whole experience of being locked up and going through a high-profile trial. It had shaken me, coming to after being gone on drugs for so long, and finding myself caught up in the kind of trouble I had never imagined.

I may have adapted to life on the inside, but I certainly didn't want to do anything that would send me back anytime soon. Instead of rushing right out to South Central, like I had originally planned, to see what was left of Billy's syndicate and get as high as I possibly could, I went home to my house in Sun Valley. I had been sober for nine months, and I had gotten used to how it felt. I wouldn't say that I had exactly made a commitment to being drug-free for the rest of my life, but it seemed like a good idea to stay sober for the time being.

Even after court costs, which nearly broke me, I still had a little bit of money. I had been smart enough to hand my finances over to my mom for safekeeping before I got swallowed up completely by the drugs. I had known that she would make sure all of my payments stayed current, and she did. She took care of my house and all of my bills for me during my time in South Central, while I was basically living my life like a vagabond. I consider myself very lucky that she was there to look out for me. Otherwise all of that money would have been spent on crack, and I would have been left with nothing.

But I was actually doing all right for myself, especially given everything I'd been through. I was finally able to take a break and relax for a little while. Becky and I were basically a fairly normal couple at that point. We hung out at the house, went out to dinner, had family and friends over, that kind of thing. We even got married a few months after I was released. My brother had gotten married while I was in jail, and because I always wanted to be just like Jimmy, I wanted to get married, too. We had a small wedding at my house, no honeymoon, and that was it; we were married. Clearly I wasn't in the best place to be embarking on a lifetime partnership. But she had stood by me through everything. And even though we still fought a lot, I was young, and I thought I knew what I wanted.

I was glad I didn't have to go back to work right away because I didn't want anything to do with acting. It wasn't like people were exactly banging my door down to offer me parts right then, but that was fine with me. Now that I had been out in the real world, I thought of acting as a fake job. On top of that, I had just come off of all of the terrible press surrounding my trial, and I was still hurt from everything they had said about me. I wasn't ready to live my professional and personal life in the public eye again. And by this time I knew I was in no condition to work anyhow. There was nothing left inside me that I could have drawn on as an actor. All of the excitement and joy I had felt as a kid had been crushed, and all that remained were depression and anger and hate. I had quit drugs in jail, but because there weren't any rehabilitation programs for prisoners, I hadn't received any of the support I needed to handle the emotions the drugs had been repressing. Without the drugs, these dark feelings took over.

I wasn't in the best emotional state to begin with. On top of that, I faced the fact that the retrial the DA had threatened was looming, at least for the third charge, on which the jury had deadlocked. My anxiety definitely made it hard to stay sober, especially when I knew the kind of euphoria that a hit of crack would instantly make me feel. The other problem was that my wife kept drinking and using drugs during this whole time. And it's not a good idea to have those kinds of temptations around somebody who's as new to recovery as I was. But she felt like I was the one with the problem, not her, and she was perfectly happy with her life as it was, so she did as she liked. I certainly knew from my own experience that there was no point in trying to convince her to embrace recovery when she wasn't ready.

Another challenge to my sobriety was that I had to drive too far to get to my AA meetings, and this meant passing by the areas where I used to do drugs. Any recovering addict who was really committed to getting sober would have seen both of these circumstances as dangerous triggers and would have tried to avoid them. But I didn't do anything to change either. Like I said, I don't think I had completely made up my mind to stay sober, so I just tried to white-knuckle it as best I could.

One day, I was driving to a meeting, and I saw the turnoff that I used to take to go buy drugs, and my car went on automatic pilot. I stopped and bought some crack and kept on driving until I got to a motel where I could smoke it.

And then, just like that, it was on.

Almost immediately, I was smoking twenty-eight grams of crack a day, just like I had in South Central, and it felt just as good as I had dreamed it would during all those long months in jail. Now that I was free from all of the pain that had come up during my sobriety, and the stress of knowing that I might be about to face another attempted murder trial, I was not about to give up drugs again anytime soon. And so I had to figure out a way to supply my habit, just like before. I had thought about this while I was in jail, and I knew exactly what I had to do.

After I was released, I never went back to Billy's drug houses in South Central, but I hadn't forgotten any of the lessons he had taught me. And my time out of the drug world had only made me realize that I wasn't ready to retire any more than I was ready to be sober. I decided to take the game I had learned from Billy in South Central and bring it to the San Fernando Valley. Only this time I would make it bigger. Once I started getting loaded again, and I wasn't in my right frame of mind anymore, the plan made so much sense that it seemed like the only way.

Using what Billy had taught me, I set up shop. I took some of the money I had, and I went out and bought a bunch of coke. I got my drugs from this group of Latino guys, and they ended up hanging out a lot and helping me with the rest of the business. We hung out sometimes socially, too. But the one time I can really remember them being over at my house in Sun Valley, they were high on PCP, which made them really out of it. As I've already said, like most addicts, I had this funny snobbery about drugs, like the one I was doing wasn't as bad as anything else that was out there. I was not down with the PCP, so I mostly kept our dealings professional. I had a few guys who worked for me, but mostly I liked to employ girls because I could have sex with them anytime I wanted. I went out and found four or five who were willing to do what I told them. Instead of selling out of drug houses, I ran my operation out of motels, and I soon had two or three sites going at once. I'd pick the girls up on the corner, and I'd drop each of them off at a different motel. I'd give them a certain amount of crack and tell them what I needed back and when I expected to have it. Then I'd stop by and pick up the money later. They had pagers on them, and if they ran out of drugs or needed protection because a situation got out of hand, they'd page me, and I'd go over to the motel and do what had to be done.

I had girls who worked the streets for me, too. Before they met me, they had been taking the money they earned turning tricks and using it to buy drugs. When I saw these girls out on the streets, I would talk to them, and if they seemed like a good fit, I'd bring them into the little family I had created. We made an agreement where I gave them a better deal on drugs than they would have received otherwise. And I helped them out with things that made their life better, like a place to take a shower. If they got into trouble, they knew they could count on me. If they got arrested, I bailed them out. If they had a run-in with somebody crazy on the street, they paged me, and I went down and helped them out. In exchange, they gave me a cut of their money. Like the money I earned dealing, this money went toward funding my business operation, which in turn was all about keeping me in all of the crack I could smoke, which at that point was a lot.

On a typical night, I would get everyone who worked for me set up and then take my drugs back to my house in Sun Valley and get high with whatever girl I was having sex with at the time. Although I was a newlywed, we were always fighting. I did what I wanted, when I wanted, and my wife pretty much did the same. Not surprisingly, the early days of our marriage were also the last days of our marriage. In addition to my wife, there was one girl I hung out with more than the others for a while, but I can't even remember her name anymore. I really didn't know how to have a relationship with a woman. I definitely didn't associate sex with love. I thought women were good for sex, and that was it. For a lot of years, I didn't have any women friends, even. I thought that if I wasn't having sex with a woman, it wasn't a good relationship. And, of course, I had sex with all the girls who worked for me, too.

I didn't ever get close to any of the girls in my life, or to anyone else. I knew plenty of people who died when I was an addict. But I never knew them well enough to really care about them. During that time there could have been people who were dead, and I would have stepped over them and kept right on walking. I was on so much crack that I was like a zombie.

For the first few months, things went pretty smoothly, considering the type of business I was running. But then trouble found me again. On the night of May 5, 1990, I was sitting in my car in North Hollywood with this guy named Daniel Mulven, who was working for me at the time. My drugs were at home, but he had three grams of coke on him. When the police came up behind us, I knew we were in for it. His coke was in his pocket, his wallet, and a bag that he tried to stash under my seat. They pulled us out of the car and arrested us both on drug charges.

Once again, my latest woes were all over the news in a flash. Luckily, Johnnie came down and got everything straightened out. I kept telling the cops that the drugs didn't belong to me. And since most of the drugs had been on Daniel, and the arresting officers had seen him hiding the rest of the drugs on my side of the car, the

Los Angeles County district attorney decided he didn't have enough evidence to bring me up on charges. In the end, Daniel got charged, but I was released four days after my arrest. That was a true crime in and of itself. They should have taken me into custody. It would have helped me in the long run. But they didn't, and I didn't have the sense at the time to realize I was headed for trouble. I was glad to be released from jail and get back to my drugs, and my girls, and my business, in that order. Of course, the headlines about the charges being dropped never seemed to be as big as the headlines about me being arrested.

That August, I was retried for the assault with a deadly weapon charge I had faced the previous year. I did not want to go through all of that again, but I felt lucky, at least, that I didn't have to go back to jail during the trial. Of course, the problem with being on the outside was that I was free to use drugs, and I was using plenty during that time. This made it very difficult for me to make it to court. I managed it for the first few days. And then, one day, I got a little too loaded. I tried to go to court, but I couldn't find the courthouse. I was driving around, up and down the nearby streets, but I was totally lost. That's how out of it I was. When I finally did make it to court, I was late by several hours. The judge, Florence Marie Cooper, was really mad at me, and she decided she was going to straighten me out.

"You're going to come to my court every single day, Monday through Friday, until your case is over," she said. "Or you can be locked up. You choose what you want to do."

I wasn't about to go back to jail. So I chose the former. I had to sit in her court, Monday through Friday, from 8:00 A.M. to 5:00 P.M. It was like a job that didn't pay. There was no way I could get high while I was there, of course, so I had to dry out in her court every day. That was really hard. It wasn't as bad as a full on detox, but eight hours without crack was enough to make me start to go through withdrawal. I had to sit there all day long, watching all of these cases that had nothing to do with mine, until my case finally came up. In the meantime I had no control over how my body was responding to the agonizing process of sobering up. I'd get pretty twitchy. And then, I'd get so tired that I couldn't keep my eyes open. Every time I'd fall asleep, the bailiff would come over and wake me up. Finally it would be my turn to go up in front of the judge, and Johnnie would come up with me, and we would do what had to be done for the day. And then I would go home at night and smoke as much crack as I could until it was time to go back to court again the next day.

Luckily, the whole trial lasted less than three weeks and I didn't have to testify. I think things began to turn in my favor when Johnnie presented the evidence that the LAPD had found bloodstains on Bradley Garcia's clothes after the shooting but not on mine. Bradley had been considered my accomplice during the first trial, but he had cut a deal and testified against me in exchange for what he hoped would be a get-out-of-jail-free card. This time around, things weren't looking so good for him.

Finally, on August 23, the jury began its deliberations. I didn't have to sweat it out for as long as I did the first time around. It took them only one day to reach their decision. When they came back, they acquitted me. It was finally over for good.

That fall, even though I was still using heavily and pretty out of it, I was supposed to make my triumphant return to TV. It had been a big deal when the actor who played clean-cut Willis Jackson had fallen from grace and ended up in the seedy world of crack and crime. And it was certainly big news when I went back in front of the cameras for the first time in years. The press made a big to-do about it.

Al Burton, who gave me my start on *Diff'rent Strokes*, was the one to take a chance on me. He was doing a TV movie, *The New Lassie*, and he gave me a part in that. It wasn't a big part, but I had a couple of lines. I played a police officer. I don't think I have to explain the irony of that. Being on the set in my uniform was so funny because Al wouldn't give me my gun right away.

"Todd Bridges with a gun will be really weird," he said. "I'll wait until the last minute, when we start filming, and then I'll put the gun in your holster."

By the end of 1990, my marriage to Becky had run its course. That winter, we agreed that it would be best if we got divorced. It was all pretty straightforward. We did the paperwork ourselves and went before a judge, pleading irreconcilable differences as the cause for our divorce. The judge asked us if we were sure we couldn't reconcile those differences and make it work. We were sure.

I got used to some pretty weird places and some pretty weird people. Someone I knew owned a storage facility in Sun Valley, so we used to sell out of there a lot. We'd hang out in one of the storage rooms, getting high all day and all night, and people would show up and buy drugs from us inside the unit. It didn't matter to me if I was sitting in a windowless box that was no bigger or nicer than the jail cell I'd called home for nine months. I was getting high, and that was all that mattered to me.

Another time, I had to buy drugs, and all of my regular people were out. So I heard about this other woman who had what I needed. I drove to the address I had been given and found myself at a trailer park. I pulled over and walked among the run-down trailers until I came to the place where she lived. I had seen some nasty drug houses in my day, and I was expecting more of the same—filthy windows, torn-up furniture, trash everywhere, the smell of garbage and backed-up sewage and crack. I knocked on the door and listened to the faint sound of music and someone moving around inside. I was greeted by this really pretty black lady with a big Afro.

I told her who had sent me.

"Come on in, baby," she said.

I followed her inside, watching her hips sway as she walked. I stopped right inside the door because it was dark and smoky, and I couldn't see to move forward. The sweet, musky scent of incense blanketed me.

"Sit down," she said.

As my eyes adjusted, I sat down on the couch and moved some satiny throw pillows out of the way so I could get comfortable. Heavy drapes covered the windows, and candles burned on the end tables, the coffee table, and every other available surface. It looked like a harem from the late '60s. Batiked tapestries were draped over the walls and furniture. She sat down next to me, and I got a better look at her. She was wearing a brightly colored African print dress, and she looked as much from the '60s as her furniture did. It was like I had stepped into a time machine.

"I'm hoping you can hook me up," I said.

"Whatever you need, baby," she said.

Her voice was a sexy purr. We smiled at each other, both knowing exactly what was going down.

She broke out a pipe and some rock, and we smoked it together. I sank back into the couch, hypnotized by the whole vibe of the place. She slid over close to me on the couch, and then I really wasn't going anywhere. I ended up hanging out in her trailer with her for a couple of weeks. We got high together, and we had sex about a million times. It was the best, and then I moved on.

A lot of the people I met during that time were street girls. I remember this one girl, she was cold one night, so I gave her my leather jacket. Of course I never got it back. I should have known. She used to buy drugs from me, but then I had to stop selling to her because she owed me money. She tried to buy drugs from another dealer in Sun Valley. Well, news of that got back to me before long.

Drug dealers had a sort of code, and if somebody owed another drug dealer money, no other drug dealers would sell to her. They would tell her that she wasn't going to get any drugs from any of them until she paid back the money she owed. This girl needed to be taught a lesson. So some of my guys went over to where she lived one night and shot her building up. She still didn't have the money, but she paid me back with what she had, which was pussy. I was happy with the arrangement, and she was too far gone to care as long as she got more crack.

I wasn't vicious, just too high to feel anything for anyone, including myself. And that's how that world worked. If someone said nasty things about me, or tried to hurt me or rip me off while I was high, then there was trouble. It was like what used to happen when I got bullied as a kid, but amplified. If someone made me angry while I was on crack, I didn't have any perspective on the situation, and I went off. Even the slightest insult fueled the rage that already churned inside me. I'd leave the person alone at first, but once I started coming down, the insult would start festering, and rolling and rolling around in my head. And then there was no stopping me until I'd had my revenge.

Here's a perfect example: I sold this guy some drugs. I knew him from around, but not real well. He was nothing more than a typical addict, but not the worst I'd seen. When he paged me, I went to his house to do the deal.

"Hey, Todd, how's things?" he said.

"Not bad, not bad," I said.

"I need a dub, man," he said.

A dub was how people asked for $20 worth of rock.

I gave him his rock. He sized it up and then handed me a $20 bill.

"Thanks, man, catch you later," he said. As soon as our transaction was done, he hustled me out of there real quick.

I didn't think anything of it. Addicts were shifty to begin with, and once they scored, they were all about getting high as quickly as they possibly could. I wouldn't have been any other way. And I didn't particularly feel like hanging out with him anyhow. I put the $20 in my pocket as I walked out to my car.

Later that night, I was back at my house, and I pulled out all of the money I had made from selling drugs that night. I had all of these small bills in my pockets and I took them out and stacked them up and counted them all out. I came across the $20 bill and opened it up. As soon as I did, I saw that it was a $1 bill. That joker had cut the ends off a $20 bill, put them on a $1 bill, folded it up so it looked like a $20 bill, and passed it off to me. I couldn't believe he would do that to me. I turned that bill around every which way, but it was definitely a $1 bill. I was pissed.

He had thought he was going to get away with it, but I wasn't standing for that kind of bullshit. I was bound and determined to teach him a lesson. I waited for him all night. When I saw him, he got what was coming to him. If he had just left me alone, he would have been fine. But he crossed me, and that was a big mistake. Like I said, the entire time I was dealing, I was so high that I was never in my right frame of mind, and that meant that there was no telling what I would do if someone provoked me.

To pay me back the money he owed me, he gave me his girlfriend, who was this Persian girl I also knew from around. I sold her to another guy, who she had sex with so I would forgive her man's debt. That's how it worked. She also had sex with me a couple of times for drugs. She had a twin sister who smoked crack, too, and I used to have sex with her in exchange for drugs sometimes, too.

It was a whole different world with its own rules and logic. Everything was for and about the drugs, and there was never a time that we weren't all high out of our minds. Get a few of us together, add in the fact that the drugs made us paranoid, and all sorts of crazy stuff was bound to happen. I was at home getting high one night, and I happened to look out the window and see this car sitting in my driveway. "Who parked a car in front of my house at two in the morning?" I asked.

Nobody knew.

Right away, I was thinking it was somebody trying to kill me. Obviously. I called 911. The police came over with their sirens going. It was probably the only time in my life I was actually glad to see the cops.

Of course, they sent these two rookie officers, which meant their logic wasn't all that much better than the crack logic I was working on. They walked around the car and looked in the windows. There was an ammo box in the front seat.

"I've seen this in my training," one of the cops said. "That case is probably a bomb."

I was very high and severely paranoid. Now they'd worked my last nerve by telling me this car could have a bomb in it. I wanted them to do whatever they needed to do to keep this car from blowing up and killing me.

In the meantime, the noise and the commotion had woken up most of my neighbors. And then the cops called for backup. When the additional officers arrived, they went around and cleared everyone out of their homes. If the bomb exploded, they didn't want anyone to get hurt. Everyone from my entire neighborhood was standing outside in the street in their robes, thinking about how tired they were going to be at work the next day, and giving me the stink eye.

Finally, the cops blew up the ammo box. I was waiting for it to make this huge explosion. Only it didn't. The blast opened the box. Inside was nothing but papers.

The cops left, and everyone went back to bed. Finally, after all this, I realized that the car actually belonged to someone I knew. I called him up and gave him hell.

"What in your right mind would make you leave a car in front of my house without telling me?" I said.

"I'm sorry," he said. "I didn't know."

"Don't say you're sorry," I said. "My entire neighborhood had to be cleared out, and now they're all mad at me."

My neighbors were pissed. They knew what I was up to at my house, and this was the final straw. They wanted me out. The next morning, when I woke up, there was a message for me on my garage door: "Get out of this neighborhood, you porch monkey."

But I didn't go anywhere, and things only got crazier at my house. Some people moved in with me, and they had their kid with them. We were all using, but I didn't really think of this as a bad thing at the time. It wasn't my kid, and I hadn't brought him into the situation. Now that I'm a father myself, the thought of having a kid in an environment like that gives me chills. But as I've said many times, I wasn't in my right mind back then. I do still talk to that kid, though, and he's doing well.

One of my neighbors, Greg Savanti, was a radio DJ and a cool guy. Even though he didn't use drugs, we became friends. We used to hang out and BBQ together. He told me that the police had called him up and asked if they could watch my house from his yard. I knew it was only a matter of time before my car got pulled over, or my house got raided. I had to be very careful not to give them anything they could use against me.

The crack already made me paranoid to begin with, and being watched by the cops made me even more freaked out. It was a weird thing to experience. Like one time I was hanging out at home, and I was really high. I scanned the mountains behind my house with some binoculars to make sure no one was out there.

That's when I saw it: There was a tent up on the hillside.

"What the hell?" I thought.

I ducked down below the windowsill, where I couldn't be seen. I hid there for a minute, and then I figured that maybe I was just being paranoid and imagining the whole thing. Real stealthily, I looked through my binoculars again. Now there was a cop in camouflage crouched outside the tent. He was looking back at me with his own pair of binoculars. That's right; I was looking at him, and he was looking at me. It was like an episode of *The Twilight Zone*. At least I knew I wasn't being paranoid.

"He's out there, the bastard," I said.

I called the guys who worked for me and told them that we'd have to be sneakier. When they came over from then on, they parked their car four or five blocks away, so that the cops doing surveillance on my house couldn't see it. And then they walked up to the house and came inside. I waited until it was dark, and I left through the back door. I had fenced in my backyard, which ran up against the mountainside, and dug a tunnel under the fence. Normally I kept the hole covered, but it was possible for me to get out to the street without being seen. After a little while, one of the guys would go into my garage and get into my car. I had tinted windows, so when he pulled out into the street, the cops couldn't tell that it wasn't me who was driving. The guy took my car and went to the movies, or the mall, and the cops followed him the whole time, thinking I was the one driving.

But I had already snuck out to the car they'd left for me, and I was long gone in some other direction, doing my thing, going by the motels, picking up my money, dropping off the girls in different places, taking care of business.

With the cops watching me, I made good use of Billy's advice about hiding my guns and my stash. When I traveled anywhere, I always made sure that whatever I had on me was put away in one of the secret compartments in my car.

I also had cause to draw on what he had taught me about holding my own in a challenge. I got a call from my guys that this fool was trying to run them off of their spot. I knew if I let this go, it'd just open the door for more trouble, so I went down there and stood up to the guy. He started talking all crazy and running off at the mouth about doing this and that to me. I lifted my shirt and showed him my gun.

"Well, whatcha gonna do?" I asked. "It's your choice."

He left. I won the challenge. My guys stayed right where they were.

Billy's lessons served me well in the valley, too. Of course, as he had told me, it only worked if I was willing to go all the way. That boldness was something that couldn't be faked. And I had it. I was willing to do anything to prove my point because I didn't care about my life at all. After using that heavily for that long, I had become so desolate that I didn't care about anyone or anything, not even life itself. All I cared about was staying loaded. If I allowed myself to ever be sober for a minute, all of my old pain came up, and it just hurt too much. So I kept myself from feeling. That was the only way I could make it through.

13

METHAMPHETAMINE BLUES

EVEN THOUGH I STAYED as high as I could, I just kept sinking lower and lower. The girl I was dating at the time took me home with her one time, and when her father saw how skinny and out of it I was, he sized me up right away.

"What are you doing with your life?" he asked me.

"I'm a drug addict," I said. "That's what I am, and I'm happy being a drug addict."

"You need to get your life together," he said.

"This is my life," I said. "I'm fine with this."

I guess he didn't like my tone because he got mad at me, and he shoved me. Of course, that was the wrong thing to do to me, and I shoved him back. Even in that moment, when I was high and angry, it all seemed so pathetic to me. But I kept having that same thought: "I'm a drug addict. That's all I'm good at anymore."

I went home and I tried to cry. But there were no more tears left in me. All that was left was anger. I was mad that I'd let myself sink this low in the first place. But I couldn't imagine any alternatives, because getting sober meant dealing with the pain, and that was way too much for me. I was angry at everything and everyone. I blamed my addiction on everyone else. I wasn't ready to start looking at myself.

That was a very dark time for me. There was nothing good left in my life. Not even God. Well, I know now that He was in my life, because that's probably all that was keeping me alive. But I didn't feel His presence. I didn't want Him in my life, either. I didn't want anything in my life. I was stuck in the depression. I was stuck in the ignorance. I was stuck in the sadness. I was stuck in the shame. And, sometimes, when a person gets stuck in all that, he doesn't want to come out of it. So I stayed under the influence of drugs, totally numb, totally isolated in my own miseries.

There were glimmers of hope. But something always seemed to happen to send me back into a tailspin. I was asked to do a part in a movie in 1991. I was honestly surprised that anyone had thought to hire me at that point. I only watched TV or movies as something to space out to when I was high, and I certainly didn't think about acting in them. I had let all of my connections go. I knew the only time people in the industry had thought of me recently was when my name had been in the news for all of the wrong reasons. But it felt good to be asked, and part of me wanted to prove I could do it. I needed the money, too. I took the part. I was too far gone to have a big emotional response to acting again, but I was glad to get paid. And it was a good paycheck. I had about $50,000 in cash at the time.

Right after that, I went on a really bad drug binge. So I called my neighbor, Greg Savanti, the one I was good friends with, who had tipped me off that the police were watching me. I told him I wanted him to take $25,000 from me and give it to my mom so I wouldn't spend it on drugs. I had this publicist named Dylanne, who was working for me at the time, and she told him that he should give the money to her, and she would give it to my mom for me. The two of them came to this motel I was at, using drugs, and they got the money from me. Only Dylanne never gave it to my mom. She took it, and we never heard from her again. My friend still feels so bad that she tricked him and ripped me off. He couldn't believe it, but I could.

Being betrayed by my publicist for the second time in my life, while at the same time having my money stolen from me all over again, did nothing for my mental state. And as I've already said, it was pretty fragile to begin with.

Right around then, I met this girl Joelle. With me, everything started with a girl, right? She ended up being real bad news for me, but I didn't know that at the time. All I knew was that she was hot, and I wanted to sleep with her. She was selling and using methamphetamine, and she told me that she thought I should start selling it, too. I didn't know anything about meth, but I was open to trying anything, especially when there was a hot girl involved.

Joelle came over to my house. We were hanging out, smoking crack and flirting, which led to sex. Like I said, when I was getting high at home, I liked to be naked. I was lounging on my bed, feeling worn out in that good way after a long night of sex. I reached over, grabbed my pipe and a rock, and took a long hit.

"Can I get me some of that?" Joelle asked.

"I don't know," I said. "What are you going to do for me?"

"I think I already done plenty," she said, laughing.

"You ain't done nothing yet, girl," I said. I handed her the pipe, slapped her lightly on her bare ass, and stood up.

"You know what I feel like?" I said.

"What's that, baby?" she asked, laying back after her hit and looking up at me through half-closed eyes.

"I feel like taking a shower," I said.

"Well, you sure is a dirty boy," she said.

"And you's a nasty girl," I said. "Maybe you'd better come with me."

I went into the bathroom and got under the hot water. A few minutes later, she came in. She climbed in with me and started rubbing up against me with her breasts. I was instantly hard. She had something in her hand.

"You got a present for me?" I said.

"That's right, baby," she said. "Some of that crystal method I've been telling you about."

She held up the hypodermic needle and gave me a sexy look. Normally, I hated needles. But I was already high and feeling good and I was into doing whatever it took to keep both going. She was a pro, and she found a vein and shot me up before I had time to register what was happening. As soon as the drugs hit my bloodstream, the high was so good, I literally had an orgasm. It was the best high I'd ever had in my entire life. Right there I had my two favorite things all rolled up into one, and I was immediately hooked.

Meth replaced crack for me. And pretty soon I was shooting about fourteen grams of meth a day. I was selling it, too, along with crack and weed. It was pretty much the same setup I had used to support my crack habit. But there were a few problems with meth. The first problem was that I really liked the way meth made me feel. Soon I was shooting more meth than I was selling. The second problem was that meth made me crazy. In some ways, I was still lucid. I had the good sense not to share needles. There were diabetics who would sell their extra needles, so I always had my own supply of clean needles, which I carried around in this doctor's bag with all my methamphetamine, crack, and pot. And I always made sure to hide my drugs very well whenever I was going anywhere in my car. The police searched me many times while I was dealing in the San Fernando Valley, and they never found anything.

I was still able to function on a basic level. But beyond that, meth was really screwing with my head. I could already tell that it was the beginning of the end for me. But I loved that meth high so much that I was determined to keep it going for as long as I could. Things weren't looking good. It was very difficult for me to eat when I was on meth. I had dropped down to about 112 pounds, and at a height of 5'11", I looked like I was in a concentration camp. But I didn't care. All I cared about was shooting more meth, so I could stay high. I stopped sleeping and spent all my time getting high and selling drugs to buy more drugs, to stay high even longer.

The longest I ever stayed up on meth was something like fourteen days. I started seeing these little creatures in my house. They looked so real to me that to this very day I could swear I actually saw them. They were these little men who looked like those Stretch Armstrong dolls, but green. They were being manufactured under my house. They came up out of the ground and ran around my living room, and I would run around my house, chasing them and shooting my gun at them. Sometimes I hit one, and it died. Then, all of a sudden, the wall opened up, and the creatures grabbed him and dragged him back inside, so I couldn't show anybody. That's why nobody else could see them but me. Other people could sure see what I was doing to my house, though. One day, my mother called to tell me she was going to come by for a visit, and by the time she got to my house, I had broken up a bunch of my furniture and was using it to nail myself into the house. Another time, she actually got inside the house, and she noticed that there were bullet holes everywhere. She acted like everything was normal, but she didn't stick around too long.

Soon after that, my phone rang, and there was a guy I had never spoken to on the other end.

"Tell me about the little green men," he said.

I was glad to have the chance to explain them to someone, and so I started telling him all about them. But then, as I was talking, I started thinking, "Wait a minute, something's not right here."

"What did you say your name is?" I asked.

"My name is Dr. . . ." he said.

I hung up the receiver right away. That was all I needed to hear. I knew that if I told this guy about the little green men, the doctors would come in white jackets to get my ass. I was not about to let them put me away. I sure could have used it, though. My mind was so shredded by the drugs that my mom actually had called that psychiatrist, and she was trying to have me committed.

I knew things had gotten a little weird, but I mostly thought everything was fine. I had made some new friends, and since I spent days and days alone shooting drugs at that point, I was glad for their company. They started working for me, so I picked them up and dropped them off at different places around the valley. We talked things over while we were driving in my car. And this one girl, Lisa, was really hot. First, we started out by making jokes and flirting when we were in the car together. Then she'd come back to my house after she was done working for the night. We'd hang out and get high. And that, of course, led to sex, a lot of sex, which, of course, made me happy.

And then, after being up on meth for almost two weeks, I finally came down and passed out for three or four days. When I woke up, I got together with the Latino guys who'd been working for me since I first started running my operation in the valley. Like I said, they were into PCP, so we didn't hang out that much, but sometimes we'd have a few drinks and get high together.

We were all sprawled out across the furniture in my living room.

"Hey, where's Lisa?" I asked them.

"Who?" they said.

"You know, Lisa," I said.

"What are you talking about?" they asked.

"You know, Lisa, that hot girl I was hanging out with last week," I said.

Finally they got it.

"Lisa's not real," they said.

"Yes, she is," I said. "I see her all the time. She was staying here."

"There's been nobody here with you but us," they said.

That rattled me. But then I shot more meth, and I saw Lisa and my other new friends again, and I forgot that they were anything but real.

I was about as far gone as a person could be and still be alive. I was starting to realize how bad off I was, and so were the other people in my life, at least the ones who were real.

Weird Ernie was still a pastor with his own congregation in Carson, and he had never given up on me. He still knew, deep down, that he was on a mission from God to help me find my way back to the right path. He came by my house all the time to check on me. I didn't let him inside, so he stuck his hand through the barred gate I had over my door. I stuck my hand out, too, and he grabbed onto it through the bars.

"Your hands feel like they're dead," he said.

That made him pray for me even harder. We stood outside like that while he prayed for me, and then I went back inside and shot some more meth.

My mom was still praying for me, too. But I had pushed her to the edge of what she could endure. Finally, she came to my house dressed in black. She started to cry, and she told me it was the outfit she had bought to wear to my funeral.

"I'm ready for you to go whenever God wants to take you," she said. "I am ready for it. I am tired of worrying about you."

I was tired, too, but I wasn't ready to stop.

I wasn't ready to stop, but I didn't know how much more I could take, either. Even as high as I was all the time, I could tell that my life was out of control. I started to get tired of being on my guard all the time.

I had good reason to think things were getting out of control. My binges and their aftermath were getting scary. Not only would I be up for two weeks, shooting at little green men and having sex with imaginary girls, but then I would come out of a drug binge and pass out for something like five days. Literally. Nobody could wake me up, and I didn't get up, even once during that time, not even to go to the bathroom. This started to take a toll on my health, and I was having seizures.

It was important to make sure I had somebody safe around me when I was out like that, but that wasn't always easy to find. This one girl I was sleeping with was at my house while I was passed out for three days. And during that time, she loaned my car to somebody. It was one of the guys who worked for me, but still when I woke up, and heard what she'd done, I was furious.

"You did what?" I said.

"It's back," she said. "Your car's back."

"Yeah, but you didn't know it would come back," I said. "Are you crazy?"

That was it for her and me; I told her straight up. "I will never pass out around you again," I said. "I will get rid of your ass out of my house so that all of my stuff is right there when I wake up."

That wasn't even the worst of it. I was in this motel with another girl, and we were having sex for hours. On coke, it was like that. I could just go and go. Anyhow, I finally finished. I got up, got dressed, and grabbed my car keys.

"I'll be right back," I said.

The last thing I remember is heading out of the motel.

The next thing I knew, I woke up on the side of the 14 Freeway, which runs between Los Angeles and Palmdale. I have no idea how I was able to lie there without some police officer or somebody coming along and seeing me. I guess I wasn't visible from the road because I was flat on my back. I came to, and I was just lying there in the dirt and the scrub grass, and I had no idea how I had gotten there. I figured I had been gone for an hour or two. I got in my car, which was parked nearby, and went back to the motel. The girl was gone. I went down to talk to the guy at the front desk, and he gave me a funny look.

"You checked out of here three days ago," he said.

"What?" I said.

"That girl," he said. "She checked out three days ago. You guys gone."

"What the hell are you talking about?" I said. "I was only gone for an hour."

"No, you check out."

I couldn't believe it. Three days had passed, and I had no clue.

Another bad thing about getting involved with meth was that I started meeting all of these meth monsters. These people were just weird, messed-up people. Methheads like to tinker. They could take apart anything and put it all right back together, only they usually lost interest partway through and went off to get high. Since I was selling speed, I saw some serious meth houses in the San Fernando Valley. And, sure, I'd done my time in some nasty-ass crack houses in South Central, but these places where people did meth were tripped out by comparison. I'd walk in the front door, and there'd be a TV in the living room, but it'd be all taken apart, with the parts strewn around. There might be a guy, all tweaked out, tinkering with it. Tweakers have always got to be doing something, so they'll break an appliance in the process of trying to fix it. Actually, they were a little bit like I used to be as a kid, when I was always pulling my toys apart to see how they worked. But the drugs meant that these people could keep at it for hours and hours—until they came down, or spaced out, or decided to get high again or "fix" something else. The TV was just for starters. There might be two or three TVs, all tore up. There was junk everywhere in those houses. They were like scavengers, and they tore everything apart. Stoves. Microwaves. VCRs. There was an upside—when the fan in my car went out, some methheads I knew got it to work again. I don't know how they did it. But other than that, they were bad news. They were in another world, like zombies. I was hanging out at one of these meth houses when one of the girls leaned over toward me and slid her hand up my thigh in way that told me exactly what she had in mind. I took one look at her. Teeth all ground down. Skin covered in acne. The bones of her skull looked like they were about to poke through her face. The girls who were on meth, those were some beat-down-looking girls. Even I didn't want to get with them. Of course, I wasn't looking so hot myself in those days, or thinking too clearly, so I took what was easy to get.

As much as I liked the high that meth gave me, I didn't like everything else that came with it—the paranoia, the delusions, the methheads. I was used to some pretty dark stuff, but this was too bleak, even for me. It was around this time that I decided I wasn't going to shoot meth or smoke crack anymore. I liked the meth way too much, and I knew that my mind couldn't take much more.

I used pot to take the edge off of coming down. It was still nasty to detox, but the pot helped with the worst of my symptoms. It was a different kind of high, but it was still being high, and it kept me from sinking as low as I had when I had detoxed in the past. I was soon smoking pot all the time, and it made me stupid. Just going to a McDonald's was about the limits of what my brain could handle. I'd be standing there, staring up at the menu, not even able to focus on the words, just looking at the pictures, until one of the employees shook me out of my daze.

"Can I help you?" the guy behind the counter asked.

"Uh, I'll take a number . . .

"No . . .

"Maybe a . . .

"No . . .

"Or a number . . .

"No . . .

"Ah, let me get . . ."

I was seriously like a bad joke from *Bill & Ted's Excellent Adventure* when I was high on pot, but that was nothing compared to what I had just been through, and I was able to finally pull it together some.

It was around this time that I started hanging out with Tiffany, who was the girl I mentioned before who was supportive of my decision to clean up. She'd come by the house, and we'd just watch TV, order in some food, that kind of normal stuff. It felt good after how crazy my life had been. Of course, she'd be having a drink while we were hanging out. And she'd go into the bathroom to smoke crack every now and again. But I wasn't tempted to go back. I was seriously done with my wild ways and how sick and crazy they had made me feel. If I was ever tempted, I'd just take a big bong hit, and that would mellow me out until the craving passed. Somehow it worked for me. I decided to start shutting my operation down. Things calmed down after that. I mostly just hung around the house, smoking pot, and trying to let my mind right itself, day by day. I still had a little money left, and I was able to get by.

My life was much more normal than it had been, but there were still a lot of drugs and drug people around me. The whole drug world had been my life for many years, and I still had a lot of ties there. People were always in and out of my house, and some of them were drug people. Some were tenants who helped me out with my expenses. And some were people who were in a rough spot and needed a little help themselves. I knew a thing or two about hitting bottom, and I liked to try to help people out when I could. Like, this one girl, she moved into my house for a few months when she was fourteen years old. I had partied with her parents and gotten to know them very well. But then they both got heavily into drugs, and the situation got messed up. I had given this girl my number and told her to call me if she ever had a problem. And so, when she did, I was glad to be able to give her a place to stay. She actually tracked me down years later and thanked me for having impacted her life in a positive way. That really made me feel good, to know that I had been able to help her. In spite of the situations I had gotten myself into over the years, and the many people I had gotten hooked on drugs, I could still do good.

Even when I could have used rescuing myself, I couldn't stand to see someone get abused or hurt, not after everything that had been done to me as a child. When I'd been high on crack and meth, I'd buried all that, along with any sympathy I might have had for anyone else. That was the only way to survive. And yes, I used and abused some people, especially women, along the way. But once I got my head clear, I always had to stand up for the weak and defenseless, even when it ended up causing me problems in the long run. Like it did on Sunday, March 7, 1993, when I was hanging out at home, and I heard a commotion going on in the room of my tenant Donald Knud. Now, I was letting Donald stay at my house for free because he was having a hard time of it, but we weren't real close; more like drug buddies. I'd found out that he'd been dating the girl who lived

down the street. She was fifteen years old, and he was twentysome-
thing. They were in his bedroom, and I heard him push her down. I
wasn't about to let him hurt a little girl, not in my house. I knocked
on the door to his bedroom, loud, to let him know I was serious.

"Hey, man, you guys can't do this in my house," I said. "She's
under eighteen."

"I'm not leaving," he said.

To show me that he meant it, he picked up this samurai sword,
which he must have taken from where I normally kept it near my
bed. He started swinging it at me.

"This ain't none of your business, Todd," he said. He was serious
about doing me harm. He hit me on my left forearm and cut me in
two places, deep enough that I was bleeding.

"That's it, man, you're done," I said.

And then my shoulder, which had a torn rotator cuff at the time,
fell out. I was in agony.

"Fuck!" I started screaming.

But I didn't have time to think about the pain, because he was
still coming at me, waving that big sword.

"I'll fucking cut you!" he yelled.

I backed down the stairs, trying to get clear of him. He kept after
me, swinging the whole time. But he kept missing and hitting the
railing of the stairs, all the way down. I ran into the kitchen and
grabbed a butcher knife. I'd been in enough fights to know a thing
about knifeplay, so even though I was high, and my adrenaline was
racing, and my shoulder was hurting like you wouldn't believe, I
knew I had to focus and wait for him to make a mistake, or else he
was going to kill me.

"Come on, motherfucker," I taunted him. I jabbed forward like I
was going to go for him. He fell for it and swung at me. But he over-
swung and left his chest open, and that's when I stabbed him in the

chest. I pulled out the knife and he fell to the ground. I called 911. Thank God I actually managed to control myself and not keep at him, or else I would probably be in prison to this day. It was one of the only times in the early part of my life when I did keep it together. Usually, the rage that had built up from all of the abuse I'd suffered when I was younger would swallow me up.

When the cops and the ambulance got there, they came rushing in. But they didn't have their guns drawn, and I didn't give them any reason to draw them. They found me sitting in my house, smoking a cigarette. I pointed them right to where Donald was and told them exactly what had happened.

Not that the news reported the positive side of the story. All anyone heard at the time was that I was up on an attempted murder charge again. It was the same thing all over. They loved nothing more than describing me as a former child star turned drug addict. But the thing was, they never told the whole story. I hadn't wanted to hurt Donald in the first place. I'd just been trying to keep him from hitting his girl in my house. Once he wasn't a threat to me anymore, I left him alone until the ambulance got there.

Now, that was lucky for me, because when the police investigated, they talked to two witnesses, who were also living at my house at the time, and the detectives decided that what had happened between Donald and me was what they called mortal combat. I was defending myself, and once he was incapacitated, I let him be. They kept me in jail for only three days, and then I was free to go. Pastor Johnson came and got me out and took me home.

The young man I had once called Weird Ernie had become a good friend now that we were older. He had never faltered in his determination to try to help me avoid destroying myself and eventually bring me back to God. I appreciated that he had believed in me, even when I was at my lowest and most far gone. Now that I was trying to get my life in order, he continued to be a great source of support to me, and I often drove to Carson to hear him deliver his sermon on Sunday mornings.

I was starting to realize how close to the edge I had been, but I knew I wasn't out of danger yet. There were times when I had cravings for crack and meth so strong I thought I would buckle and go back to my old ways. And there were moments, like during my run-in with Donald Knud, when my anger almost got the best of me. I was sure that all this trouble had started back in my childhood, when I was a little boy longing for a father figure to care about me and help bring me up. This emptiness had made me vulnerable to Ronald Rayton and to drugs.

Right as I was making these connections in my life and figuring out how I'd ended up where I had, the entire city of Los Angeles erupted in violence. On April 29, 1992, the four LAPD officers who had been videotaped beating Rodney King were acquitted, and thousands of people rioted. I would have been following the case closely anyway, but my own history with the LAPD made me particularly interested. When I saw the footage of people looting and rioting in the same South Central neighborhoods where I had added to the problem by selling crack for years, I started to take responsibility for what I had done. And I started to think even more about how I had ended up there. I didn't want other kids to feel the same pain that I had felt and get caught up in the same bad decisions I had. I was talking with Pastor Ernie about this one day, and he encouraged me to use my name and influence to make a difference. And so, with his help, I founded the Todd Bridges Youth Foundation in June 1992 to help at-risk kids get a better start in life. It was a lot of work to get things up and running, but Pastor Ernie found us a building to use as our headquarters, and he enlisted the staff of his church and members of his congregation to volunteer their time to help us set up programs and reach out to the kids.

I was still shaky at that point, but Pastor Ernie continued to be a great source of support, and I found myself energized by my efforts. It felt good to go back to the same South Central neighborhoods where I had been a drug dealer, only now as a force for good. I got Johnnie and Conrad Bain to support the cause, and organizations such as Motorola and Cross Colours sponsored us. I was glad to use my Hollywood connections for something positive. I especially loved working with the kids, who could hardly believe that a famous actor cared enough about them to spend time with them. I hoped to teach them just how much value they had. We soon had all sorts of programs, including tutoring sessions and acting classes.

I had the desire to live a better life and help others, but I had a lot going against me. I hadn't ever really gotten my head straightened out over what had happened to me as a child, or the things I had experienced as a drug addict. So when my old life came calling in the form of that sexy former flame Joelle, who wanted me to buy her a sixteenth of speed, I wasn't strong enough to resist. That's when I had my last big run-in with the cops, in December 1992, and almost ended up committing suicide by cop before allowing myself to be taken into custody.

Looking back, I can see that getting arrested that day was probably the greatest blessing of my life. At the time, it sent me into a tailspin. I had been proud of the progress I had made toward getting my life in order, and it devastated me to lose ground again. I resigned as the head of the Todd Bridges Youth Foundation. I went in for my arraignment on January 14, 1993, and pled not guilty to one count of possession of a controlled substance and one count of transporting a controlled substance while armed with a handgun. I found out that I was looking at nine years in prison if I was convicted on both counts. That knowledge, on top of the fact that Johnnie had said this was the last time he would represent me if I didn't get clean, were more than I could handle. I went right back to using crack and meth again, and I used heavily for the next six months until I had to go back to court, in July. At that appearance I changed my plea from not guilty to guilty on both counts, and that's when I was given the chance to go to rehab.

For me, the sixth time was the charm. Even though I had been to rehab five times before, CPC Westwood was finally just what I needed. Even with the Depakote and the counseling, it was still a really hard path back from the painful, shameful place where I had been living for most of my life. But I had an advantage this time that made all of the difference: I was finally ready to make a change. I was determined that I would never again let things get as bad as they had been during those past few years. This didn't just mean quitting drugs and alcohol, it also meant changing my whole approach to everything. For so many years, I wasn't happy, I was always sad about something. I was sad about being in my shoes. I was sad about being black. I was sad about what had been done to me by my dad and Ronald Rayton. And because, as a little kid, I couldn't understand why such bad things had happened to me, I figured it had to be my fault. I blamed myself for my bad relationship with my dad. I blamed myself for what Ronald Rayton did to me. I assumed I was the one who brought everything bad on myself.

But after God touched me in rehab and helped me to get out of my own way so I could listen to everything my counselor, Judy, and everyone else had to say, I stopped blaming myself. I started learning other, more positive, ways to approach my life. I read "The Big Book," which is like the Bible for people in Alcoholics Anonymous, again and again. I read it backward and forward. What I learned was that most of what had happened to me was not my fault. The only thing I had to take responsibility for was my drug use and the bad decisions I made while I was on drugs. It was such a relief to put down the heavy weight of blame. I had done some terrible things while I was high, and in the service of getting high, but it was so much less than everything I had been carrying on my back for so long. I could handle my own mistakes. I could be responsible for myself.

By the time I had been in rehab for thirty days, I was feeling better than I had in years. It was time for me to leave, and I was ready to go home and rebuild my life. And then I got a visit from a well-known singer and actor who also was in the program. He sat down across from me in my room and got serious.

"Look, man, I don't recommend that you go home," he said. "In fact, I don't recommend you go anywhere near that house. That house is bad for you."

Now, I'll admit there was something weird about that house. My mom had rented it out while I was in rehab. The tenants were people she found herself, and the whole thing had nothing to do with me. But then, the female tenant overdosed on heroin at my house and died. It turned out she was someone I used to date years ago. The really sad part was that she OD'd in front of her daughter. My mom got a call when it happened, and she went over to the house to make sure everything was okay. The cops hadn't forgotten whose house it was.

"Where's Todd Bridges?" one officer asked. "We know he lives here."

"He hasn't been here in years," my mom said.

"Well, sure, but this is his house, and we'd like to talk to him," he said.

"You're not going to talk to him," she said. "He has nothing to do with this."

But I didn't care what had happened there or what the cops thought about my involvement in it. That was my house, and I wanted to go home.

236

My visitor knew how much was at stake, though, and he was determined.

"You should go into sober living," he said.

"I'm not going into sober living," I said. "I want to go home."

"No, you should go into sober living," he said. "Trust me, it will work."

I thought about how God had told me that if I finally shut up and listened, He would bring people into my life who could help me. I had listened in rehab, and everyone there had already helped me so much. So I decided that I would listen to what He was telling me and not do what I wanted to do.

They found me a sober living place, which is basically a supervised living situation where people who have just completed rehab can go to be supported while they try to find a job and get their life on track. The only problem was that I didn't have any money left, and I couldn't afford it at the time. But I got really lucky. Someone else agreed to pay for it for me, and they ended up taking me anyway.

Since God had spoken to me, I could see His hand in my life all over the place. I have to think it was at work here, too. The house they chose to put me in was full of gay men. I was seeing a psychiatrist at the time, and it was really the first time in my life that I was dealing with the fact that a gay man had molested me as a child. So my first reaction was that this was not where I needed to be. But, of course, it was exactly the lesson I needed to learn right then. I came to see that not all gay men are child molesters, which may seem obvious, but when you've been through something like I went through, it can give you all kinds of screwed-up ideas about things. It also was good for me for another reason. I was still working out my anger issues, too. If they had stuck me in a different kind of house, with guys like myself, I would have been fighting the whole time. But these guys, they were kind of soft, almost, and they were able to nurse me back to health. And basically that's what they did. They loved me back to health. They were very patient with me. When I got angry, which I did plenty, they didn't rise to the bait at all.

"Now, Todd, you don't need to be angry," they said.

And they were right. I didn't need to be angry anymore. It was finally safe for me to put aside my anger and stop fighting.

I stayed at that house for about six months before I was moved to another house. By that time I was under better control, and I didn't have a single fight.

I made a lot of progress. I was determined, by this point, that I was never going to use drugs again and that I was going to find a way to live a good, positive life. But I still had to pay for the charges on which I had been arrested. I went back to court, and the judge told me I had to do a ninety-day observation at the Chino Men's Correctional Facility, to make sure I had really learned my lesson and wasn't a further threat to society. The last thing I wanted to do right then was go back to prison. And I was nervous about giving up the good thing I had going at the sober living house, but I knew I didn't have any choice, and that if I could just make it through this one final ordeal, I'd be able to put my old life behind me.

14

BACK ON THE CHAIN GANG

So I WENT TO THE PERSON who ran the sober living house, and I told him what was happening and asked him if my space would be available when I got back. I was told there would be a spot for me, and that at least made me feel better.

The time came when I had to turn myself in, and my mother came and picked me up. She took me out for a pancake breakfast, and then we went to Pasadena, and I went to the courthouse, where they took me into custody. It was a really difficult moment for me. I had vowed that I would never go back to prison, and yet there I was.

I went back up to my old floor, and a lot of the same guys were there. That was the first time I met Eric Menendez, because we had been kept on different floors at different times during my last stint in jail. He and Lyle were both still in there awaiting their trials, which didn't take place until 1993. There were a lot of familiar faces from when I'd been moved there the last time, and they all laughed when they saw me.

"Welcome back, Todd," they said.

"Yeah, welcome back," I said. "I promise you, when I get out of here this time, I won't be coming back."

"Yeah, sure," they said. "You said that the last time, and you're back now."

I had plenty of time to think about that. I was back on the row, waiting for the chain. That's what they called it when they came to take you away to Chino, which is a state prison. They never told a prisoner when he was getting moved, so every day when I woke up, I wondered if that was going to be the day it happened. I was nervous about going to prison. I didn't know what it would be like, but I had to go. I was six months sober. I was starting to feel like I knew what my life was all about, and I knew where I wanted it to go. I knew what I didn't want: I didn't want to use drugs anymore. I knew that. And now I was about to experience something totally different, something I didn't want. Now I'd made it to the big leagues. It was only temporary, but I still had to get through it.

The judge wanted to show me what my life would be like if I kept fooling around like I had been. They didn't send me to Chino right away. They let me sit in a county jail for a couple of months. And so, even though I had made a lot of big changes, my life was right back to where it had been before. I passed the time as I had before, watching TV and following the usual routine.

That's when I got to know Eric Menendez. Whenever I talked to my mom on the phone, Eric would get real quiet. It must have been because his mom was gone. I know he was found guilty of killing her in the end, and so it might seem like he couldn't have cared much about her. But I can only imagine how hard that must have been, knowing he had killed his parents and could never talk to them again, because he killed them, not somebody else, but him.

Even if he did feel bad, though, he really thought he would get away with it.

"I'm going to get manslaughter and go home," he said. "I'm going to get out of here."

"You're going to get life, dude," I'd think. "They're not letting you go. You killed your parents. How do you get away with that?"

Even so, Eric and I had fun together sometimes. We figured out this trick that worked on the doors to our cells. We'd put these little cardboard tabs in the doors, so when the guards came around and closed them, we could just hold them from the inside. When the guards checked the doors, they seemed like they were shut. And then, when the guards left, we'd come out of our cells and talk to each other and do all this crazy stuff in the corridor between the cells. One time, we were having these water fights, throwing water at one another, and Eric got too close to me. I forearmed him, and he flew back against the wall. He ended up getting hurt and going to the infirmary, and the truth about how it happened came out. They wanted to charge me with a crime. They were going to accuse me of trying to escape and injuring another inmate. But then they realized how bad it would look if people knew we were out of our cells. So they ended up dropping everything and letting it blow over. They watched us more closely after that, though.

And then, all of the sudden, at two in the morning, they came to the door of my cell.

"Chain's here," the guard said. "Chain's here."

"Oh, shoot," I thought. "This is it."

I was real nervous then.

Now I was in transition, so I had to put on what they called a fish uniform. They chained me up and took me downstairs, where they put me on a big bus with everybody else who was getting moved that night. They drove us all out to Chino, which took about ninety minutes. When we got there, my life felt like it was a movie all over again. We drove up to a big gate with barbed wire all over it. And there were guys with guns on guard towers. That's when it really hit me.

"Oh, my God," I thought. "This is prison. This is real."

The gate opened up. We drove inside, and the guards came up onto the bus.

"Let's go, everybody off!" they shouted at us.

All of us new guys climbed down off the bus, and as we were getting off and lining up, all of the resident prisoners were yelling at us.

"Yeah, motherfucker!"

"I'm going to fuck you!"

"Oh, my God," I thought. "I'm going to have to fight."

I knew I could handle myself if I needed to, but I was still scared

First off, they had us all strip down and get in this big, long line. There were fifty guys, all naked, all different sizes—fat, skinny, big, small—all waiting to get our clothes. I got up to the front of the line and stood there while they checked my paperwork and got my uniform together. This black officer came up to me. He was kind of cockeyed, and so he gave me this funny look.

"Well, well, well, Willis Jackson smoked his ass all the way to prison," he said.

"Great, this is just what I need right now," I thought.

"Can I just have my clothes, please?" I said.

He gave me my clothes, but he was still laughing.

"Get your ass over to your clothes and get over there," he said.

Then they took me and locked me in this place, which was basically like a big cage, for holding prisoners they were moving. They handcuffed my arms behind my back and left me there for something like eight hours. I was next to a guy who looked really tough, but there was nothing else to do, so we started talking.

"What's up, Todd?" he said.

We talked for a little while, and that seriously opened my eyes.

"I'm in the Bounty Hunters," he said.

I knew they were a Blood gang from my days in South Central. I had dealt with the Bloods often, but that was many years and, hopefully, another lifetime ago.

"Man, what you got to do?" he asked.

"Man, I got to do a ninety-day observation." I said.

"That ain't shit," he said. "I got three consecutive life sentences."

"Damn, I guess mine ain't that bad," I thought.

"I ain't never getting out of this motherfucker," he said.

At least, then, I realized I didn't have it so bad. But then my arms started hurting, and my legs got tired, and I was trying to sort of lean against the cell wall so I could rest. Finally this guard came by and saw me.

"Oh, yeah, that's right," he said. "We forgot about you."

They locked me up in this place where they put all of the serious offenders who couldn't be out with the regular prison population. It was maximum isolation, just like being back in the hole. I was only out of my cell for an hour every day to shower, and that was it. The rest of the time, I was alone in my cell. It was awful, and I knew I was going to start losing it. I never want to go through that again.

I asked for a meeting about getting moved.

"Look, I want to be on the main yard," I said.

"No, we can't risk it," the warden said. "Someone's going to hurt you."

I knew I was going to have to fight, but believe me, that was better than the isolation, which was seriously wearing me down.

"Dude, I have a reputation coming in here," I said. "I can survive the main yard. I do not want to be locked up like this for my remaining time. It's too hard. This is hard time. I don't want to do hard time."

"Well, we'll see what we can do," he said.

They finally came and said they would let me go on the main yard if I signed all of these releases. I signed. I couldn't get out of solitary confinement quick enough.

Meanwhile, I would not sign the release for my mother and brother and sister to come visit, even though they really wanted to see me. I hadn't minded them seeing me when I was in jail before. But things had changed. I had changed. I didn't want them to see me when I was in Chino. Besides, it would have been such a hard thing to go through. I didn't think I could stand to have them come see me, and then have them leave, and know they were going out and have steak sandwiches, or whatever, while I was going back to my cell to be locked up. I couldn't do it.

I finally got to go to the main yard. First, they put me back in another fish uniform, and they put me on another bus. That bus took me out of one gate and back into another gate, where the main yard was. That's where the shit got scary. I was about to hit the main yard, and they were yelling, and cussing, and screaming, and spitting at us.

"Shit, here it goes," I thought. "I asked for it, and they gave it to me, and now I'm going to have to fight right away."

All of a sudden, this big black dude comes up on me. Of course, it had to be the biggest, baddest-looking guy in sight. My heart was just going crazy in my chest while I sized him up. "Damn, I'm going to have to fight this big black dude right now," I thought. "As soon as he says something crazy, I'm just going to connect, and start fighting, and not stop."

He was sizing me up, too. I was really worked up by this point. I knew a lot was riding on how I handled myself in this fight. He leaned down near to my face, but I was afraid to get too close to him in case he hauled off and hit me. Instead of going nuts on me right away, he started talking so only I could hear him.

"Man, let me talk to you for a minute," he said.

I was freaked. I had absolutely no idea what was going to come next.

"Yeah?" I said.

He looked around to make sure no one could hear.

"My last name is Bridges, and I told everybody I was your half brother," he said. "Just go along with it and I'll take care of you."

I wanted to laugh; I was so relieved.

"Sure," I said, trying to play it cool.

But on the inside, I was elated. God had sent me a protector. It had to be.

I turned around and made a big show of being glad to see him.

"Hey, man, where you been?" I said. "Good to see you, man."

I turned around to one of the guys who had gotten off the bus with me.

"It's my half brother," I said. "He's been locked up for a long time."

After that, I started to relax a little bit.

When I got to my dorm that first night, I did get challenged by this other black guy. As soon as I walked in, he was all up in my face.

"What the fuck are you doing?" he asked.

He started talking trash. I knew I had to shut him down right away.

"Look, man," I said, my voice intense, "you've got to close your eyes sometime. When you close your eyes, I'm going to fucking stick you with something."

I made myself look as big and scary as I could, and I didn't back down for a second. He was looking at me like I was crazy. Well, what did he expect? He started it. He ended up leaving me alone after that. I guess he wanted to see what I'd do. But at that point, I was no joke. I was into defending myself completely.

Another time, this Latino guy did say something crazy to me.

"Hey, man, what's up with that?" I said, squaring off against him.

Again, I would not back down because I knew I couldn't if I was going to protect my reputation.

"Come on," he said, challenging me.

We both stood and stared at each other, neither of us making the first move to fight or to walk away. It got really tense, but thankfully we never got into a fight because he ended up letting it go. That was lucky for me, as I realized when I found out who he was. Someone came up to me and told me that I had talked trash to one of the biggest Mexican gang leaders in Chino, who could have me killed just by giving the word. I got nervous then that he might be planning to get me back when I wasn't expecting it.

But the guy actually ended up having a real conversation with me instead.

"Let me tell you something, man," he said. "You're going through a lot. And I respect you because you're not a punk, and you're not going to let people push you. You'll fight back, no matter what happens. I know who you are. But you have no idea who I am. I respect you for the fact that you stood up for yourself anyhow, even though it could have meant real trouble for you. No inmate will lay a hand on you while you're in this prison. If they do, they'll lose their life."

, So I had his protection, too.

While I was in there, I actually didn't need as much protection as anyone expected I would. I was able to do things that ordinary blacks weren't able to do. I was able to hang out with the Mexican gangs, the black gangs, and some of the white guys. Most of the races did not mix at all, and there was a lot of violence between the different groups. But because people knew me from TV, and because I knew how to deal with all different kinds of people from my days with Billy, I got along. The only time I had to pick a side was if a fight went down, and then I had to go with the blacks; otherwise I would have been put out by my people. That's just how it was.

And just like when I was in jail before, my life settled into a routine. I was given a great job in the shipping and receiving department. That helped out my standing in prison because I could get pens for people. I sold pens. I sold food. I sold pretty much anything I could think of to sell. I had people do drawings for me, and I would sell those, too. That's what keeps guys going in prison, anything they can do to make a little money and earn the other inmates' respect.

The other inmates and I found ways to pass the time. We played cards and dominoes. A group of us guys used to pray together at night. We all took turns leading the prayer group different nights of the week. We all prayed that our cases would go well and that we would have the strength and wisdom to turn our lives around.

Some aspects of Chino actually weren't that bad. The food was good. The only thing was that we had to eat quickly. We had a five-minute window, and if we didn't finish everything in that time, and get out of there so the next prisoners could come in and be fed, they'd throw our food away and we'd end up hungry. That's where I learned to eat really fast, and I still eat fast to this day.

We used to try to sneak oranges back to our cells by hiding them in our clothes. If a guard saw a bump where there shouldn't be one, he called me over.

"Come here," he said.

"Yeah?" I said as I walked over to him.

"What's in your pocket?" he said.

"Nothing."

But he knew what it was. And he knew that I knew that we

weren't supposed to have it, either, because some prisoners would try to make juno, which was this homemade fruit wine. He reached over and smashed the orange in my pocket, laughing the whole time. He thought it was hilarious. He knew I didn't have that many clothes, and now I had sticky pulp all over my underwear and pants.

"Now, go throw that orange away," he said.

It may have seemed mean, but he was just messing with me, almost like a brother. That was a first, actually having authority figures be decent to me. But there was this one female officer who just couldn't stand me. She was always looking for a reason to give me a 115, and that was serious. If I received a 115 while I was in there for observation, it would have affected my court case. I was going to have to go back to court at the end of the observation, and if I had a 115, the judge might then decide to recommend that I go to prison for an extended time. The probation department was all about sending people to prison. I didn't want to give them any ammunition, so I tried to steer clear of her, but by now, we all know how I used to get when someone started with me.

Part of being under observation was that I had to see a psychiatrist for an evaluation. This was a big deal because his report would help the judge decide whether I had been rehabilitated and could be released, or if I needed to be sent to prison for a full sentence. I was really nervous when I went to meet the psychiatrist.

But when I sat down, the psychiatrist smiled at me.

"I know you," he said.

"You do?" I said.

"Yeah, you were in the Northridge Mall about thirteen years ago," he said. "And my son came up to you and asked for an autograph. Not only did you sign an autograph for him, you sat and talked with him, and took a picture with him. That made me realize that you are not a person who deserves to be in prison."

I couldn't believe I was hearing all of this.

"I'm going to write a recommendation that you need a second chance," he said.

I thanked him like a thousand times and vowed to myself that I would prove him right. That moment showed me that it really does pay to be nice to people. And it made me feel lucky that my mom raised me with some manners. Otherwise I might have been rude to his son, and then I would have been in trouble. I saw that doctor a bunch of times after that, and he did end up recommending that I be released.

That was a huge relief for me and for my family. The whole time I was there, my mother kept trying to see me, but I never signed the release. I just couldn't face her while I was in there. I needed a break from my life on the outside around then, too, because I had just found out that Tiffany, the girl I'd left at home, was pregnant. That was really stressful. I wanted to do the right thing, but I knew I wasn't in any condition to be a father. She had a miscarriage, and as cold as it may sound, it was probably a blessing.

It was getting close to my court date, but they weren't quite ready to release me yet. I ended up doing six months in there, total. Finally it was time for me to go. The day before I was scheduled to leave, I was walking across the grass. The female officer who had it in for me happened to see me pass by.

"Get off the grass, you bastard," she said.

"All you had to do was tell me to get off the grass," I said. "Nobody ever told me that before."

"What?" she said.

"Nobody ever told me not to walk on the grass before," I said.

"Like I said, get your fucking ass off of there," she said.

"You don't have to be an asshole about it," I said.

"That's it, I'm writing you up," she said.

"I don't care," I said. "I'm getting out of here tomorrow, anyway. You can't stop me from getting out of here."

"That's it, you're going to be 115," she said.

I guess I hadn't totally dealt with my anger issues yet. I was working on it. But after all those years of taking abuse at the hands of the police, I couldn't stand to be told what to do by someone in authority. I had to make my point.

But I sure didn't want to go to prison.

I called up Johnnie right away.

"You need to get me out of here," I said. "Like tomorrow. They're trying to write me up for this 115."

All of the sudden, the whole mood of the place switched over immediately. She was nastier to me, and the other correction officers all started being real jerks to me, too. I lost my job in shipping and receiving. My last few days there were really rough. They tried to write me up, but I got out of there just in time.

The correction officers didn't look too happy on the day I finally got out.

"So you made it out, huh?" one of the guards said.

"Yep," I said. "Well, you know what they say, right?"

"What?" he said.

"Nobody likes pigs that don't fly straight," I said, referring to *Scarface*.

He gave me a hard look; he thought he had me all figured out.

"You'll be back," he said. "We'll be waiting on you."

"No, I won't be back," I said. "This will be my last and final time. I learned my lesson."

This time I knew I really meant it.

They sent me back to county jail for a few days, and then I had to go in front of the judge. Johnnie was there with me, and my mom, and my brother, and sister. I knew that the psychiatrist had said he was going to recommend that I be released, but I was still nervous. I really wanted a second chance.

The judge got right down to it.

"I'm going to tell you something, Mr. Bridges," he said. "I've read the report from the psychiatrist. I've read the report from the prosecutor. I've read the report from the probation department. The probation department is saying that you need five years in prison. But the report from the psychiatrist is interesting, and I believe what he's saying. I believe that you need a second chance. And I do believe, if I give you a second chance, you will turn your entire life around."

"Judge," I said, "that's what will happen. Trust me, I will end up turning my life around. I won't continue what I was doing. I will never use drugs again. I promise."

"Well, I'm going to give you this second chance," he said. "I'm going to order you released to go home immediately."

I was so happy.

"Did you bring all of your stuff here?" he asked.

"Yeah," I said.

"I'm going to release you here then," he said. "You don't have to go back to county."

That was the happiest moment of my life. No matter what else happened to me, I knew that all the pain and the shame were finally behind me. I knew I would never go back to using drugs again. That same day, my mom took me back to the sober living house where I had been staying, and I went right back to my new sober life. When it was time for me to move out, I ended up moving in next door and getting a job running the place. I just loved being there. I loved being around addicts and helping them. I loved being around people who were working the program and the twelve steps of recovery. Finally, I loved just being alive. It had been a long time coming.

15

SEVENTH HEAVEN

IF IT HAD BEEN UP TO ME, I never would have left the sober living house. It was such a safe, supportive place, and that was just what I needed. My life made sense there, and I was able to establish a routine. That was really important because I had plenty to deal with at the time. Just being sober and facing all the emotions I had kept buried for so long was hard. Plus, I had to do all of this in the public eye, with everyone well aware of what my crack addiction had done to me, since it all came out during my trials. I had fallen about as far I could fall. It was all pretty humbling.

It didn't help that the court had taken away my driver's license, so I had to take the bus everywhere I wanted to go for two years. I wasn't ashamed to be riding the bus. If I had to get somewhere, I took the bus. It was fine. I had a little bus pass and everything. The only bad part was that people made fun of me pretty much every day. I'd be sitting at the bus stop, just doing my thing, and a car full of people would drive by and see me waiting there, and they just thought this was the funniest thing they'd ever seen.

"Hey, Willis, fuck you, you fucker!" they'd yell at me.

Or they'd flip me off out of their car window as they drove by. I'd look at them and laugh. Sure I got mad. Sure it was a reminder of how much had changed since the days when I was driving my BMW to the set of *Diff'rent Strokes* and out to the hottest nightclubs in the city. But I knew what I had to do, and I didn't care what other people thought about it. That was my whole thing. Once I got my head straightened out, I didn't care about anybody else's opinion of me. I realized it didn't make any sense to care. They didn't know the real me, or the real story of what I had been through, and I didn't have to prove anything to them. After that, I felt a lot better. I focused on getting up every day and trying to do the right thing.

It wasn't always easy. My anger still flared up sometimes. I did end up having one incident on the bus. But it wasn't because someone was giving me a hard time. It was because I still hated to see people get taken advantage of, just like when I'd stood up for the kids who got harassed by the bullies back in school. This old guy was sitting in one of the seats on the bus, and this young guy came in and made the old guy get up. That's not something a person wants to do in front of me, especially not back then, when I was still learning to manage my emotions. I was hot. I gave the old guy my seat, and then I went and stood right next to the young guy. I wanted to beat him up so badly. All of my anger and hostility just flamed right up. But since I'd gotten sober, I had learned some things about not letting my emotions run me, so I didn't go for him right away. I just stood over him, breathing on his neck like a wolf, waiting for him to make one wrong move so I would have an excuse to kick his ass. But he never gave me one. He got nervous and hopped off at the next bus stop. I let it go and went on with my day. It felt good that I was able to hold it together like that. It was definitely a learning process for me.

With the substances gone, the pain came up. And now it wasn't only the torment from my childhood—the abusive father who didn't know how to love me, the substitute father who betrayed my trust by molesting me, the police who harassed me—it also was the pain of acknowledging all of the torment I caused myself and others—the fights I got into, the people I screwed over, the women I dead-ended so I could have sex with them. It was tough to accept that there was no one else to blame in the end but myself. Even if I didn't create what happened to me as a child, I chose how I dealt with it. It was time to take responsibility for all of that mess.

Luckily, I was going to see a psychiatrist at the time, or I don't honestly know how I would have managed to process everything. I can see now that I should have gone long before that to talk to a therapist about the abuse I received from my father, and Ronald, and the police. But I couldn't bring myself to admit that anything was wrong. Today, everybody sees a psychiatrist. But back in the '80s, people who went to a shrink kept quiet about it, especially the people I spent time with.

Even with a doctor's help, it took me years to really come to terms with what had happened to me and what I had lost. But in the early days of my recovery, I was given some information about addiction. It helped me to understand what I needed to do to stay sober and build a new life for myself, and why it was so hard to do both of these things. I learned that when I started using drugs and alcohol, I basically stunted my growth as a person. So when I sobered up, even though I was a twenty-seven-year-old man, I was still wired to behave like an eighteen-year-old kid. I actually had to learn how to be an adult. I had to learn responsibility. I had to learn basic things, such as social skills, because I only knew how to act around other addicts. Most important, I had to learn to filter some of the things my brain told me. I would walk into a room, and the newly sober addict inside me would think everyone hated me. When I had been using drugs, that paranoia and self-consciousness would have been enough to make me rush out and get high. But I didn't want to do that anymore. And, with my new resolve and my newly acquired tools for handling life, I managed to stay clean.

In addition to seeing a psychiatrist, I did a lot of meditating during that time. But the thing that helped me the most was Alcoholics Anonymous. For the first three years, I went to meetings every day. I was careful to keep my social circle connected to people who were in the program, too. I didn't want to have people in my life who weren't a part of the program because it was too dangerous for me. Not everyone in the program was a safe bet, either. It was important to stay away from the people who were relapsing a lot and stick with those who wanted to make sobriety work for them.

I had a great sponsor who helped me so much during my early recovery. When I chose my first sponsor, I knew myself well enough to realize that I needed to pick someone who wouldn't tolerate my crap. He was too big and tough for me to even try to pull any nonsense on him. I did exactly what he told me to do. And that was just what I needed right then. One of the biggest lessons all addicts have to learn is that they need to stop doing what they want to do and start doing what they're told by the people who have actually succeeded at sobriety. That's the toughest thing in the world for an addict. I know it was really hard for me.

There were aspects of my past that it was harder to make peace with than others. While I was living in Venice Beach, I saw my dad for the first time in several years. By that time, he was sick. He had chronic obstructive pulmonary lung disease, and his body was ruined from drinking for so many years and smoking too many cigarettes.

But I needed a car. He let me use his in exchange for driving him to the hospital every day. I would have almost rather taken the bus. Old age had not mellowed him at all. And spending time with him drove me crazy. He still didn't know how to act or treat people right. He wasn't willing to accept responsibility for anything, and he was always blaming my mother. He never seemed to have a nice thing to say about anyone or anything. I used to sit there listening to him complain, and I'd find myself hoping that his car door was unlocked, so that when I hit a corner, he'd fly out and roll into the street. That fantasy is all that got me through some of those car trips. But at least we were spending time together, which was more than I could say for a lot of years of my life. I was making progress.

As a drug addict, I had left a lot of wreckage behind. One of the first steps of my recovery, when I was just getting out of rehab, involved apologizing to everyone I had hurt while I was using. My dad was the only person who didn't receive an apology. I said I was sorry to everyone else in my family, and I really meant it. And I gave them the chance to tell me how hard it was for them when I got arrested, and they had to hear about it everywhere and worry themselves. I owned up to all of that.

I didn't just make amends to my family, either. I had to try to get in touch with all of the people I had hurt. When I ran into people from my past, I apologized for what I had put them through. For those people I couldn't just approach, because they weren't in my life anymore, or it would have been too upsetting for them, I wrote apology letters. I wrote a lot of apology letters.

The thing I regretted most was all the people I had gotten strung out on drugs. Now that I could understand how becoming an addict could ruin a person's life, I felt terrible that I had brought all of that on girls just so I could sleep with them. It was hard to look back and see the lack of caring I had for the people in my life during my drug years. It took me a long time to come to terms with everything I had done. Finally, with help from my psychiatrist, and my sponsor, and the program, I came to see that the only reason I behaved liked that was because I didn't care about myself. But that was changing.

My recovery was going well, and I was feeling better and better about myself and my life. And then the people who ran the sober living house finally told me I had to go home. They felt like I was ready to transition into regular life, and they wanted my bed for someone who was fresh out of rehab and really needed it. This scared me for a couple of reasons. I wasn't sure I was ready to maintain my sobriety in the real world. And I thought I was going to get in trouble and have to go back to jail because one of the terms of my probation was that they wanted me in sober living. I was all about doing whatever I was asked to do by the Los Angeles court system. I was even okay with the fact that they gave me drug testing for longer than they should have, even though I was one of the only ones I was in probation with at that time who never tested dirty in two and a half-years. After six months of that, I should have been free and clear. But if peeing in a cup would keep me out of prison, that was just great with me. And so, when they no longer had space for me in sober living, I was really worried that it was going to screw up my probation. That was a very stressful transition.

I went to stay at my mom's house in Canoga Park for a few months while I figured out what to do next. One night, I was resting in the downstairs area that she had done up for me, and an ambulance drove by with its siren on. I didn't think anything about it until my mom came running downstairs to see if I was there. She was still haunted by the fear that I was in the back of every ambulance and police car she saw, even after I had been sober for several years. I felt awful when I saw how upset she was. That was a really important moment for me. Before that, I had made amends to my mom and everyone else in my life, but I don't think I really understood why I was apologizing. Even once I sobered up, I never truly realized how much harm I did to my mom during all of those times I vanished for six months, and she knew I was out on the streets of South Central Los Angeles, feeding my addiction by any means necessary, and she couldn't stop fantasizing that I was dead in a ditch somewhere. Seeing the pain I had caused her was hard, but it was good for me, too. It finally helped me to take responsibility for the choices I had made and the damage they had caused.

I also started to feel really bad about the pain and suffering I had put my brother through, the pain and suffering I had put my sister through, the pain and suffering I had put all my friends through. It wasn't easy to take responsibility for all the hurt I had caused all of these people who had done nothing but love me, even when I was at my lowest and most despicable. But accepting what I had done was an important part of making peace with my past and letting it go so I could finally move forward.

I wasn't sure what to do next with my life, so I couldn't have been happier when I got an offer to run another sober living house, in Venice Beach. Being in charge of the sober living house meant I had a purpose and a place to stay. But it didn't pay anything, so I had to find a job. Gone were the days in the final seasons of *Diff'rent Strokes*, when I made $30,000 a week and had a Porsche with a vanity license plate. I didn't have any money left. I didn't have anything. I wanted a car that wasn't my dad's, and I had to figure out a way to pay for it. So I started looking for a job. That was a harsh reality check. During the years when most people were going to school and working their first jobs, I had been acting on *Diff'rent Strokes* and traveling the country with the Hollywood Teens. I had a high school diploma, but I had never gone to college or held down a "real" job, and I had a lengthy criminal record. I was not exactly most people's ideal applicant.

I could have been mad at myself for ruining my career and throwing away everything I'd worked so hard to achieve. But luckily, in the first year or so of my recovery, I wasn't able to think about the big picture. That's a good thing, because it probably kept me from losing my mind or becoming too overwhelmed by everything I had done and the hard road ahead of me. I was taking it one day at a time, just like the program told me to do. I didn't care about what had happened before. That was gone. I was glad to be alive, and I wanted to work. I still had all of the same qualities that had made me a successful actor and probably even helped me to be a good drug dealer. I mean, it *is* a job, right? I was determined. I had a good work ethic. I always arrived on time. With the help of therapy, I liked people again. Well, most people.

I finally got a job at Washington Medical Center. It wasn't easy. I worked twelve-hour shifts, from 7:00 P.M. to 7:00 A.M. But I didn't mind. It ended up being the best job in the world for me. It helped me through a lot of my own stuff. I worked with other addicts who were in rehab. I processed them, took their vitals, filled out their charts, and all of that stuff. Just like my work at the sober living house, it was very healing for me to help people who were in the early stages of getting sober. They were struggling through all of the same things I had recently struggled through. Being able to show them, through my own example, that there was a way forward, that it would get easier, felt really good. It also reminded me that this was true for myself, too.

Like I said, I was still learning how to manage my anger better. But that was actually a good thing in this job. All of the nurses loved working with me because I didn't take any crap from any of the patients, and so the nurses knew they were safe when we were on a shift together. Patients got angry and out of hand all the time because they wanted medication, and the nurses wouldn't give it to them.

So they'd yell at the nurses and threaten to beat them up. But when I was there on duty, nobody threatened to beat anybody up. They knew I'd throw their ass out. A lot of them were working on their own anger issues, so it could get pretty heated.

"I'm going to get you fired," this guy said to me.

"Do you think I care about this job?" I said. "I'm doing this job to help you. This job, it don't mean crap to me. I make nothing here."

That was probably the hardest thing for me to accept about entering the working world. When I saw my first check, I couldn't believe it.

"Holy crap, is this what real people make?" I thought. "How am I supposed to live on this?"

I was making something like $400 every two weeks. It was enough to cover my car payment and that kind of stuff, but it wasn't what I was used to making. I got by, though. And I was actually starting to feel pretty lucky. Running the sober living houses, I didn't have to pay any money for rent or utilities or food. Whatever money I had left over after my car payments was mine, free and clear.

I worked at the sober living house for three years, from 1993 to 1996. It was rewarding work, but it ended up being one of the hardest jobs in the world. I quickly found out that not everybody wanted to be sober. In fact, most people didn't care about sobriety because they weren't ready for it yet. They were there because the judge had put them there. I actually started working with the court system in Santa Monica, and I would go to the courts and get people, just like the guy my mom found to get me into CPC Westwood. I'd talk to the district attorney and convince him to let me try to straighten them out instead of sending them to jail. I had a pretty good rapport with the DA's office. They used to give me a lot of people out of the Santa Monica courts. So I had people in and out of my sober living houses all the time. The two houses I ran had sixteen beds between them, and I would guess that I had about three thousand people go through there in those three years. And out of all those people, I know of only one person who stayed sober. That's the reality. A very small percentage of people who try to get sober actually succeed. It made me want my own sobriety even more.

I wanted to be sober, and I was working the twelve steps, but it still took a long time to get myself back to what any regular person would consider normal. It took about a year just for the drug fog to go away. And during that time, my mind was really fuzzy. When I was first in rehab, I fell in love with this girl, and I thought she was the most beautiful girl I had ever seen. And then, once I had been sober longer and my mind cleared, I couldn't understand what I had been thinking. And that was only one little thing in my life. I had to relearn and rethink everything.

Like I said, it was very much an ongoing process. I was doing really well, I was working, I had a car, I was back on my feet. And then I found myself in trouble again, in 1996. I was in an arcade in Marina Del Rey, hanging out and playing video games, and this guy I had seen hanging out there came in and started getting into it with me. As we all know by now, that was the wrong thing to do to me, and I was not going to let it go, anger management or no anger management. It got heated. I was seriously mad by this point. He hauled back and punched me in the face. The blow startled me, and by the time I shook it off, he had taken off running. I pushed my way through the crowd and chased him out of there. He got in his car and drove away. I jumped into my Jeep Grand Cherokee and started following him. All I could think about was teaching him a lesson. I was easily going sixty miles an hour, and I lost control of my car. I hit a parked car, but I kept going. By the time I finally crashed to the point where I couldn't drive anymore, I had hit a bunch of cars, including his car, and they arrested me for assault with a deadly weapon. When I found myself in court again, I was really frustrated with myself. But it had happened, and there was nothing to do but deal with the consequences. Luckily, my probation from my last arrest had recently ended, so I didn't end up getting into even worse trouble. And the charges were dropped to vandalism, so I didn't have to serve any time. I took that as a warning sign and haven't been in trouble since.

It was around this time that I started thinking about acting again. I'd done a few bit parts since I decided I'd had enough of making the little money I was earning at Washington Medical Center. I was ready to get back to where I could make some real money. The only problem was that no one would hire me. Not only that, but they were always making jokes about me. It was that same old story about the former child star turned crack addict, which just seemed to tickle everyone so much. It sure wasn't funny to me. It was my life. But just like when I was looking for a regular job before, I was persistent. I made sure the people I met with understood how much I wanted to work, and now that all of my past problems were behind me, how hard I intended to work. Slowly but surely, people started trusting me again and giving me work.

My first project was a TV movie called *Circle of Pain*, which aired on Showtime in 1996. The producers were Bobby Mardis and T'Keyah Crystal Keymah, who had been on *In Living Color* and *Cosby*, and they both acted in the project with me as well. I was excited about the part because I could really relate to it. I played a guy who had just gotten out of jail and was trying to get his life together but kept running into a bunch of bad elements that were making it hard for him. It was a meaty role, and it made me glad I wasn't having the same problems in my own life. It felt great to be acting again, to be on the set again, just to be doing everything that was so familiar to me. I knew right away that it was what I was supposed to be doing.

I had taken a detour, a ten-year detour, but I was back. It gave me hope that my career would start back up.

That was a special project, too, because I had the chance to work with Rosalind Cash again. It was wonderful to see her after so long, and having come through the darkness that overtook me after she and I worked together when I was first starting out. I don't think she was really honest with any of us on the set about how sick she was during the filming because she passed away a few months later.

I worked on *Circle of Pain* for about four weeks, and during that time I became certain that acting was still my first love. This was a big relief for me. When I first got sober and discovered that I didn't want to return to acting right away, it definitely felt scary to turn my back on something that had been such a major part of my entire life. It felt great to know, for sure, that I was back where I belonged. When I returned to the sober living place I was running, I quit so I could focus on getting my acting career back together. I rented my own place in Venice Beach.

I was cast in a play that Lisa Wu Hartwell was doing in Atlanta. This was back when she was married to the R & B singer Keith Sweat, and she still went by Lisa Sweat. I arrived in town with plans to be there for a few months to rehearse and perform the play. When we showed up for the first day of rehearsal, I noticed one of the other actors right away. Her name was Dori Smith. I had never met her before because she wasn't from Hollywood. She lived in Atlanta, near where she had grown up. Well, we got really close during the time we worked together on that play, and by the time I was due to go back to LA, we had fallen in love. I asked Dori to move to LA with me, and then I went back, ready to make some more changes in my life. Dori moved out to LA a few months later, and we started building a relationship. It was hard for me to be trusting and open at first, after everything I had been through and all the shallow relationships I'd had with other addicts that were only based around drugs and sex. But Dori was very patient, and we were both committed to making it work. We got married on May 25, 1998.

My son Spencir was born that same year. It was while Dori was pregnant with Spencir that I finally came as close to forgiving my father as I could. The whole time I was in rehab and working on my recovery afterward, my counselors and sponsors kept telling me I needed to make peace with my father. If he died, I was going to be stuck with all those bad feelings from my childhood without any way to release them. My mom always used to tell me the same thing, that I needed to go and talk to him before he died. They were all telling me this for years, but I couldn't do it. I was still too angry at my father, and I wasn't ready to forgive him. Finally, when he was in the hospital and I knew he was very ill, I went in and said what I had to say to him. I sat down by his bedside and looked at how frail he was, and it was hard to believe that this was the same man who used to hit my mom and me. He looked really sick, and old, and worn out. I knew it was now or never. I told him how much he had hurt me by not being there for me when I was a kid, and by taking Ronald Rayton's side over mine, and how I felt like I had gotten into drugs to escape the pain he had caused me.

While I was talking to him, I heard this funny noise next to me. I looked over and saw that my dad was lying there, looking up at me, and crying.

"I'm sorry," he said.

I'd like to say we shared a tender moment then, but the truth is that I didn't believe him. I didn't know how genuine he was really being. But that wasn't important. I had done what I needed to do. And I knew, from working the program as vigorously as I had, that it didn't really matter if he said he was sorry, or if it was sincere. What really mattered was me and how well I was able to make peace with my own past. Once I realized that, I was able to forgive my father. And when he died a few months later, I was glad I had resolved everything when I did.

I do, honestly, feel like I've finally forgiven my father. I think a big part of it had to do with letting go of my anger. Once I did that, I could better understand where he was coming from. In the end, I felt bad for him. It must have been so hard for him, having to leave school and go to work at fifteen. I think that's what made him such a bitter person. Even though I was working at the same age, my mother made sure I had a normal childhood, so I never felt like I missed out on anything. But my dad never got to be a kid, and I think that seemed really unfair to him, and it poisoned him against the world.

Even after I forgave my father, I had to live with his legacy. I struggled for a long time to find a way to become a good man, a responsible husband, and a caring father without the love and support he was supposed to give me.

But as hard as it was to forgive my dad, the most difficult thing I had to do was learn how to forgive myself. It took years after I got sober. It was the worst when I was first rebuilding my career, and I was broke, and I was having trouble getting anyone to hire me. I couldn't stop thinking about all the dumb stuff I had done to myself and all the mistakes and horrible decisions I had made. I kept having the same thoughts over and over again: "You should have been careful. You should have been watching. What were you thinking? What were you thinking? What were you thinking?"

But I could see that, slowly, things were getting better, and that kept me going.

Around this time, my ability to make peace with my past was tested. A girl I had dated about five years before got in touch with me and told me I was the father of her daughter. When she became pregnant, I had asked her if the baby was mine. She had said no. So it was a shock to find out that she had lied to me and that I had a daughter I had never met who was a full year older than Spencir. This was a lot to take in, especially as Dori and I had worked hard to create a family unit based on all the values that were important to us. I didn't know how I would work another child into that mix. But having known the pain of having a father who didn't express his love for me, I was determined to do right by any child of mine. After a paternity test revealed that Bo was my daughter, I had the chance to meet her for the first time. Of course, I loved her right away. And she has become an important part of my family. It can be a juggling act, but Bo often stays with Dori and Spencir and me, and goes on vacation with us. As both of my children grow up, I make a point to give them all the attention and affection that I always longed for from my own father. I don't want them to know the pain I did.

When I became a dad, I gained an all new understanding of how much suffering I had caused my mom when I was an addict. Once I knew firsthand how hard it was to watch one of my kids be sick, and know there was nothing I could do to make them stop hurting, I understood that there's nothing in the world parents want more than to protect their children from danger. Parents don't want to see their children hurting, or doing wrong. When they have to watch their children struggle with something as dark as I did, it's probably the worst thing they can go through, short of losing that child. And to realize that I intentionally caused my mother this pain, even if I wasn't in my right frame of mind at the time, was awful.

But instead of trying to bury my hurt, as I had done in the past, I had better tools for handling my emotions after rehab, so I talked to my mom about how I was feeling, and I took responsibility for what I had done. Because ultimately, as I've said, no matter what I've gone through in my life, I made bad decisions, and I'm the one who took my life to where it was. No one else did that. I did that.

Around the time I was finally moving beyond the mistakes I had made when I was younger, and building an ever more positive present with my family and friends, I lost someone who had a huge role in helping me grow up. My TV sister and longtime friend Dana Plato died of an accidental drug overdose on May 8, 1999. I was devastated when I got the phone call, but I can't say I was entirely surprised. Dana had been using drugs and alcohol since she was thirteen years old. The last time I had seen her, a few years before she died, when she and Gary and I were asked to make an appearance at a parade in Orange County, she was clearly still using. She disappeared into the bathroom for a long time. Gary and I just looked at each other with that old way of "That's just Dana being Dana." But I was sober then, and I felt like I had to at least say something when she finally came out.

"Is everything okay, Dana?" I asked.

"Yeah, of course," she said.

"Really?" I said. "You were in the bathroom a long time."

"I'm not doing anything," she said.

But she looked worn down by then. She had gotten into as much trouble as I had over the years. Along with all the problems that Gary had, it caused some people to say that the *Diff'rent Strokes* kids were cursed. Of course that's just stupid.

Even though I didn't see her again after that, I knew that Dana had a problem, and I was trying to help her in her final days. The last time I spoke to her on the phone was three days before she died, and I tried to get her to consider rehab.

"I found a good place for you to go," I said.

"Todd, I don't have a problem like you do," she said.

I could remember when I had said the same thing to people who had tried to help me, so I was still hoping she would come around like I had.

The day before Dana died, I heard her make an appearance on the Howard Stern show. When he asked her if she had ever done cocaine, she said she hadn't. I knew this was a lie, and so did everyone else who was listening. The callers beat her up pretty badly. I couldn't understand why she didn't just admit it. Who cares?

But Dana was never good at handling questions or pressure from people. She just couldn't deal with it when people had any kind of expectation of her. I don't think facing that kind of ridicule when she was already in a weakened state helped her at all.

I spoke at Dana's service, which was held in Los Angeles a few days after her death. It was a really hard experience to get through. Dana was such an important part of my life. She really was like a sister to me. She taught me so much about the ways of the world, and she never judged me, no matter what kind of bad choices I made or how low they brought me. And even when she was using drugs heavily herself, she always maintained something of the bright, bubbly girl I first met years ago when she came in to audition for *Diff'rent Strokes*.

It was also difficult because Gary and I still weren't speaking, and seeing him at Dana's funeral just reminded me that I had lost him as a friend, too. He and I didn't say even one word to each other at Dana's service. It was hard to believe how much things had changed from the first two seasons of *Diff'rent Strokes*, when we were great friends who played practical jokes and built cardboard forts together. It was good to see Conrad Bain, though, and he and I remain close friends.

Of course, when Dana died, the press had to bring up all of my past problems. And that was upsetting for me, too. It seemed like no matter how long I stayed sober or how much good I tried to do, they would never let me live down a few years of bad decisions. The same was true when my brother, Jimmy, and I were able to help someone because we were in the right place at the right time in April 2001. We were just hanging out, fishing and relaxing, at Lake Balboa Park in Encino when we saw this woman's wheelchair roll into the lake. Apparently her fishing line had jammed on the joystick of her wheelchair, and she lost control. Well, she was a paraplegic, and she was strapped into her chair, so when her chair tipped over and her head went underwater, she could have drowned. But as soon as I saw what was happening, I jumped into the water. And then Jimmy jumped in, and we saved her life. At the time, I was just happy that she wasn't hurt. But then, when the paramedics arrived, I could tell that one of the guys recognized me. I knew right away that it would be all over the news. I didn't even mind that it was, except that they always had to bring up the bad stuff, too. I was watching Fox News, and I swear their coverage started something just like this: "Actor Todd Bridges saved a woman's life today. But he wasn't such a hero in 1989." I just remember thinking, "Can't a guy get a break?"

It helped a lot when my brother, Jimmy, and I started our own production company and began developing material together. I realized that it was going to take a long time for people in Hollywood to forget my past, so if I wanted to rebuild my career, I had to do it for myself. Our first project had the same name as our production company, *Building Bridges*, and it was a short film about my life. That was a lot of fun to do because not only did Jimmy and I write, direct, and produce the project together, but also most of the cast was made up of our family members. My sister played our mom back in the '70s. Other than that, everyone pretty much played themselves, including Dori and Spencir.

Jimmy and I have since done four more projects together, and we have a bunch of stuff in the works, including the script for a full-length feature film of the story of my life.

As my career started to pick up, it brought a whole new set of challenges. Just like I had to relearn how to be an adult and socialize when I first got sober, I now had to handle the pressures of the industry for the first time as a person in recovery. Even though my drug and alcohol use had never gotten to the point where I used on the job when I was working, I had gotten used to partying with the people I worked with when I was younger. Years later, everyone in the business was still partying, except for me. It worked out well for the other people when I was doing movies, though. Being in Hollywood is really a great, easy job except for the fact that the hours are incredibly long, and so everyone always wants to go out for a drink after a day of shooting. Well, since I got sober, I've always been the designated driver, and everyone loved that.

I've always loved the camaraderie that is created on a set, and I still have so many good friends who are involved in entertainment. But to this day, I don't socialize very much within the industry. I will sometimes, when I'm feeling strong or feeling like I can resist the urge to use. Otherwise, I mostly stay away from all of it, just to keep myself safe. I don't want to put myself in a bad position. As a recovering alcoholic, I have to be aware of always being careful, no matter how long I've been sober. Temptation is a dangerous thing. It's like how a married guy's not going to go hang out at a whorehouse every day. It wouldn't make sense. But as long as I've been mindful of the people I surround myself with and things we spend energy on, I haven't ever been seriously tempted to use again. I've never found myself at a liquor store, about to go in, or at the turnoff to an old dealer's house. My body has craved the feeling of getting high. But giving in to those urges is something that is the farthest from my mind that it can possibly be.

I lost so much before I got sober, and I'm not willing to go down that road again. Having jeopardized everything, and knowing how hard it was to get it back, I'm not going to throw it all away again. If I was to use drugs now, I know what would happen to me. I would lose everything I have. It would be gone. And then I'd be back on the news and the TV entertainment shows for using drugs, and nobody would trust me again. I'd be out of work, and my whole life would be miserable.

One of the hardest things about my recovery has been how much I've had to struggle to get my career back when other actors who had similar problems have had a much easier time of it. Sure, people such as Robert Downey Jr. and Drew Barrymore have had to earn trust again, but they've been given the opportunity to do so, and by working hard and proving that they're not the people they used to be when they had substance abuse problems, they've achieved even greater success than they had before. I know some people are going to object to this, but I have to be honest about the fact that I think there is a racial divide in the industry that makes it much harder for black actors to get a second chance. Once they've disappeared off the scene, they're likely to disappear for good.

I think that the real problem behind this situation is a lack of unity among blacks in Hollywood. It's not like when I was starting out, when veterans such as Redd Foxx and Sammy Davis Jr. welcomed the younger generation with open arms and everyone socialized and took an interest in each other's career. For some reason, we don't look out for each other anymore. I think this is a real shame, and not only because I feel like this kind of unity could have helped my own career, but also because I think we would be making more of an impact on the industry if we did a better job of working together.

I don't think this is true only in the entertainment industry, either.

Most racial and ethnic groups in our country support each other, whether it's the Jewish community or immigrants from Brazil or Poland, or anywhere. But blacks aren't like that. We don't have many community centers, no retirement homes, no sense of coming together for a unified goal. This is something I want to draw attention to and help to change.

I know that some of my fellow blacks won't take me seriously because I happen to be married to a white woman. But that's exactly the kind of backward thinking we've got to change. We can't control who we fall in love with, and the fact that I fell in love with Dori doesn't make me or my son any less black.

I don't mean to sound ungrateful or like I'm judging anyone, but I think it's very important for us to talk about these issues and keep them out in the open. I honestly believe that part of the reason my life has followed this path was so I would be humbled and made to see the difficulties facing many black Americans and be in a position to help us to come together to make the situation better. If I had stayed on my path of being a huge movie star, I never would have thought about these things. I would have been too busy counting my money. But that's not the purpose I was given, and I really want to make a difference.

Also, having experienced the racism and harassment I did as a child, I am committed to helping make sure that the next generation doesn't have to experience that kind of hatred and then grow up hating themselves because of the color of their skin. Obviously, having Barack Obama elected president is a huge step in the right direction. I can feel the positive change already, but it is up to us to do more in our immediate communities and daily lives. No matter how much my career continues to improve, I will continue to be committed to this mission. I will just use my greater visibility to reach more people.

My career has continued to pick up steam, and for this I am extremely grateful. In recent years I've also had some amazing experiences that have helped rebuild my confidence. So many of my fans have been so nice and supportive, just coming up to me on the street and acknowledging me. Everybody seems to have a sense that I'm trying to change my life, and as I have changed things for the better, people have acknowledged me for that, which means so much.

Getting support from the public has been amazing. But nothing could have been better than the moment when I got one of the greatest compliments I have ever received, at the TV Land Awards in 2003. I was there giving out an award with Conrad, and we were waiting backstage during the ceremony. We looked over and saw Halle Berry standing there, whispering to her friend, and looking at me. Well, she kept looking at me. I was happily married at this point, and Dori was in the audience, so I wasn't going to go talk to her. But Halle Berry is one of the most beautiful women in the world, and such a talented actress, so it definitely got my attention that she was staring at me.

"Halle Berry is checking me out," I thought. "She's checking me out."

Conrad noticed, too.

"Halle Berry is looking at you," he said.

Finally, I guess her friend convinced her to come over to me.

"Hi," she said.

"Hi," I said, feeling pretty excited and nervous by this point.

"I have something I need to tell you," she said. "When I was growing up and you were on *Diff'rent Strokes*, you were my boyfriend. And when you kissed Janet Jackson, I wanted to scratch her eyeballs out. I was going to beat Janet Jackson up if I ever saw her on the street."

I was floored. I didn't know what to say. And that wasn't even the best part.

"And you're still sexy," she added.

So that was definitely good for my confidence, and then, finally, in the past three years, the business has come around and really allowed me to do what I do best. I was asked to be part of Chris Rock's very funny show *Everybody Hates Chris* in 2007, and that was just a fantastic experience. It felt so good to be back on a series again. And my character, Monk, was this great eccentric military man who was really enjoyable to play. They even paid homage to my TV past with a "Whatcha talkin' about, Monk?" in one of the first episodes.

Most recently I've been doing commentary for the show *The Smoking Gun Presents: World's Dumbest*, which is pure fun. Plus it makes me feel a lot better about my past. Even at my most screwed up, I never did anything half as asinine as these people.

At this point, with sixteen years of sobriety, a happy marriage, and two beautiful children who are growing up to be strong and independent young people, I can definitely say that I've made a lot of progress. On average, I now have six days of happiness. And the seventh day is turmoil, as I fight my same old inner fight and work on trying to love myself and forgive myself for my past. But that's okay, because I now know that even the bad days don't last forever. And with God's grace and a whole lot of patience, we all get to where we're supposed to be in the end.